The Heirloom Gardener

CAROLYN JABS

Sierra Club Books
San Francisco

*To Kent Whealy
& The Seed Savers*

The Sierra Club, founded in 1892 by John Muir, has devoted itself to the study and protection of the earth's scenic and ecological resources—mountains, wetlands, woodlands, wild shores and rivers, deserts and plains. The publishing program of the Sierra Club offers books to the public as a nonprofit educational service in the hope that they may enlarge the public's understanding of the Club's basic concerns. The point of view expressed in each book, however, does not necessarily represent that of the Club. The Sierra Club has some fifty chapters coast to coast, in Canada, Hawaii, and Alaska. For information about how you may participate in its programs to preserve wilderness and the quality of life, please address inquiries to Sierra Club, 530 Bush Street, San Francisco, CA 94108.

LIBRARY OF CONGRESS CATALOGING IN PUBLICATION DATA

Jabs, Carolyn.
    The heirloom gardener.

    Bibliography: p.
    Includes index.
        1. Vegetables—Varieties. 2. Fruit—Varieties.
    3. Vegetable gardening. 4. Fruit-culture. I. Title.
SB324.73.J33 1984   635   83-4755
ISBN 0-87156-803-9

Jacket/cover design by Larry Ratzkin
Book design by Wilsted & Taylor
New illustrations by Mary Foley Benson
Composition by Wilsted & Taylor
Printed in the United States of America
10 9 8 7 6 5 4 3 2 1

Contents

PART FOUR
Plants for the Future

PART FIVE
Resources for Heirloom Gardeners

Preface

IN 1980, I WAS ASKED TO WRITE AN ARTICLE FOR the *New York Times* about a group of people who were saving and exchanging seeds from old vegetable varieties. Though I had been gardening for several years, I knew little about old varieties. Yet, like a newly learned word that suddenly appears in everything you read, information about heirlooms began to surface everywhere I looked. Catalogues from small seed companies specializing in heirloom varieties appeared in my mailbox. Rumors about collectors who had accumulated hundreds of heirloom beans or apples came in over the gardener's grapevine. One editor sent me to investigate a "heritage garden" at a nearby living history museum, and on another assignment, I found myself in Colorado within visiting distance of the National Seed Storage Laboratory.

As I talked to these gardeners, scientists, collectors, seed companies and historians, I found that most had the same goal—the preservation of old and endangered fruit and vegetable varieties. Yet, despite their common purpose, they knew little about each other. Gardeners were poorly informed about government programs to preserve old varieties. Scientists at the National Seed Storage Laboratory were ignorant of efforts to plant authentic gardens in living history museums. And historians knew virtually nothing about the new seed companies that had come into being to sell old varieties. Worst of all, the average gardener had never heard of heirloom varieties, much less the movement to keep them alive.

This book was written with all these groups in mind. It has two purposes. One is to explain why the survival of heirloom varieties matters and to describe the preservation efforts of private collectors, seed exchanges, living history museums, government facilities, and seed companies. The second is to provide how-to guidance for those who are inspired to seek out and grow heirlooms of their own.

The marginal illustrations, which come from nineteenth-century horticultural sources, also do double duty. Their elegant details and eloquent captions may kindle the interest of gardeners who have never considered growing heirlooms. In addition, they should be an aid to collectors who have difficulty locating original nineteenth-century source materials.

Many of the illustrations are the work of Isaac Sprague and first appeared in *The Field and Garden Vegetables of America* by Fearing Burr, Jr., published in 1863. Most of the other illustrations are taken from the D. M. Ferry catalogue of 1881, though a few come from Messrs. Vilmorin-Andrieux's *The Vegetable Garden*, the Burpee catalogues of 1888 and 1916, the Northrup, Braslan & Goodwin catalogue of 1891, the Parker & Wood catalogue of 1886, the H. W. Buckbee catalogue of 1909, and the Peter Henderson & Co. 1878 catalogue. Fruit illustrations come from *The Fruits of America* by Charles Hovey (1851), S. W. Cole's *The American Fruit Book* (1849), and Green's Nursery Co. 1910 catalogue.

In most instances the descriptive captions come from the

same source as the illustrations. Sources for the captions are identified with initials as follows:

FB	Fearing Burr, Jr.
AV	Vilmorin-Andrieux
DM	D. M. Ferry
BP	Burpee
PW	Parker & Wood
PH	Peter Henderson
HWB	H. W. Buckbee
NBG	Northrup, Braslan & Goodwin
GR	Green's
AFB	*American Fruit Book*
HOV	*The Fruits of America*

Much of the material for the book was gathered directly through interviews, correspondence, and questionnaires. To help readers trace sources, the verb "says" is used to identify material that comes from direct communication with the author. The verb "writes" indicates that materials come from published sources, which are generally cited in the text. Readers who want fuller citations are directed to the bibliographies at the back of the book.

Acknowledgments

THIS BOOK EXISTS BECAUSE A FEW REMARKABLE PEOPLE have chosen to make heirloom fruits and vegetables an important part of their lives. Kent Whealy of the Seed Savers Exchange, Robert Becker of the New York State Agricultural Station, Jan Blum of Seeds Blum, Dr. Louis Bass of the National Seed Storage Laboratory, Tom Woods of the Oliver H. Kelley Farm, and Dr. David Percy of the National Colonial Farm deserve special thanks for their willingness to help me with my research as well as their thoughtful comments on the manuscript.

Much of the information for the book was gathered through questionnaires and correspondence, and I am grateful to all the representatives of seed companies, curators for living historical museums, and individual collectors who responded. The following people were particularly generous in sharing what they know about heirloom fruits and vegetables: Carl Barnes, Lynne Belluscio, Will Bonsall, L. J. Butler, Tom and Judy Butterworth, Kim Cary, Russell Crow, Desmond Dolan, Craig and Sue Dreman, Glen Drowns, Elwood Fisher, Richard Grazzini, Lawrence Hills, Jim Johnson, Rob Johnston, Thomas

Knoche, Robert Kurle, Robert Lobitz, O. J. Lougheed, Gary Nabhan, John Rahart, Darrell Rolerson, Eric Roos, William Ross, Leroy Schmidbauer, Terry Sharrer, Willis Skrdla, Ralph Stevenson, Ted Telsch, Albert Vasquez, James Whitman, and John Withee.

Finally, I must thank Joan Faust, garden editor of the *New York Times*, who first asked me to look into the Seed Savers Exchange; Rosalind Creasy, for loaning some of the valuable old seed catalogues from which illustrations are reproduced; my editor, Diana Landau, who shepherded the book through the publication process; and other Sierra Club Books staff and freelance personnel: copy editor Linda Gunnarson, book designer Christine Taylor, and production supervisor Susan Ristow.

PART ONE

A Heritage
of Fruits and Vegetables

I

Living Heirlooms

INDIVIDUALS IN EVERY GENERATION MUST DECIDE what they will preserve for those who follow. Some hope to leave fortunes, homes, or works of art. Others want to pass on peace, freedom, or religious faith. Today, growing numbers of people are trying simply to save the other living things that populate our planet. They want their children to know whooping cranes and blue whales, Esopus Spitzenburg apples and Hopi blue corn.

Apples? Corn? How did they get on the endangered list? We see apples in every market; many of us grow corn in our gardens. Yet these two varieties, prized only a hundred years ago for their unusually fine flavor, have come close to extinction. Although they were rescued and are now being preserved as heirlooms, hundreds of other old fruit and vegetable varieties have quietly disappeared.

Why should we mourn the passing of these old varieties? Does it really matter that no one will ever again taste Red Narragansett corn, Alma Gem melons, or Mr. Topp tomatoes? More to the point, why should we mobilize our efforts and resources to save the old varieties that still exist?

Though there are many answers to these questions, most can be distilled into a single word: choices. The essence of freedom is the opportunity to choose among alternatives. When choices are unnecessarily limited, so is freedom. In a world that is changing so rapidly, one of the most meaningful things we can preserve—for ourselves as well as future generations—is a full range of possibilities, so that we—and they—will be able to make good choices in situations we cannot yet foresee.

By keeping heirloom fruit and vegetable varieties alive, we preserve choices in food, our most essential commodity. Many of the old varieties were extraordinary in one way or another. Red Narragansett corn was popular in the 1860s because it matured extra early and its reddish kernels were particularly tender. Alma Gem melon was so delicious that it brought prosperity to the entire town of Alma, Illinois. Mr. Topp tomato produced fruit even in the coldest seasons. However, despite their unique qualities, these varieties and countless others like them have disappeared.

Vanishing Varieties

Kent Whealy, founder of the Seed Savers Exchange and one of the whistle blowers on the loss of old varieties, describes seed lists from the turn of the century: "The names of bean varieties covered six standard-sized pages of single-spaced typing paper. Pea varieties covered four similar pages. It's estimated that less than 20 percent of these varieties have survived to today." The situation is just as serious for fruit. At the turn of the century, a scientist compiled a list of 8,000 apple varieties available in the United States. In 1981, when the U.S. Department of Agriculture prepared a new list, only 1,000 of those varieties could be found.

Some of the old varieties fell out of favor because tastes changed. Others have been neglected because they are not

Narragansett corn. *The plants of this variety are slender of habit, and produce but little forage. The ears, which are put forth low on the stalk, are eight or ten rowed, and quite small, seldom measuring more than five inches in length; the kernel is large, and, like other sugar varieties, shrivelled or wrinkled at maturity; the cob is red. It is tender, and of excellent quality, and, as a first early, is recommended for cultivation.* FB

suited to the mechanized conditions of contemporary agriculture. Still others are ignored because they are narrowly adapted to the growing conditions in a specific place or the tastes of a particular ethnic group.

Whatever the reason, each time we permit an old variety to become extinct, we sacrifice part of our heritage. Those who ask why we need more than a few varieties of beans or corn might as well wonder why a library needs more than one book on a subject. Each heirloom variety has distinctive characteristics. One grows in clay; another in sand. One tolerates drought; another does best in humid conditions. One keeps well; another is resistant to disease. The list of characteristics is endless. As many as 10,000 genes combine to make each variety unique.

Not all of the old varieties can be cultivated today. Many do not meet modern production standards; others are not attuned to contemporary tastes. Some are particularly susceptible to disease or spoilage. Yet even flawed varieties are worth preserving, if only as a bundle of genes. Many plants that seem undesirable on the surface have been found to contain specialized genes that control everything from flavor to disease resistance. Indeed, genes for disease resistance are often found in weedy plants that don't have particularly good flavor. In the past, scientists preoccupied with flavor or yield or some other characteristic may have allowed the extinction of varieties that could, today, supply downy mildew resistance in cucumbers or smut resistance in corn.

GENETIC RESOURCES

Just as important, the varieties that are being allowed to die out today may contain characteristics needed in the future. As humans alter the environment, we will need food crops that can produce despite new stresses. In the future, breeders may be looking for plants whose leaves are unaffected by acid rain, crops that can tolerate high levels of carbon monoxide, or varieties that provide essential nutrients that haven't yet been identified. It is impossible to know just which characteristics we will want in our future crops; so it is foolish to deplete any source of genes. At the simplest, heirloom varieties represent a reservoir of genetic possibilities.

Thanks to modern plant breeding, scientists can dip into that reservoir and recombine the genes. By crossing parent varieties that have desirable characteristics, scientists create new varieties superior to the parents because they incorporate only the parents' desirable traits. Plant breeding has produced dozens of improvements that consumers take for granted—lettuce enjoyed year-round because it tolerates shipping, tomatoes that are cheaper because less of the crop is lost to disease, oranges that have no seeds, and so on. Gardeners, too, have benefited from new varieties that resist disease, grow more compactly, and yield more abundantly.

There may be even more remarkable innovations ahead. With the new techniques of bioengineering, scientists can lift a single gene or a cluster of genes from one plant and embed it in another. When perfected, these techniques will accelerate plant breeding. The traditional breeding process is time-consuming because cross-pollinating two plants combines their genes at random. Breeders must "grow out" thousands of seedlings to get a plant that has the right combination of genes and then must make more crosses to breed out undesirable characteristics. As a result, breeding a new vegetable variety takes several years; breeding a new fruit variety may take a lifetime. By enabling breeders to be more selective about the genes they combine, genetic engineering should drastically reduce the time needed to develop new varieties.

Scientists are even more enthusiastic about the possibility of transferring genes from one species to another. Breeders have never been able to breed the cold-hardiness of cabbage into to-

Egyptian Blood Turnip beet. *A variety from Europe. In form, like the Flat Dutch Turnip. Color deep blood red. Of medium size and cooks remarkably tender and sweet. The seed is very small and sparingly produced.* DM

matoes because tomatoes won't set seeds from cabbage pollen. However, scientists now believe that it may be possible to lift specific genes from one species and insert them into another. The implications of this process would be nothing less than revolutionary. Corn, for example, requires large infusions of expensive nitrogen fertilizer. Legumes such as beans and alfalfa have the capability of taking nitrogen from the air and "fixing" it in a form that can be used by plants. Scientists now speculate that someday they may be able to make corn a self-fertilizing crop by transferring the nitrogen-fixing gene from beans to corn.

Endangered Genes

Bioengineering enables scientists to manipulate genes more easily, but it does not enable them to create new genes. Though scientists can cause genetic changes or mutations with radiation, the chances of coming up with a gene for some useful characteristic, such as disease resistance, are remote at best. For the foreseeable future, we will continue to be dependent upon nature's reservoir of genes, a reservoir that we are draining at an alarming rate. Both wild and domestic plants are imperiled, though in many ways the distinction is academic. Domestic plants are nothing more than wild plants that commanded attention, often from primitive people, because they were more edible than other plants. At first, people sought out these plants during their nomadic travels; then they began to arrange for them to grow in more convenient places. Naturally, the plants that produced the largest edible parts or had some other advantageous characteristic received preferential treatment. In this way, the Incas "bred" plump tomatoes, Middle Eastern gardeners fattened the root of the carrot, and Chinese farmers in the eleventh century shortened the growing season of rice from 180 to 100 days.

In other words, while wild plants were evolving in response to natural pressures, domestic plants were changing in response to human pressures. Just as wild plants that grow in a valley are subtly different from plants of the same species on a neighboring hillside, so crops grown by a valley farmer who saves seed year after year have slightly different genes from the crops grown by a hillside farmer, even if both start with the same variety.

The genetic variations in wild and domesticated crops are a precious resource. Both are endangered; yet wild species often grab the headlines. In his disturbing book *The Sinking Ark*, Norman Myers points out that the earth's supply of species is being depleted more rapidly than several of its most precious mineral deposits. "Of the planetary stock of 5–10 million species, one species disappears each day," he observes. "By the end of the 1980's, the figure could be as high as one an hour." Myers's figures refer to both plants and animals. The situation for plants has also been documented by the International Union for the Conservation of Nature. The IUCN's Threatened Plants Committee estimates that 10 percent of the world's known flowering plants are "dangerously rare or under threat."

Both of these reports concentrate on species, which, in the biological hierarchy, are plants that share common characteristics. In a botanical name such as *Phaseolus vulgaris*, the second word refers to the species, in this example common kidney beans. Yet, as most gardeners know, the species *Phaseolus vulgaris* can be further subdivided into hundreds of varieties. Some varieties evolve in nature; others, called *cultivars*, are deliberately bred to have useful horticultural characteristics. Since the origins of many heirlooms are uncertain, they are usually described as varieties. As such, they often do not attract the attention of scientists who are concerned about saving species. Though many bean varieties may be imperiled, *Phaseolus vulgaris* is in no danger of extinction.

Improved Golden Wax bean. *One of the best dwarf beans grown; pods are large, long, brittle and entirely stringless, of a rich golden wax color, and six days earlier than the ordinary wax; very fine both as a snap bean and a shell bean for winter use.* NBG

Focusing on wild species leaves many Americans with a sense of impotence since most endangered species are located in underdeveloped countries. Though North America has some endangered plant species, the native flora is limited compared to that of other continents. The Mississippi River Valley, for example, has only one-eighth the native plant species to be found in the Amazon Basin. The continent is particularly poor in wild relatives of cultivated food crops. If we were required to eat only crops which originated in North America, our diets would consist of little more than Jerusalem artichokes, cranberries, blueberries, strawberries, pecans, and sunflower seeds.

The Evolution of Heirlooms

It is the shortage of native North American food crops that has led to an influx of plants from other places. From the beginning, immigrants to this country brought their plants with them— corn from Mexico, tomatoes from Peru, carrots from the Netherlands, peas from France, onions from Portugal, cabbage from Germany. Today, this rich collection of domesticated plant varieties is as much in need of preservation as the wild species in other countries. Some of these "folk" varieties have found their way into seed catalogues, but many are heirlooms, passed from one generation of gardeners to the next. Presently, all are vulnerable to economic and agricultural forces that are driving them into extinction. Though the need to preserve wild species in foreign countries is urgent, Americans are faced with the equally formidable challenge of salvaging a rich heritage of domestic heirlooms.

Most heirlooms have been replaced in common use by "improved varieties"; yet heirlooms themselves have often been improved by gardeners who reserved only the finest plants for seed stock. Gradually, their varieties changed genetically to adapt to local climates as well as to the tastes and preferences of particular families. Although the process of selecting the best plants for seed was largely intuitive, it received scientific validation from Charles Darwin's theories of natural selection. Armed with those theories, nineteenth-century plant breeders began selecting not only to enhance crops but to alter them. The sugar content of the sugar beet, for example, was tripled through their efforts. Other improvements were made by observant gardeners and farmers who noticed plants that were different from all the rest and saved their seed. These kinds of "discoveries" were responsible for some of our finest heirlooms, including Henderson's bush lima bean and Golden Bantam corn.

In the late nineteenth and early twentieth centuries, improving plants by selection was possible because all the crops being grown were open-pollinated. An open-pollinated crop produces seed when its flower accepts pollen from itself or from another representative of the same variety. Open-pollinated plants of the same variety have many genes in common, but each plant is slightly different from its neighbor. Through cross-pollination of neighboring plants, genes are constantly being shuffled and reshuffled. Occasionally, the reshuffling results in an extraordinary new variety, but usually it produces minor modifications. Though these variations may go unnoticed by the gardener, they work to his or her advantage. A gardener who saves seed from the best plants year after year will gradually produce a variant strain that is perfectly adapted to the local climate and soil, not to mention the gardener's own taste.

PLANT BREEDING COMES OF AGE

Selection was the only sort of breeding being done until the turn of the century, when Mendel's laws of genetics were rediscovered. (Mendel had started his painstaking observations of peas in 1843, but when he presented his conclusions in 1865, his contemporaries did not grasp their importance. In 1900, three other botanists confirmed his findings.) With a clearer understanding of genetics, scientists began making deliberate crosses to marry the desirable genes in two parent varieties. One of the first success stories was that of a Swedish scientist who raised the productivity of Swedish wheat 25 percent by combining the winter resistance of Swedish field wheat with the high yield of English square wheat. This accomplishment stimulated other breeders, and soon dozens of new varieties of other grains and vegetables were appearing in seed catalogues.

Some of the new varieties were open-pollinated but many were hybrids. Unlike open-pollinated crops, which have slight genetic variations between individual plants, each plant of a hybrid variety is identical to its neighbor. To produce such uniformity, breeders start with promising open-pollinated varieties. Instead of allowing the plants to cross-pollinate with each other as they would in a garden, the breeders hand-pollinate each flower, using pollen from the same plant. This process, called *selfing*, is repeated for as many as ten or twelve generations. The inbreeding results in many weak or deformed plants, which are weeded out, until the breeders have a generation of acceptable plants that are genetically uniform. When seeds from the inbred line are planted, they produce identical plants.

Having assured the purity of the inbred lines, breeders begin crossing them until they hit upon a combination that produces a new variety superior to either of the parent varieties. Because the parent plants are genetically identical, the hybrids are uniform too. They also display a characteristic known as *hybrid vigor*, an unusual productivity that appears only in the first generation. Seeds harvested from hybrids are often sterile and never display the productivity of their parents.

Seed companies benefited from hybrids because the company that developed a new variety could keep its parentage secret and be the exclusive source of seed. Though farmers and gardeners could save their own seed from open-pollinated va-

Early Sugar Loaf cabbage. *The color of this variety and the form of its head, distinguish it from all others. The plant, when well-developed, has an appearance not unlike some of the varieties of Cos lettuce; the head being round and full at the top, and tapering thence to the base, forming a regular inverted cone.* DM

rieties, with hybrids they were obliged to buy fresh seed from the company each year. Most farmers willingly paid the premium prices because the increased yields from hybrids more than offset their cost. During the first fifty years of the twentieth century, hundreds of old, open-pollinated varieties were dropped in the rush to hybrids. In 1930, 1 percent of Iowa's corn cropland was devoted to hybrids; by 1943, farmers were planting nothing but hybrid corn varieties. The advantages were obvious—with hybrids, farmers could grow 50 percent more corn on 25 percent fewer acres. The story has been the same for other crops. Potatoes went from 61 bushels per acre in the 1930s to 251 in the 1970s. Tomatoes increased from 61 bushels per acre to 166 bushels. The improved crops weren't always hybrids, but as long as they increased yields, farmers and gardeners gladly abandoned the old in favor of the new.

The Risks of Uniformity

It is, of course, impossible to criticize such gains in productivity. The success of plant breeders has made the United States the best-fed nation in the world, with plenty of extra to sell or share with others. Yet the very success of the breeders has created dangers. For one thing, the mass planting of new crops that are genetically uniform is an invitation to epidemics. Because all the plants are alike, a disease or insect that attacks one, attacks them all. This fact was tragically illustrated by the Irish potato famine in the 1840s. The Irish depended upon a single strain of potato, called Lumper, which had been imported from the Caribbean in the 1600s. Because potatoes are propagated from tubers, all the plants in the country had the same genetic background. When a new blight appeared, none of the plants had genes for resistance and the entire crop was wiped out.

More recently, the same problem occurred in the United States. In the late 1960s, corn breeders began using Texas (T) cytoplasm because its genes rendered the male plant sterile, eliminating the expensive process of detasseling the corn crop to ensure proper pollination. A proliferation of variety names concealed the fact that a large proportion of the corn crop was based on the same genetic combination. In 1970, a blight attacked plants with the Texas (T) cytoplasm and wiped out 15 percent of the U.S. corn crop. In a report on that epidemic entitled "Genetic Vulnerability of Major Crops," the National Academy of Sciences warned that many U.S. crops depended on a narrow genetic base. The report, issued in 1972, noted that one variety of sweet potato accounted for 69 percent of the acreage devoted to that crop; 76 percent of the bean crop was made up of three varieties; and virtually the entire pea crop was comprised of just two varieties.

The report noted that the demand for uniformity comes from both consumers and farmers. In the marketplace, consumers associate quality with particular varieties. "The lettuce breeder must produce a Great Lakes heading type, the pea breeder an Alaska or Perfection type, the snap bean breeder a Tendercrop or Blue Lake type and so on," the report pointed out. Uniformity is also attractive to farmers because it means they can use machinery to plant, cultivate, and harvest the crop. "Plants which lag behind by as much as a day or two often act as 'weeds' to the main crop," the report observed.

ABANDONED VARIETIES

Old, open-pollinated varieties rarely display the uniformity desired by consumers and farmers; so hundreds and perhaps thousands were allowed to disappear. Scientists have been most concerned about the loss of varieties in foreign countries where primitive varieties, grown for centuries by native farmers, have been replaced by the new crops. Since breeders often used the

Early Frame carrot. *Root grooved or furrowed at the crown; roundish or somewhat globular; rather more than two inches in diameter, nearly the same in depth, and tapering suddenly to a slender taproot. Skin red, or reddish-orange; brown, or greenish where it comes to the surface of the ground. . . . the earliest of all varieties.* FB

primitive varieties to infuse vigor into modern varieties, their loss has been felt most keenly.

The same process has been occurring in this country, encouraged by seed companies that find it more profitable to promote and sell large quantities of a few new exclusive varieties than to stock small quantities of many old traditional varieties. Seed companies insist the varieties that are being dropped from their catalogues are inferior. "A return to the heirloom varieties by the American home gardener would be equivalent to us returning to medieval medicine," says Larry Hollar, president of Hollar and Company, a seed-growing firm. "I would rather have leeches stuck to my forehead and blood let out of my veins to heal me than to plant any varieties that have not been produced in the last twenty to forty years."

The same idea is echoed by former Secretary of Agriculture Robert Bergland. "The prediction that by 1991 three-fourths of all vegetable varieties grown now will be extinct may prove to be correct," Bergland is quoted as saying. "Obsolete varieties are being replaced by improved varieties which are adapted to extended areas of agriculture." Statements like these from public officials reveal a distubing lack of understanding. First, extinction means that even the genes of old varieties are unavailable for breeding, and, as we have seen, planting the same varieties over "extended" areas is nothing less than an invitation to epidemic.

Certainly, some of the new varieties represent significant improvements that benefit both commercial growers and home gardeners, but many other introductions are, in the words of the National Academy of Sciences, "minor modifications" that do not justify the elimination of old varieties. Kent Whealy makes a distinction between varieties dropped before and after World War II. "Many of the vegetables that were dropped during the first half of this century *were* replaced by superior varieties, but that hasn't generally been the case for the last twenty years," he explains. Whealy points out that most breeding being done today is tailored to commercial growers, so the new varieties are less suited to the needs of the home gardener. As a vegetable gardener, he believes that the heirloom varieties still available today are best for home gardeners.

Why Gardeners Grow Heirlooms

More and more gardeners seem to agree with Whealy. Acting individually and cooperatively, they have built a grassroots network to save the old varieties. Why do they care? If new varieties are better than the old, why keep the old? First, when it comes to food, "better" is a subjective term. A mere hundred years ago, people preferred green cantaloupes and white roasting corn. Today, our tastes have changed, just as certainly as the tastes of the next generation will be different too.

The idea that old varieties taste better than new ones is hotly contested by breeders who insist that old peas are starchy, old radishes are woody, and old beans are stringy. Yet heirloom gardeners are just as adamant in insisting that they like the old varieties better. And perhaps that's the point. As the old saying goes, "There's no accounting for taste," and heirlooms enable gardeners to indulge individual preferences even when they are eccentric.

Other gardeners are drawn less by taste and more by curiosity. Most long-time gardeners appreciate a challenge and find their curiosity piqued by names such as Hundredweight pumpkin, Ice Cream watermelon, and Blue Queen beans. Many are intrigued by the fact that the varieties have been around for so long. "If a vegetable variety has survived a hundred and twenty years, it has something good about it," says one heirloom enthusiast, "and a gardener may as well have a look."

Some gardeners find themselves caught up in the history of old varieties, which, in many cases, is entangled with the history

Sugar pumpkin. *Fruit eight or nine inches at its broadest diameter, and six inches in depth; form much depressed, usually broadest near the middle, and more or less distinctly ribbed; skin bright orange-yellow when the fruit is well ripened, hard and shell-like, and not easily broken by the nail; stem quite long, greenish, furrowed and somewhat reticulated; flesh of good thickness, light yellow, fine grained, sweet and well flavored . . . The variety is the smallest of the sorts usually employed for field cultivation. It is, however, a most abundant bearer . . . For pies, it is not surpassed by any of the family.* FB

of their own families. Many of the oldest heirlooms have survived because they were passed down from generation to generation. Taking responsibility for some of those varieties gives gardeners a feeling for their roots in every possible sense. Unlike dry facts and dates, heirloom varieties provide an opportunity to taste and touch a genuine part of the past. Still other gardeners use heirloom vegetables and fruits to recapture a past that is more personal. They may seek a particular sweet corn that evokes memories of childhood cookouts, or a great-aunt's turnip that tasted better than any of the catalogue varieties, or an apple tree like the one raided in adolescence.

Nostalgia may motivate a gardener to experiment with old varieties, but the relationship is usually cemented by the fact that old varieties perform well in home gardens. Heirloom varieties were grown before gardeners had access to sprays or fertilizers or techniques for irrigation. They made do with whatever nature provided and often produced bountifully on those rations. By contrast, modern varieties are often bred to meet the needs of commercial growers, who think nothing of spraying apple trees fifteen times a season.

OLD VS. NEW VARIETIES

The concerns of commercial growers are often at odds with the needs of home gardeners. Uniformity, the sine qua non for commercial growers, is at best a nuisance for home gardeners. Commercial growers want everything to ripen at once so they can harvest the lot when their mechanical pickers go on search-and-destroy missions through the fields. Most home gardeners would rather have their beans ripen gradually so they can pick just enough for dinner every other day. Commercial growers want uniformly sized vegetables so they can be processed more easily. Home gardeners do better with tomatoes in several sizes so that some can be used for for sandwich slices, some for salad wedges, and others for stuffing or sauce. Commercial growers like tough vegetables that ship well. Home gardeners are perfectly willing to coddle their vegetables on the trip from garden to kitchen.

The interests of commercial growers usually take precedence with breeders. Breeding is tremendously expensive, and companies rightfully feel that they are most likely to recover their investment by producing a supermarket variety. On the other hand, many gardeners raise their own vegetables because they are dissatisfied with the quality of supermarket produce. When they turn to the glossy seed catalogues, however, they often find the same standardized varieties. In contrast, heirloom varieties offer a cornucopia of choices. Instead of standard green beans, heirloom gardeners can raise beans with pods of any color from ice white to royal purple and seeds ranging from the ebony of Black Valentine to the swirling browns of Missouri Wonder.

Heirloom varieties are also more likely to be adapted to regional variations in climate and soil. Seed companies are impatient with these regionally adapted varieties, preferring to stock a few all-purpose varieties that do reasonably well everywhere. Selling ten common-denominator varieties is more efficient than selling a hundred heirlooms. But heirloom gardeners know that nature thrives on messy diversity. The bean that grows best in the garden on a southern slope fertilized with manure will be subtly different from the bean that grows best in a valley garden enriched with leaf mold. Heirloom varieties that have been cultivated in the same place for decades or even centuries are fine-tuned to the conditions of that place in a way that common-denominator vegetables can never be.

A GARDENER'S LEGACY

Finally, heirloom varieties appeal to some people simply because they offer a concrete opportunity to do something about

Improved Red Valentine bean. *In some sections, the Valentine bean is considered to be the best snap variety in existence. They bear tender and fleshy pods, while for a pickling bean it is one of the best. The introducer says this new variety is fully ten days earlier than the old sort, being more prolific and retaining all the excellent qualities of its parent.* PW

an increasingly urgent problem. "The one process ongoing in the 1980's that will take millions of years to correct is the loss of genetic and species diversity," writes Edward O. Wilson, professor of comparative zoology at Harvard. "This is the folly our descendants are least likely to forgive us." Although individuals may not be able to save the Bengal tiger or the California condor, each gardener can commit him- or herself to saving one or two fruit or vegetable varieties. If a quarter of America's gardeners made that commitment, thousands of endangered varieties would be preserved.

Gardeners are not alone in their struggle to save heirloom varieties. Museums have begun to preserve old varieties as seriously as they preserve old buildings and tools. Small seed companies have stepped in to sell varieties dropped by the multinational giants. Even the federal government has renewed its commitment to preserve plant materials in the National Seed Storage Laboratory in Fort Collins, Colorado.

These efforts, as described in succeeding chapters, require the back-up of gardeners who will simply grow the heirloom varieties year after year. A 1978 report from the National Academy of Sciences entitled "Conservation of Germplasm Resources" concludes that "after weighing all available measures for preserving endangered species under controlled conditions, we are repeatedly forced to the conclusion that the only reliable method is in the natural habitat." For fruits and vegetables, that habitat is home orchards and backyard gardens.

Some gardeners will grow the old varieties because they believe they are genuinely better than modern varieties; some will grow them just to perpetuate their genes so they will be available for future use. Either way, heirloom gardeners are part of the self-reliant American tradition of pitching in to save a heritage of choice and freedom. Caught between the past, which often seems quaint but irrelevant, and the future, which bears down on us with unseemly speed, many of us grope for something that we can accept from our ancestors and pass on to our children without apology. For more and more gardeners, heirloom seeds are just such an inheritance.

PART TWO

Who Is Saving the Seeds?

2

One Thousand Different Beans

EVERY SPRING, JOHN WITHEE OF LYNNFIELD, Massachusetts, picks up his hoe and heads to the garden to plant his beans. Like other gardeners, he marks out rows, loosens the soil, and makes shallow furrows. Unlike other gardeners, he plants several hundred different beans—the huge, red and green Christmas lima and the tiny, black Bird Egg bean, early American favorites like Lazy Wife and ancient Native American beans like Jacob's Cattle, pole beans like Uncle Quimby and bush beans like Nova Scotia.

John Withee may have the country's largest private collection of old seeds—he has more than a thousand named varieties of beans—but he is not the only collector of heirloom varieties. Dozens of collectors share his fascination with beans, and other gardeners are collecting old varieties of corn, tomatoes, carrots, squash, apples, grapes, and other crops. Unlike scientists who are paid to maintain collections of germplasm for their breeding potential, private collectors are self-appointed caretakers for varieties that are old, unusual, and neglected.

A few collectors are scientists who have united vocation and avocation, but most are amateurs who make a living in some other way. A few are farmers, but many make do with a garden plot behind the house. Most start innocently with a single variety that piques their curiosity. Somehow that first variety leads to another and another. Soon, to the amusement of friends and the amazement of mates, the cellar shelves are lined with jars, each containing the seeds of a unique and sometimes irreplaceable variety.

Not everyone can be a collector of heirloom fruits and vegetables. The work requires the persistence to ferret out rare old varieties, the patience to keep accurate records, and the commitment to keep the varieties alive by planting them year after year. Yet despite its demands, collecting heirloom varieties can easily become a sort of calling. Though others may think them eccentric, most collectors are tremendously dedicated to the preservation of the old varieties they've accumulated. Without waiting for anyone else to confirm the need, they have plunged in to save a heritage few others know about, much less appreciate. They are invisible heroes, who will receive the gratitude owed them when the varieties they've been saving from oblivion turn out to resist new diseases or to contain new nutrients. In the meantime, their example is an inspiration to anyone who still believes that individuals can make a difference.

The Bean Man

John Withee's story is as typical as stories about such remarkable people can be. He started gardening in 1927 when, as a boy, he contributed to the family finances by selling market vegetables. His family lived in Maine, where a staple dish was beans baked in a hole lined with hot coals, and it was John's job to dig the bean hole. Years later, when Withee had a home of his own in Massachusetts, he decided to revive the tradition.

Lazy Wife's Pole bean. *The pods, of a medium, dark-green color, are produced in great abundance, and measure from 4 1/2 to 6 inches in length . . . they retain their rich, tender and stringless qualities until nearly ripe, and at all stages are unsurpassed for snap—shorts being particularly luscious. Many persons have testified that they never ate a bean quite so good in rich flavor.* BP

The hole was easy, but he couldn't find the Yellow Eye beans that he remembered from his childhood. He went searching in Maine, where old-timers had heard of Yellow Eye beans but didn't grow them anymore.

Withee quickly expanded his quest to include other old and forgotten bean varieties. Whenever he had time off from his job as a medical photographer, he would travel, visiting food stores in ethnic neighborhoods and talking to anyone who expressed the slightest interest in beans. Gradually, the beans began accumulating until, today, his collection numbers about 1,200, including several baking beans remembered from his childhood. Withee readily acknowledges that the total includes duplications. "Scientific varietal names mean nothing to me," he explains. "If somebody sends me a bean and calls it Uncle Quimby's baking bean, so be it. I'm not about to change it." He also argues that a bean from Massachusetts has adapted to the climate in subtle ways that make it genetically different from a bean of the same name that has adapted to conditions in New Mexico.

The sheer size of Withee's collection distinguishes him from other collectors. Around 1975, he realized that he needed help to keep alive all the varieties he'd collected. "It's one thing to plant two hundred varieties," he explains, "but it's another to care for them, take notes, tie them up, and do everything else that needs to be done." So Withee started Wanigan Associates, a nonprofit organization whose name referred to the cooking shacks used by loggers in Maine. Members of the organization could order beans from Withee's collection if they agreed to return increased seed. Only 10 percent of the people who joined Wanigan Associates kept that agreement; many gardeners simply treated Withee's book of beans as yet another seed catalogue. In 1981, floundering in correspondence and unsorted beans, Withee decided to turn over the collection to the Seed Savers Exchange, where Kent Whealy promptly absorbed many of the rarer varieties into a Growers Network whose members keep them alive.

Today, Withee has small samples of each bean variety and grows one plant from each of five hundred varieties every year. "The risk of failure is evident," he says, "but the back-up of the Seed Savers reduces the odds on complete loss." Each seed is presprouted in optimum conditions and stored in a gelatin solution in the refrigerator until the ground temperature reaches 55–60°F; then it is planted. In the fall, Withee harvests the bean plants and threshes them in a large, funnel-shaped sack that he designed. After tying off the narrow end of the sack, he loads plants into the wide end and beats the sack with a stick. When the plants are broken, he hoists up the bag and unties the narrow end. The heavy bean seeds fall out of the hole and, if there's a breeze, the debris from the plants blows away.

Much of what Withee knows about beans is now in a book called *Growing and Cooking Beans*. Though he makes passing references to other species of beans, Withee, like most bean collectors, concentrates on the common, or kidney, bean because, as he writes, "their diversity in form, texture, color and taste [satisfies] every growing and eating requirement or desire among bean lovers." In the first half of his book, Withee shares his considerable knowledge about growing beans and offers a helpful table describing and giving sources for nearly two hundred beans that were available from seed companies in 1980. The second half of the book contains bean recipes that Withee has collected with the same enthusiasm as the beans themselves, including the famous recipe for bean-hole baked beans that inspired his collection in the first place.

MORE BEANS

Withee is not the only collector to become fascinated with old beans. Undoubtedly, part of the appeal is the fact that though many old bean varieties are rare, they do exist. Beans are difficult to hybridize—all the effort of hand-pollinating a flower produces only a few seeds—so most seed companies sell open-pollinated varieties, and more of the old-timers have survived. Home gardeners have also found it easier to keep heirloom bean varieties pure because the plant is self-pollinating, making crosses between varieties less likely. Finally, beans make a satisfying collectible because their seeds come in a beguiling array of colors and sizes.

"There's nothing you could get more good out of than growing beans," says Ralph Stevenson, a Michigan collector who finds bean collecting the ideal retirement hobby. "In the summer you got 'em growing, and in the winter you got 'em to look at." Stevenson's collection started with Jacob's Cattle bean, which was reportedly found in Native American ruins in the Southwest and dates back to 1200 A.D. Fascinated by the handsome seed with its maroon streaks, Stevenson started to look for other unusual old beans. His collection now numbers more than five hundred old varieties, but he continues to correspond with gardeners in hopes of finding varieties he doesn't have. Unlike Withee, Stevenson doesn't keep every bean he finds. If two beans with different names have identical seeds and growing habits, he combines the seeds and notes the names as synonyms.

Even with that attempt at keeping the collection manageable, Stevenson finds that propagating his beans is a staggering task. "I try to replenish half the collection every year," he says. "The beans are pretty much self-pollinating; so I don't need much space. Occasionally, the hummingbirds will cross the larger beans, but that just keeps things interesting." Although Stevenson plants a few crosses just to see how they'll turn out, his main concern is obtaining true seed, loyal to the characteristics of the parent plant. To do that, he plants short rows, carefully identifying them with numbered markers. Throughout

Dwarf Horticultural bean. *A most popular market variety; very productive and furnish green shelled beans as early as any and about equal to the Lima in quality. Pods medium in length, round, curved, with splashes of bright red on a yellowish ground.* NBG

the growing season, he takes notes about the progress of each variety.

In the fall, he picks the pods when they turn straw-colored, without waiting for the plants to dry. Each variety is spread on its own ventilated tray and left to dry outdoors for several weeks. Then Stevenson stuffs the plants into a gunny sack and pummels them with a stick. "I use a wooden stick on a wood floor so the bean seeds don't break up," he says, "and then I pour everything in front of an old electric fan to get rid of the chaff." Each variety goes into a numbered baby-food jar and spends thirty-six hours in the deep freeze to kill weevil eggs. Stored in a cool, dark place, the bean seeds will keep for three to five years, Stevenson figures.

The fact that bean seeds can be safely stored for several years was one of the reasons that Mark Fox, an Iowa insurance adjuster, started his collection. His first step was to go through seed catalogues looking for old varieties. Today, with 300 of the known 1,200 varieties, he continues to collect for the thrill of finding something new. "People think I'm not playing with a full deck," he says. "It *is* a lot of work, but I have great pride in the collection." Fox collects, in part, because he is disturbed by the loss of genetic diversity, and he finds that the easiest way to explain the concept is to take people into his bean patch. "Most people don't believe in the diversity—until they see it," he explains. "Then they are amazed that so many types of beans exist."

Fox also finds it challenging to identify the beans he collects. "This is obviously the real chore," he says. "You try and match description with bean and vice versa. But because of the unstable nature of the collectible, I am sure that today's Trout Bean is not exactly like it was fifty to a hundred years ago." Like other bean collectors, Fox depends heavily on *The Beans of New York*, a book containing thorough descriptions of cultivated varieties that was published in 1931 by the New York State Agricultural

Station. Now, however, he's planning his own book on beans, which will be a field guide with pictures and descriptions of different varieties.

Russell Crow, a bean collector from Illinois, has already compiled *A Hill of Beans*, a short booklet describing the beans in his collection. The copies he printed were quickly distributed to other gardeners, making Crow think that he should start a small seed company that would sell only beans. However, "the thing that cured me was trying to grow half an acre of beans for seed," he says. "There's so much involved, and you can always be wiped out by the weather." So Crow kept his job in a local auto plant and collects beans in his spare time. During the summer, spare time usually means three hours a day spent in the garden.

One of Crow's goals has been to find all the beans described in *The Beans of New York*. Several years ago, he drew up a list of varieties he hadn't been able to locate and requested them from the National Seed Storage Laboratory in Fort Collins, Colorado. Though the facility is supposed to be a kind of savings bank for old varieties, the staff was able to supply only seven of the eighty requested varieties—Wonder Wax, Corbett Refugee, Tiny Green, Seminole, Rival, Uniwalled Wax, and Full Measure. Crow, however, was not discouraged. "What amazes me," he says, "is that this far down the road in this century, there is still even this much, that people have bothered to keep this much alive."

Collecting Corn

Carl Barnes, an Oklahoma farmer, is equally surprised to find that so many heirloom varieties still exist, particularly for corn, the crop that he has been collecting since 1946. Unlike beans, hybrid corn varieties have been the norm for many years, and saving corn seed at home is more difficult because the crop cross-pollinates so easily. Though he is pleased that so many

Ellm's Early Yellow Field corn. . . . *without doubt the best variety of field corn for cultivation in the New England states. Ripens in ninety to a hundred days. The bright yellow ears measure ten to twelve inches long; they set low on the stalk, the cob is small, while the kernel is large. It is a very showy and handsome corn. In 1882 it took the first premium at the Hingham Agricultural Society Fair; being exhibited by Mr. Ellms.* PW

have survived, Barnes has a sense of urgency about saving open-pollinated corn varieties because he believes the world will need the genetic diversity they contain. "The hybrid corn in this country is developed from six basic lines," he observes, "and three of them are closely related. If something happens to those hybrids, we'll be in the lurch."

Barnes is so concerned about the problem that he founded an organization called CORNS, whose members are dedicated to preserving old, open-pollinated varieties, including teosinte, pod corn, flint corn, sweet corn, popcorn, and dent corn. "We have members who are preserving one variety and members who are preserving several dozen," says Barnes. "Altogether, we're keeping about a hundred open-pollinated varieties alive."

Three of those varieties are descended from the corn carried by Barnes's Cherokee ancestors over the infamous Trail of Tears in 1837. An even more ancient variety is Anasazi Corn, which was found in a dry Utah cave and estimated, by carbon dating, to be as much as eight hundred years old. Barnes's personal favorite is Yellow and White Old Hickory, which, he says, "tastes like corn, not sugar." Eventually he hopes to start a corn museum, displaying sample ears from as many varieties as possible. "I would really enjoy developing a traveling museum to educate people," he says. "I'd like to increase awareness about corn and spread the word about the work that all of us are doing."

Corn is a collectible that needs great patience since a breath of wind will cross-pollinate a variety and dilute the genes Barnes is trying to preserve. He notes that the pollen from sweet corn is particularly light. "Pollens from [field and dent corns] are more granular and heavy. They usually drift fifteen to twenty feet and then hit the ground," he observes. "Sweet corn pollen seems like it will sail forever."

As a result, he doesn't plant sweet corn and hand-pollinates most of his field corn. As soon as ears form, but before silks appear, he covers the seed ears with paper bags fastened at the bottom with rubber bands. Every other day, he checks to see whether the silks have emerged. When they do, he cuts off the tassel of each seed plant and shakes pollen onto the silk. Often he pollinates the ears again the next day. "You may not get perfect pollination with this method," says Barnes, "but at least you know the seed is true."

Not all corn collectors are trying to keep old varieties pure. Ernest Strubbe, a corn breeder in Minnesota, starts with old varieties and refines them to obtain brilliantly colored strains that he uses in unique corn mosaics. He's been collecting colorful corn since 1929, when he crossed a black popcorn with a yellow field corn. Some of the kernels were a beautiful bronze, so Strubbe patiently picked them out and planted them the following years. Each year he picked out the kernels with the purest bronze color and replanted them until all the kernels on each ear were a rich and uniform bronze.

Using the same technique, Strubbe has produced corn in every color of the spectrum. Though many display unusual solid colors, such as turquoise and orange, some have caps or stripes of contrasting colors. He is particularly proud of a green variety that he's been working on for nearly forty years. Strubbe's goal is to preserve as much variety as possible. "Back in the old days . . . you'd go to the county fair and people would exhibit all kinds of garden vegetables, all different kinds of corns," he recalled in an interview with Kent Whealy. "Today, you go down there and one or two hybrid companies show off some of their yellow corns, brag about their yields and that's your corn exhibit."

"WATCHING THINGS GROW"

Thomas Knoche is another collector who remembers the old-time fairs. In fact, his collection of unusual squashes and pumpkins began at the Circleville Pumpkin Show in Circleville,

Darling's Early corn. Stalk five feet in height and of slender habit; the ears are from six to eight inches in length, an inch and a half in diameter, and, when the variety is unmixed, uniformly eight-rowed; the kernels are roundish, flattened, pure white, when suitable for boiling—much shriveled or wrinkled and of a dull semi-transparent yellow, when ripe; the cob is white; best sorts for planting for early use, as it seldom . . . fails to perfect its crop. FB

Early Bush Scallop squash. *An early flat scalloped variety; color yellow; flesh pale yellow, tolerably fine grained and well-flavored; very productive; used when young and tender for boiling, and at maturity for making pies.* DM

Black Spanish watermelon. *Round, very dark green, with scarlet flesh and black seeds. It is not so large as some of the other sorts, but has a very thin rind, and a rich, sugary flavor.* DM

Ohio. As a child, he'd wander up and down the aisles, marveling at the size of one squash or the markings on another. Occasionally, he'd buy a particularly wonderful squash and keep the seeds. "As time went on, I just got more and more different kinds," he says. Some of those kinds include Estem squash, which dates back to 1888; Tennessee Sweet Potato pumpkin, which has unusually handsome markings; and Hundred-weight pumpkin, which is particularly tasty.

Keeping those varieties pure requires extra effort since squashes cross almost as easily as corn. To keep insects from cross-pollinating his collection, Knoche started by planting a single variety in each of five gardens. When his collection became so large that he had to replenish more than five varieties each year, he began pollinating by hand. The day before they would open naturally, Knoche clamps shut the female flowers on his squashes. Then he selects an appropriate male flower as a pollen donor and opens the female flower just long enough to dust the donated pollen inside. The female flower is sealed shut again so that the fruit that develops contains true seed.

Though squashes remain his first love, Knoche has expanded his collection to include beans, tomatoes, watermelons, potatoes, and corn. In total, he figures he's keeping about four hundred varieties. "I've always liked watching things grow," he muses. "It's interesting to see the different ways they develop. They all have their merits."

Learning the subtle distinctions among varieties is also part of the pleasure for James Whitman, a psychologist in Washington state who collects carrots. "I started because I like carrots," he admits, "but I'm finding great satisfaction in watching their patterns of growth." Carrots are a challenging collectible because they don't produce seed until their second year of growth, and then the flowers must be protected from foreign pollen. Whitman assures seed purity by using cloches, or hot caps, to cover the plants when they flower.

For Whitman, verifying the names of old varieties is "half the fun." Though he started collecting only a few years ago, he already has thirty-one carrot varieties. Some, such as Black Afghan, Little Finger, and Red Elephant, are old or novel; others are commercially available varieties that have desirable characteristics.

ECLECTIC COLLECTORS

In contrast, Albert Vasquez, a West Virginia collector, grows only varieties that are no longer available commercially. Vasquez, who has a background in economic botany, looks for domestic varieties that are "scarce and interesting," and he persuades friends who are visiting foreign countries to bring back seeds for unusual vegetables. "A friend, traveling in India, obtained Tinda, Kakri, black carrot, and brown chickpea, all in one lucky purchase," he enthuses. (Although the U.S. government has strict laws about importing trees, shrubs, and other plant materials, small quantities of vegetable seed can legally be imported from foreign countries. For more detailed information, request circular #Q37–4 from the U.S. Department of Agriculture, Animal and Plants Health Inspection Service, Federal Building, Hyattsville, MD 20782.)

To maintain his collection, Vasquez has devised several homemade implements for cleaning seed. For example, he makes small flails by attaching a short, hardwood dowel to a longer handle with a 100-pound test fish-line swivel. He also keeps his eyes open for sieves in various sizes to be used in cleaning seeds. These simple techniques enable him to maintain a collection of more than 224 varieties, including beans, tomatoes, potatoes, peppers, melons, and squashes. "There's a wealth of material people don't know about," he explains, "and once you get started, it's a sort of mania, like stamp collecting."

Ted Telsch is another collector who started accumulating

unusual varieties and can't seem to stop. His business takes him around the world, so he collects wherever he goes—tomatoes from Egypt, radishes from the Orient, squashes from Italy. "I try everything," he says. "It's a challenge to see what will grow here." For Telsch, "here" is Houston, where the weather is hot and humid, encouraging what Telsch calls "fungus amongus." He looks for varieties that will thrive under these conditions, particularly tomatoes. He's learned, for example, that the varieties most resistant to blight and fungus are Manapal and Manalucie, introduced by the University of Florida. Another favorite is Texas Ted, a tomato he developed by crossing Beefsteak with an unnamed variety. The tomato is just what Telsch likes—big, productive, and thin-skinned, unlike commercial tomatoes, which have thick skins for shipping.

Each year Telsch plants half of his collection and raises a dozen plants of each variety. He allows the strongest plant of each type to set fruit, but only from one flower cluster. He pinches off other blossoms and, eventually, all but one fruit from the cluster. "That way, the plant puts all its energy into making seed in one fruit," he explains. Telsch often gives tomato seedlings to neighbors or coworkers in exchange for a promise that each will save him a single tomato so that he can replenish his seed. He also likes the idea of spreading good varieties around. As he puts it, "Seed should be raised and swapped by individuals."

Spreading Seeds Around

John Wyche, a retired dentist in Oklahoma, has a philosophy similar to Ted Telsch's. Each year he distributes free seed to thousands of gardeners, particularly those who are needy or elderly. His collection of more than two hundred varieties includes some that are still sold by seed companies and some that have been passed from generation to generation by his Cherokee ancestors. One of these varieties is a purple and white Squaw corn, brought by his ancestors over the Trail of Tears in 1834. "I have kept the seeds of my fathers," he says. "I gave seed to my people so they would have food to eat, and I give seed to old people to bring a little happiness."

Getting seeds into circulation is also the goal of Darrell Rolerson, who thinks of himself as a curator of old seeds. Among other things, Rolerson distributes a "germplasm specimen kit," which includes starter packets for twelve heirloom varieties. "This kit includes a whole garden," says Rolerson. "Corn, beans, squash, cucumbers, tomatoes, and melons selected for the greatest variety and companionability—none of them will cross-pollinate." As a bonus, the kit also includes the Rugosa rose, which bears hips the size of plums.

Rolerson's own collection includes more than a hundred varieties. He is particularly interested in native strains of corn, beans, and squash—"the three sisters of the earth." One of his most prized varieties is the Aztec bean, which came to him as four seeds that had been rescued from an Aztec tomb. The huge bean has a startling purple color, and Rolerson distributes several hundred samples each year. Another find is a subarctic tomato that self-sows, enabling gardeners to have a perpetual tomato patch simply by turning plants under at the end of the growing season.

Rolerson lives off the coast of Maine on an island that he describes as an "ark for genetic preservation." Unlike many collectors who feel isolated in their interest, Rolerson has infected his neighbors with his passion for heirloom varieties. "Enthusiastic neighbors help me keep my collection going, even if they keep only a variety or two for me in their gardens," he explains. His ultimate goal is to develop an indigenous agriculture; so his want list includes "the hardiest strains with the broadest genetic base, which are already resistant to disease and insects, which bear early and abundantly, and whose flavors are pleasing even to a fussy gourmet."

OLD-TIME TOMATO FLAVOR

Flavor is a preoccupation for many collectors, including Leroy Schmidbauer, a New Jersey teacher who has been searching for tomatoes that epitomize the old-time flavor he remembers from his childhood. "The new hybrids may be disease-resistant and they may ship well," he admits, "but they just don't have that slightly acid taste of a good tomato." Schmidbauer's collection of nearly fifty varieties includes some especially flavorful finds, such as the Lapp tomato given to him by an Amish gardener. "The tomatoes handed down from generation to generation are often the best," he says, "but you really have to look for them." Another favorite is a nameless Italian sauce tomato that is shaped like a "giant banana pepper." Though he thinks this variety is unrivaled for size, meatiness, and flavor, Schmidbauer doesn't ever expect it to be commercially available because of its unorthodox shape.

Each year, Schmidbauer plants a third to a half of his collection in a sixty-by-sixty-foot space. For each variety, he takes seed from the third or fourth tomato of the first plant to set fruit. When the tomato is ripe, he cuts it in half, scoops out the pulp, and washes the seed clean in a sieve. Then he transfers the wet seed to a paper plate to dry thoroughly. Each seed variety is placed in a labeled envelope to winter in a cabinet in Schmidbauer's dry cellar. One of his dreams is a long-term storage program for old American tomato varieties.

Dr. John Rahart, a Colorado collector, is also concerned about storage. His goal is to develop a network of small, volunteer seed-storage facilities that would store locally adapted varieties. Dr. Rahart became aware of the value of such varieties

Apple-shaped tomato. *Fruit somewhat flattened, inclining to globular, depressed about the stem, but smooth and regular in its general outline. The size is quite variable; but if well-grown, the average diameter is two inches and a half, and the depth two inches. Skin deep, rich crimson; flesh bright pink, or rose-color—the rind being thick and hard, and not readily reduced to pulp when cooked. The Apple-tomato is early, hardy, productive, keeps well, and for salad and certain forms of cookery, is much esteemed; but it is more liable to be hollow-hearted than any other of the large varieties.* FB

when he moved to the Rocky Mountains. "Getting any tomato to grow at our location is near impossible with commercial varieties," he says. "So I was forced to seek local and specially adapted varieties, such as the Pink Meat tomato, which consistently produces golf-ball-size tomatoes even in our cool climate." Varieties grown by Native Americans in the region also interest him, and he has spent considerable time on reservations seeking out old varieties. "The more you collect, the more it intrigues you," he says. "You're always on the lookout for something old or interesting."

Dr. Rahart is also concerned about keeping the varieties he has found. With the help of Dr. Bruce Bugbee of Utah State University, he is trying to devise a simple, effective storage system that will allow home gardeners to safely keep seed for twenty to thirty years. "There are two ways to increase seed longevity," he explains. "You can control the temperature or the humidity. We've chosen to concentrate on humidity." To reduce the moisture content of seeds, Dr. Rahart combines equal weights of seed and silica gel in an airtight container. By experimenting, he has determined that small seeds such as tomatoes and peppers are ready for storage after twelve days, and larger seeds such as beans and corn are ready in fifteen days. At that time, the seeds are transferred as quickly as possible to airtight storage containers. Though Dr. Rahart hopes to organize several small storage depots using these techniques, he believes varieties have the best chance of survival if they're grown. "We assume that people won't deposit the seeds and forget about them," he says. "We expect that people will be growing these seeds. Long-term storage is back-up."

COLLECTING HEIRLOOM FRUITS

Fruit collectors don't worry about seed storage since most trees and berry bushes are propagated from cuttings. Once they have

Napoleon (Royal Ann) cherry. *Of fine appearance and the very largest size; yellow and amber, with bright red blush; flesh firm, juicy, delicious.* GR

acquired and rejuvenated an old variety, they can count on it living for several decades with minimal care. As a result, fruit collectors can and do amass enormous collections. Dr. Elwood Fisher, a professor of biology, maintains what is believed to be the nation's largest private collection of heirloom fruit varieties. His 2,000 fruit cultivars include 840 apples, 166 pears, 52 cherries, and smaller samplings of plums, almonds, jujubes, currants, gooseberries, peaches, nectarines, and many other nuts and berries.

Dr. Fisher had a head start because both sides of his family had always maintained large orchards in West Virginia, where he still lives. "When I was a boy, we grew our own fruits and vegetables," he recalls. "I figured 'Why stop?'" Because fruit trees survive even when they are neglected, Dr. Fisher has sought out old varieties in the mountains between New York and Georgia. Many of his best leads have come from people who were in charge of fruit displays at county fairs or from old-time circuit-riding ministers.

When he finds a variety that is not represented in his collection, he takes scions that are later grafted onto rootstock from trees of known reliability. He keeps careful records about where each tree was rediscovered, when it was grafted, what rootstock was used, how much fruit it produces, and whether it is susceptible or resistant to disease. As a biologist, Dr. Fisher has an interest in preserving genetic diversity, and he tests old varieties to compare them with modern cultivars. Finally, though, he collects fruit varieties because, in his words, "Gardening is the shortest way to happiness."

Though collecting old varieties is a rewarding avocation, it can be expensive. Most heirloom collectors pay for their efforts out of pocket; yet Dr. Roy Renfro of Denison, Texas, obtained a small grant to fund his collection of grape varieties. The Thomas Volney Munson Memorial Vineyard includes seventy-

Niagara Hardy White grape. *Bunch very large and handsome, often shouldered, compact; berries large, round; skin thin, tough, does not crack and carries well; has not much pulp when fully ripe, melting, sweet, with a flavor and aroma peculiarly its own, and agreeable to most tastes; ripens with the Concord, sometimes a little earlier.* GR

five varieties that Munson would have known when he wrote his classic *Foundations of American Grape Culture* in 1909.

Dr. Renfro assembled the collection with the help of state agricultural schools, the U.S. Department of Agriculture, and collectors around the world. He keeps careful records on the production of each variety and distributes detailed descriptions. He notes, for example, that America, a variety known in 1885, "endures the severest drought with ease" and "has passed through 27 degrees below zero without damage." An 1883 variety called Rommel has flesh like "sprightly melting jelly of the most delicate flavor."

FIELD CROPS

What Dr. Renfro is to grapes, O. J. Lougheed is to field crops such as wheat, oats, barleys, soybeans, peas, and flax. "Everyone else is collecting vegetables or fruits," he observes, "but field crops are at least as important." Lougheed became interested in grains in 1977, when he was living in the Pacific Northwest and heard about Marquis wheat. "It was considered an excellent variety for where I was living," he recalls. Indeed, 150,000 acres of Marquis had been grown in 1974, but by 1977 it had been replaced by semidwarfs and was considered obsolete. Lougheed finally obtained a sample of the wheat from an agricultural station and found that it lived up to its reputation.

Today, his goal is to acquire dependable varieties that are well suited to small farms with special climatic conditions, such as a short growing season, high altitudes, or low rainfall. To determine which varieties will thrive in such conditions, Lougheed grows his crops without fertilizer, and he weeds "if I get to it." He believes that his benign neglect allows varieties that are truly suited to a region to "show their stuff." Lougheed backs up his casual growing techniques with detailed records. For each

New Japanese millet. *Grows from four to seven feet tall, but is not harsh and woody, as other grasses are. This is one of the most profitable and valuable seed crops . . . Cows, calves and Heifers look with pleasure upon a field of Japanese Millet, and feed in happy contentment and flourish upon its luxuriant swath.* HWB

variety, he records the original source, the amount harvested, the year grown, and a full description of the plant, the seed head, and the individual seeds. His seeds are stored in glass jars with diatomaceous earth or wood ashes, which, he claims, keeps them dry and viable for five to thirty years. But Lougheed is impatient with long-term storage. "I plan on growing everything at least every five years because after five years one forgets what it looked like and how it grew," he writes in an entry in the *Seed Savers Yearbook*. "The seed is just setting [*sic*] there and it wants to grow . . . To deprive it of that, to stuff it in a tin can for the next 60 years seems to me the height of human arrogance. Let it grow!"

POTATOES IN EVERY COLOR

Robert Lobitz likes the growing but sometimes wishes he could put part of his collection in storage for a year or two. Lobitz collects potatoes, and each of his three hundred varieties must be planted every year if the variety is to be kept alive. As a "collector, experimenter, and breeder of potatoes," Lobitz also saves seed whenever a potato blossom sets fruit. Each seed produces a different variety, so he plants several hundred each year just to see what will develop. If a new variety has exceptional characteristics, such as disease resistance, a high yield, or an unusual color, it is added to the collection.

Lobitz's interest in potatoes started when he saw an advertisement for a blue variety. "The color is what caught my interest," he says. "Potatoes can have skins and flesh of black, buff, pink, brown, blue, purple, lavender, russet, red, yellow, or white. I have just about every color." One of his favorites for color is All Blue, once called Canadian Purple. His collection now includes wild relatives of potatoes as well as rare nineteenth-century varieties such as Early Rose, Bliss Triumph, Irish Cobbler, Burbank, and Rural New Yorker. His oldest variety is Garnet Chili, which was the first potato to resist the blight that caused the Irish potato famine.

Lobitz likes Hudson and LaSalle potatoes because they are so productive—one hill of LaSalle produced more than fifteen pounds of potatoes. Green Mountain, a variety dating back to 1855, is another Lobitz favorite because it keeps so well. In fact, Lobitz finds that many of the old varieties are better suited to the conditions home gardeners can provide. "The new potatoes are bred for commercial growers," he says, "so they may not store that well in the less-than-desirable conditions available to most home gardeners." Lobitz notes that many of the new potatoes cannot compete with the old. As an example, he cites two potatoes called Snowflake in his collection. One dates back to 1873 and one was released in 1961. "They are both white potatoes," he says. ". . . [but the 1873 variety] has a bigger plant and is a much better yielder."

Lobitz plants nine 700-foot rows of potatoes and grows six hills of each variety. It takes three months of part-time effort to harvest all the potatoes, which are then stored in an unheated cellar in marked wooden bins. The large potatoes are eaten during the winter, and the smaller ones are planted, uncut, in hills. Disease, which can be a problem for a potato collector, hasn't troubled Lobitz because he pays careful attention to the soil and rotates his crop each year. If he spots a diseased plant, he pulls and destroys it immediately. Convinced that other gardeners could have the same results, Lobitz wishes there were more potato collectors. "There are so many good varieties," he says. "It's a shame for any of them to die out since some grow best in one place and some in another."

STARTING YOUNG

Lobitz's sentiment is echoed by Glen Drowns, who says he collects simply because "I hate to see anything become extinct." As

Garnet Chili potato. *Plant of medium height, rather erect, sturdy, and branching; flowers abundant, white or pale purple, showy, and generally abortive; tubers large, roundish or oblong, purplish-red or garnet-colored; eyes not abundant, and of moderate depth; flesh nearly white, dry and mealy when cooked, and the size of the tubers considered, remarkably well flavored. Not early, but hardy, healthy, productive, and recommended for cultivation. Originated in 1853 by Rev. Chauncey E. Goodrich of Utica, N.Y. from the seeds of a variety received from Chili, South America.* FB a college student, Drowns is undoubtedly one of the youngest seed collectors. He started gardening at the age of two-and-a-half and took over the family vegetable garden at eight. Early in his teens, he noticed that some of the varieties he liked were no longer being carried by seed companies. He also came across a reprint of Burpee's catalogue from 1888 and was distressed by the number of varieties that were no longer available.

So Drowns started collecting and is, today, preserving a cornucopia of varieties. A recent catalogue of his collection lists 147 squash and pumpkin varieties, 42 kinds of corn, 40 bean varieties, 11 muskmelons, and several varieties each of parsnips, turnips, and peas. To assure the purity of his collection, he hand-pollinates everything except beans, peas, tomatoes, parsnips, lettuce, potatoes, and peppers. His careful records include information about size, days to maturity, taste, quality, and uniformity.

Like many collectors, Drowns often saves seeds because they have personal significance. One bean variety came from his grandmother, who gave him several seeds before she died. Only one bean germinated, but it produced the hundred seeds Drowns needed to keep the variety alive. Drowns also has the sense of mission that characterizes so many seed collectors. "I enjoy a challenge," he notes. "It isn't much of a challenge to order all of your seeds from some million-dollar corporation." He is also worried that changes in the seed industry will result in even fewer varieties being available. "The way seed catalogues are changing really scares me," he wrote in a recent entry in the *Seed Savers Yearbook*. "In a few years, people are going to wish they hadn't been so hasty in destroying part of our heritage."

THE COLLECTOR'S MISSION

As these thumbnail sketches suggest, collectors of heirloom varieties are a diverse group. They resemble other collectors in the

Early Horn carrot. *Root six inches in length, two inches and a half in diameter, nearly cylindrical and tapering abruptly to a very slender taproot. Skin orange-red but green or brown where it comes to the surface of the ground. Flesh deep orange-yellow, fine grained, and of superior flavor and delicacy. The crown of the root is hollow and the foliage short and small. . . . as a table carrot, much esteemed, both on account of the smallness of its heart and the tenderness of its fiber.* FB

eagerness with which they search for new acquisitions, the patience they exercise in caring for their treasures, and their willingness to educate themselves so they can recognize the truly rare when they see it. Yet for those who collect heirloom fruits and vegetables, the avocation is often tinged with urgency.

They usually start their collections for personal reasons. Some try to recapture the flavors of childhood; others want to find varieties that live up to adult standards of perfection. Most quickly find themselves reveling in the diversity of varieties. Then, quietly, they come to the realization that, without their intervention, some of that diversity would disappear. Most don't shout about their discovery. In the best tradition of American self-reliance, they simply take it upon themselves to save what they can. They willingly do the exacting work of record-keeping and hand pollination so they can keep their varieties pure and properly identified. They make space in their freezers and on their pantry shelves to accommodate their precious seed supplies. And they make a commitment to keep their varieties going, year after year.

This is not to say that collectors don't take pleasure in their work. Some weave a web of correspondence with new-found friends who share their concern about old varieties. Some use the quest for old varieties as an opportunity to indulge a passion for travel. Others discover a taste for historical research and spend long hours combing old publications for clues about mystery varieties. Still others find their greatest happiness in the garden, surrounded by evidence of nature's imagination and generosity.

Nevertheless, for all their differences, collectors of heirloom fruits and vegetables are united by their fundamental goal of preserving as many of the old varieties as possible. To outsiders, it may seem that their efforts are haphazard and redundant, but like other kinds of collectors, those who collect heirloom fruits and vegetables perform several valuable functions. For one

Early Frame cucumber. *One of the oldest of the garden sorts . . . Plant healthy and vigorous, six to ten feet in length; fruit straight and well-formed, five inches and a half long, and two inches and a half in diameter; skin deep green . . . flesh greenish-white, rather seedy, but tender and of an agreeable flavor. The variety is universally popular, and is found in almost every vegetable garden.* FB

thing, collectors do the field work that uncovers treasures over-looked by so-called authorities. Most major museums owe choice acquisitions to private collectors who had the patience to seek out and preserve objects that were fine or rare. In the same way, seed collectors develop an eye for varieties that are remark-able and worth preserving. Often these varieties are not repre-sented in "official" seed-storage facilities; so the collector be-comes the vehicle for their survival.

Even when private collectors duplicate varieties held by public seed-storage facilities, they perform an important role. Ironically, collectors of antiques are praised when they acquire a rare old piece, particularly if it is like one held by a major in-stitution. The efforts of seed collectors, on the other hand, are often dismissed because the varieties they are saving are also in public collections. The truth is that precious things are best pro-tected when they are held in several places. No one would sug-gest that all copies of the Gutenberg Bible should be preserved in the same place. It makes just as little sense to count on public seed-storage facilities to hold all our specimens of rare and valu-able old varieties. Private collectors provide layers of protection, ensuring that a variety that may be lost by one collection will still exist somewhere else.

Happily, unlike Gutenberg Bibles, seeds can be multiplied; so collectors also become distributors, sharing their stock with other gardeners who further multiply rare varieties. Here, too, private collectors have an advantage over public institutions, which are usually governed by exclusionary rules about who may obtain seed. Collectors are free to share with whomever they please. Through their generosity, collectors further broaden the base for heirloom varieties and increase the odds of their survival.

The work of seed collectors doesn't make headlines. The world still sees them as dentists, teachers, and factory workers.

Yet those who value plants and their diversity owe a debt of gratitude to John Withee, Carl Barnes, Robert Lobitz, and all the other collectors who have, without fanfare or tribute, dedicated themselves to the preservation of an irreplaceable living heritage.

3
Seeds To Share

WHEN THE NEWLYWEDS PLANTED THEIR FIRST garden together, her grandfather gave them seeds for a large Pink Potato-leaved tomato, a prolific pole bean, and a deep purple morning-glory with a red star in its center. All three had been brought from Bavaria when the family emigrated four generations before; so Kent Whealy dutifully planted them in his vegetable garden and harvested seed in the fall. That winter, the grandfather died, and Whealy suddenly realized he had been entrusted with a precious heirloom. "I simply knew," he says now, "that it was up to me to carry on the tradition by keeping those seeds alive."

So Whealy planted Grandpa Ott's seeds again, and this time they grew into a mission. Now in his thirties, Whealy is prophet, publicist, scribe, and den mother for the Seed Savers Exchange, a grassroots organization whose gardener members save and swap seeds from heirloom vegetable varieties. So far, Whealy estimates that his band of seed savers has arranged for 250,000 plantings of no fewer than 3,000 old varieties, many of which might have died out entirely were it not for their efforts.

The History of Home-grown Seed

Whealy didn't invent the idea of exchanging seeds, but he's given it new meaning for this century. A hundred years ago, most gardeners grew their own seeds and willingly exchanged with friends, neighbors, and fellow gardeners. This self-reliant habit began to die out in the mid-1800s, when the United States government started handing out free seed to introduce and establish new varieties. Worthy as that goal may have been, the government also began telling gardeners that home-grown seed was inferior. Distribution of free seed stopped around the turn of the century, but the notion that growing good seed was beyond the capability of ordinary gardeners persisted. Seed companies stepped in and gladly reinforced the idea. Soon many gardeners—though fortunately not all—thought the only way to get good seed was to buy it in packets.

The idea that growing your own seed was a backward habit was reinforced by an explosion in the number of hybrids. The process for hybridization was perfected early in the twentieth century, when plant breeders found that crossing two inbred varieties boosts vigor and productivity in the next generation. For some vegetables, notably corn, hybrids have increased yields dramatically. They also produced a dramatic increase in business for seed companies, partly because the company that discovered a hybrid jealously guarded its parentage and partly because seed gathered from hybrids is usually worthless. If the seeds are not sterile, the plants they produce revert back to one or the other of the original parents; so the exceptional vigor vanishes. As a result, farmers and gardeners who started planting hybrids had no choice but to purchase new seed year after year.

In contrast, heirloom varieties are open-pollinated, and seed gathered from a variety will be true to its parent as long as it doesn't cross-pollinate with another variety. Open-pollinated varieties were the rule a hundred years ago, but today, as anyone

White Silesian lettuce. *One of the largest of the cabbage-lettuces. Head golden-green, tinted with brownish red about the top, regularly, but not compactly formed. The exterior leaves are large and broad, yellowish-green bordered with brown, wrinkled and coarsely blistered. When well grown, the entire diameter of the plant is eighteen inches, and its weight twenty ounces. The seeds are white.* FB

who reads seed catalogues knows, most of the seeds being offered are for hybrid varieties. What happened to all the open-
pollinated varieties? Whealy estimates that 80 percent have disappeared, and he is digging in to save the remaining 20 percent,
not as artifacts in a museum or subjects in a laboratory, but as
living alternatives for gardeners.

An Exchange Is Born

Whealy has many reasons for wanting to save old varieties.
First, he notes that many hybrids, for all their vigor, are not particularly delicious. Others won't produce high yields without
infusions of fertilizer and pesticides. In contrast, a variety that
has been grown by the same family in the same place for 150
years performs well simply because it has adapted to local climatic conditions and resists local diseases and pests. "I am a vegetable gardener," Whealy says simply, "and I believe that the
standard varieties that are available today are the best home garden varieties that we will ever see. The vast majority of the vegetable breeding being done today is for commercial application,
and such varieties are seldom suited to the needs of the home
gardener. The old varieties are the vegetable gardener's heritage."

Whealy is also concerned that varieties dying out today may
be just the ones needed in the future. What, he wonders, will
happen if the earth's temperature becomes a few degrees
cooler—or warmer? What plants will be resistant to the diseases of the future? What plants will grow in soil that is contam-
inated or air that is polluted? "We really don't know what we'll
need," he concludes. "So we can't let anything go down the
drain. A plant that doesn't look terrific to us now may have just
the qualities that will allow it to thrive in the conditions of the
future."

Whealy didn't have all these concerns in 1973, when he took

responsibility for saving Grandpa Ott's tomato, bean, and
morning-glory. Then he was simply curious about whether
other gardeners were saving family heirlooms also; so he put notices in gardening publications, asking to correspond with other
seed savers. That first year he heard from six gardeners, including Lina Sisco, an elderly Missouri woman who had been raising a Bird Egg bean brought to the Great Plains by her grandmother in the 1880s. Whealy liked Lina Sisco's Bird Egg bean—
"It was a flavorful little bush variety"—so he started raising it in
his own garden. Sisco's death the following winter renewed his
determination to save such old and rare varieties.

Whealy started reading everything he could about endangered plants and was especially influenced by the writings of Dr.
Garrison Wilkes, a scientist who had witnessed the loss of old
varieties around the world. "Extinction of a native variety can
take place in a single year if the seeds are cooked and eaten instead of being used as seed stocks," writes Dr. Wilkes in a much
quoted article. "Quite literally, the genetic heritage of a millen-
nium in a particular valley can disappear in a single bowl of por-
ridge. The extinction of these local land forms and primitive
races by the introduction of improved varieties is analogous to
taking stones from the foundation to repair the roof." Though
Dr. Wilkes is preoccupied with the loss of varieties in the Third
World, Whealy applied his ideas to the United States and took
to heart his admonition that "the only place genes can be stored
is in living systems."

A Catalogue of Heirloom Varieties

By 1975 Whealy's grapevine of gardeners had grown to include
twenty-nine correspondents; so he printed up a six-page circular listing the varieties each person was willing to share or trying
to find. Today, the *Seed Savers Winter Yearbook* has grown to
more than two hundred pages, crammed with single-space list-

Robin's Egg bean. *A
rather branching kind,
with stems about 16
inches high, forming an
airy-looking clump.
Leaves medium-sized,
and of a lively green
color, those at the top of
the stem being small and
long-stalked; flowers
white; pods green, turn-
ing yellow when ripe,
each containing five or
six egg-shaped seeds of a
sulphur-yellow colour,
with a more or less bluish
circle around the hilum
. . . This variety is one
of the most widely culti-
vated in different parts of
the world.* AV

ings from nearly five hundred members. Happily, it still has the folksy feel of neighbors chatting over the back fence, largely because Whealy quotes freely from letters in which members share stories and information, gardening advice and homespun wisdom.

The rules governing the Seed Savers Exchange are simple. Anyone who has seeds to exchange can be a member, and each member has a yearbook entry listing seeds available and seeds wanted. Members can order seeds from each other for the price of postage. Those who do not qualify for membership because they don't have seeds to exchange can still participate by listing seeds they would like to locate in the yearbook's Plant Finder Service. They can also order seeds from members, though the prices are deliberately high—$1 per sample for small seeds and $2 for large—to discourage gardeners who might be tempted to treat the yearbook as a seed catalogue.

Though it doesn't have the glossy pictures associated with most seed catalogues, the yearbook is a fascinating compendium of old varieties. Many have tantalizing names, such as Fat Horse bean, Aztec Gold corn, Snowflake potato, and Brandywine tomato. Some entries trace the genealogy of varieties that have taken on the name of the family that saved them. One Californian has seeds said to be descended from a cache of 12,000-year-old wheat found in an Aztec tomb. Another is saving Mescher lettuce, given to him by an eighty-six-year-old teacher who had gotten it from "Granny Wallace," who had gotten it from her granny, who had been saving it from the early 1800s. A member who is offering top-setting onions brought by his great-grandmother, a widowed mother of eleven, from Indiana to Iowa by covered wagon in 1853, asks that the variety be called the Fleener Top Set onion in her honor.

Other members brag affectionately about the old varieties they have to exchange. A North Carolina member describes the White Cornfield bean, whose pods "hang in bunches of four to

eight like bananas and are very tender." An Ohio gardener recommends the Christey bean, a pole variety that has been in his
family for two hundred years and "grows good with no known
ills." An Arkansas gardener offers seed from an unnamed corn
given to him by an old man "who said it was the best eatin' corn
he ever had." "I'll agree with that," says the member, "and I also
know it makes the finest flour, hominy, and 'gritter' meal."

Other gardeners tell heartbreaking stories about lost vegetables. A woman from Arkansas wants to find Macedonia, a
green-fleshed melon that was "out of this world." "We were so
foolish to let the seed get away," she writes, "because when we
ordered it again, they [the seed company] had lost the seed." A
Minnesota gardener tells the story of the Stovewood bean,
which had seeds more than two inches across. "The pods were
so large you could put three or four fingers into the cut end of
it," writes the gardener. "My father raised them in Tennessee,
but in 1923, we moved north of Osakis, Minnesota, and a frost
got them but good. He never seemed able to get any more seed."
A breeder from Canada writes to lament the loss of the Mr.
Topp tomato, which was frost-resistant. "It had valuable characteristics that surpassed anything I have ever seen in other tomatoes," he writes wistfully. "I would give anything to secure
that one tomato gene again."

FINDING "LOST" VEGETABLES

For Whealy, the biggest reward of the Seed Savers Exchange is
finding varieties for people who have been looking for them, in
some cases for half a century. Though the Mr. Topp tomato, the
Stovewood bean, and the Macedonia melon are still to be found,
the Exchange has had successes with what were thought to be
extinct varieties. One of these is the Moon and Stars watermelon, which was on the "want" lists of several members and on

Mammoth Long Red
Mangel Wurzel beet. *A
large long variety, grown
for stock feed. It stands a
good deal out of ground.
The roots are uniformly
straight and well-
formed.* DM

a Lost Vegetables List compiled by Whealy. When, in a television interview, Whealy mentioned the variety as an example of a "vanished vegetable," a Missouri gardener promptly called to report that the melon could be found in his garden. Whealy paid him a visit and saw, for the first time, the dark green melons with their characteristic bright yellow spots, some as small as a pea and others as large as a silver dollar.

The Moon and Stars watermelon is now being protected and distributed through the Seed Savers Exchange, but Whealy worries that for each variety the organization finds, two are being lost. In one recent yearbook, he relays a story told by a North Carolina member about a neighbor who claimed to have a brown and white pole bean that had been brought over on the *Mayflower*. "A few years later, the man died of a heart attack," the member writes. "When I read that this bean was on the Lost Vegetables List, I got in touch with members of his family, but by that time his possessions were either dispersed or discarded."

Whealy believes that the same story is being repeated hundreds, if not thousands, of times each year across the country. He is particularly concerned about older gardeners who have been loyal to old varieties all their lives. "Every year I locate elderly bean or tomato collectors who are keeping literally hundreds of varieties," he explains. "But often their health is failing, and their collections will soon be lost."

To illustrate, he tells the story of Burt Berrier, a combine serviceman who traveled through the Midwest during the 1930s, when farmers were still combining fields of dry beans. He started collecting beans and over the next forty years accumulated nearly 450 varieties. Not wanting the collection to be lost, he asked the National Seed Storage Laboratory to take charge of the varieties after his death. The Laboratory, however, was unwilling to accept less than five pounds of bean seed per variety; so it turned the collection over to John Withee, the Massachusetts bean collector profiled in Chapter 2. Withee tried to replenish the seed, but by that time a third of the varieties were no longer viable.

Despite the loss of many varieties, Berrier's collection fared better than most seeds that sit on a shelf or are discarded after their owner dies. "Seed hoarders often amass impressive collections," says Whealy, "but when they die, there is often no transfer of seeds or knowledge about the varieties because they haven't prepared anyone to carry on." Among other things, Whealy's Exchange distributes seeds to people who are willing and able to keep the old varieties alive.

Berrier's case also illustrates the need for a private organization to supplement government storage facilities, which are ill-prepared to handle the small quantities of seed typical of private collections. Whealy believes his own organization can catch some of the varieties that fall through the cracks at large official collections such as the one in Fort Collins. "Government collections cannot perform our function," he explains. "They haven't the time or the funds to distribute seed to individuals. They also aren't making any systematic effort to locate heirloom varieties or to save varieties being dropped by commercial sources."

A LIFE'S WORK

Whealy's effort is nothing if not systematic. Trained as a journalist, he has arranged for stories about the Seed Savers Exchange to appear in newspapers, gardening publications, and other media. He worries, however, that the gardeners most likely to be saving old varieties are least likely to be touched by contemporary media. He is, for example, particularly interested in acquiring seeds from clannish groups such as the Mennonites, Amish, Cajuns, and various Native American tribes. "People who are living traditional lives and honor the ways of their ancestors are more likely to save seed," he observes. "Sometimes they are reluctant to share their reserves because they feel—and rightfully so—that seed is a sacred gift from Mother Earth." Whealy sees part of his work as convincing such groups that he is a reliable steward for their heritage.

Whealy feels his stewardship so strongly that he expects to spend the rest of his life protecting what remains of an already depleted supply of vegetable varieties. From his home base, recently moved from Missouri to Iowa, he orchestrates a growing number of projects. One is the *Vegetable Variety Inventory*, a computerized list of every open-pollinated variety available from 150 American and Canadian seed companies. Whealy undertook this intimidating task out of fear that many gardeners are being lured into a false sense of complacency because their old favorites are still listed in seed catalogues. "Most of my members would buy up varieties if they knew they were endangered," says Whealy, "but most gardeners have no idea a favorite variety is in danger until it simply doesn't show up in a catalogue one year and they are unable to get it from any other source."

The inventory, which includes more than 3,500 varieties, will alert members to endangered varieties, which, by Whealy's definition, are those being carried by fewer than three companies. As the inventory is updated each year, Whealy expects it to show that more and more varieties are being discontinued by seed companies. "These varieties are being dropped, not because they are obsolete or hard to grow, but because they may not be as profitable as other varieties," he complains. "Most seed companies can't afford to offer any variety that sells less than five hundred packets per year; so small-time cultivars are simply discontinued."

Whealy feels that the problem is being accelerated by consolidation in the seed industry. When large agricultural firms buy out small companies, they tend to drop locally adapted varieties and replace them with all-purpose hybrids or patented varieties. In the past, Whealy concedes, many discontinued va-

White Japan melon. *A recent introduction, roundish, medium sized or rather small variety; skin cream-white and very thin; flesh thick, remarkably sweet and fine flavor—if the fruit is well matured, almost rivalling that of the Green Citron. It ripens early and is quite productive. Of the numerous new sorts that have been offered to the public within the past two or three years, this appears to be one of the most desirable.* FB

rieties really were inferior to their replacements, but he feels that hasn't been the case during the last twenty years. "Far from being obsolete or inferior, the varieties being dropped today are the cream of our vegetable crops. . . . " he contends. "But they are being allowed to die out due to the economics of the situation, with no systematic effort being made to keep them alive or store them."

THE GROWERS NETWORK

Originally, Kent Whealy's purpose was simply to help gardeners exchange seed by putting them in touch with one another. Gradually, he began to feel that something more than random exchange was needed to guarantee the survival of the heirlooms offered in each yearbook. So, in 1981, he organized a Growers Network of experienced gardeners willing to multiply and return seed from endangered varieties. "The Growers Network has three purposes," he explains. "First, it multiplies endangered collections that might be lost without our help. Second, it offers aid to any gardener who is unable to maintain a variety. Third, it allows us to start building an inventory of unique and outstanding vegetables that we will protect and maintain on a permanent basis."

In its first year the Growers Network included 351 gardeners, and Whealy distributed 2,400 packets of seed. Many of them were beans from John Withee's collection. "There's no way we can thank John for giving us his incredible collection except by working together to keep the entire collection alive," says Whealy. Though beans account for about two-thirds of the nearly 2,500 varieties presently in the Growers Network, peppers, lettuce, potatoes, and tomatoes are also well represented, and Whealy hopes to build up those collections. He's also keeping varieties of corn, squash, melons, and cucumbers, which he distributes only to gardeners who have demonstrated their skills in hand pollination.

Gardeners who want to multiply and return seeds of beans, tomatoes, lettuce, or peppers simply write to Whealy to ask for the varieties they'd like to grow. He doesn't promise that everyone will get what they request because he distributes only a few packets of each variety. In general, Whealy recommends that gardeners study his computer print-out of the available varieties to find those that were originally grown in their regions. "Those should do best for you," he writes. "Ones that you have read about or ones whose names you simply like may not do that well in your area."

Though Whealy wants to accommodate gardeners in search of old varieties, he is ever mindful that the purpose of the Growers Network is the preservation of as many varieties as possible, and he tries to impress upon members the seriousness of their work. "In many cases, you are being entrusted with rare and endangered varieties and there is great responsibility involved," he writes in his instructions to Network volunteers. "John Withee recently told me, 'When there is only a handful of seed left in the entire country, you must make your growers realize that they have to treat them like diamonds.'"

Storage for the Long Run

Samples sent to members of the Growers Network usually include about twenty-five seeds, and Whealy hopes to get two hundred or more back. The replenished seed is available to other gardeners through the Growers Network, but some of it is also placed in frozen storage. Whealy sees the frozen seed bank as simply another layer of insurance to preserve seeds that might slip through gaps in the Seed Savers Exchange or be lost during a particularly poor growing season. "I always tell my members never to plant all of a particular seed because any

Phinney's Early watermelon. *A very early variety; medium and uniform size, and of beautiful form. One of the best croppers we know of. The skin is smooth, with uniform, narrow, white mottled and dark green stripes. Flesh light red or pink, very sweet and delicious. For an early melon for family use, it has few superiors, but does not bear carriage well, on account of its thin brittle rind.* DM

growing season could be so short or so dry that it could wipe out many of the remaining heirloom varieties," he says.

The seeds in Whealy's frozen collection are carefully dried to a moisture content of less than 8 percent. Whealy then puts some into jars that have rubber gaskets under their lids. "I twist the lids on as tight as possible," he says. "Questionable lids are taped with black electrical tape." Whealy is even more enthusiastic about seed bags like those used by the National Seed Storage Laboratory. The bags consist of layers of paper, plastic, and foil laminated together. They can be sealed with an ordinary clothes iron, opened with a scissors, and resealed. Most important, they take up less space than jars do.

At one time Whealy planned to invest in canning machines and other seed-storage equipment. He gave up the idea when he realized that the high cost of such equipment—between $3,000 and $5,000—would lead inevitably to a centralized storage facility run by the Seed Savers Exchange. "It seemed better to develop an inexpensive technique that anyone could use in their own homes," he says now. "That way we could have small, frozen seed banks in basements all over the country."

As those words suggest, Whealy encourages and welcomes diversification. His Seed Savers Exchange has become so influential in large part because he has resisted the temptation to turn it into a fiefdom. "It's terrific when individuals take reponsibility for something that really matters to them," he says. "Three of our members are building collections of squash, half a dozen others have impressive bean collections, and there are several unique tomato collections. Others are specializing in peas, cucumbers, peppers, limas and cowpeas, small grains, potatoes, high-altitude varieties, and traditional Southwestern food crops. Several members have started their own seed companies, one is developing a system of trial gardens, and another has proposed a nationwide network of small, volunteer storage facili-

Bell pepper. *The pods which are remarkably large, and often measure near four inches deep and three inches in diameter, are pendant, broadest at the stem, slightly tapering, and generally terminate in four obtuse, cone-like points. At maturity, the fruit changes to brilliant, glossy, coral-red. The Bell-pepper is early, sweet, and pleasant to the taste, and very much less acrid or pungent than most of the other sorts.* FB

ties. And there are small regional seed exchanges springing up all across the country!"

REGIONAL SEED EXCHANGES

One regional seed exchange is the Blue Ridge Seed Savers, whose Virginia members get together twice a year to swap seeds. "I started by putting up posters in the local country stores," says organizer Kim Cary, "but most people showed up by word of mouth." Participants share food, conversation, and, of course, seeds. At one meeting, the seeds available for swapping included two unnamed corns saved by a great-grandmother in Kentucky, seeds collected by one member while visiting mainland China, as well as seeds from the Candyroaster squash, Currant tomato, Crookneck pumpkin, Birdhouse gourds, Purple tomato, and many other varieties.

Exchange meetings are also an opportunity to learn new things about gardening, as local experts share their knowledge about such subjects as seed saving, grafting fruit trees, and extending the growing season. Between meetings, members keep in touch with a newsletter that lists seed companies, recommends books, and offers tips on seed saving. Though the main goal of the Blue Ridge Seed Savers is to circulate local heirloom seeds in the region, members also put together a collective listing of seeds to be offered through Kent Whealy's Seed Savers Exchange. So far, the Blue Ridge Exchange has stimulated concern for old varieties among people who never knew they were saving heirlooms. "If every state had a few local exchanges," enthuses one member, "think how much consciousness would be raised."

Local exchanges often spring from the concerns of one or two individuals. The Scatterseed Project, for example, is the brainchild of Will Bonsall, a Maine farmer who is committed to vegetarianism and self-sufficiency. "We started growing our own seeds and became aware of the paucity of crop varieties available from commercial sources," Bonsall explains. "So we began searching for and preserving crop germplasm." His search took him to the National Seed Storage Laboratory as well as to seed-storage facilities in other countries.

Because Bonsall agreed to take careful field notes and to return replenished samples of seed, he was able to obtain rare varieties that are not usually available to private gardeners and farmers. "I would like to act as a liaison between the government collections and the seed savers," he says, "to get some of the more interesting stuff into circulation." For Bonsall, "the more interesting stuff" includes vegetables that he feels have been neglected by other seed savers, such as cucumbers, peas, and biennials such as carrots, cabbages, and onions.

The Scatterseed Project is Bonsall's way of assuring that the 1,000 varieties in his collection will be replenished. He recruits growers who are "willing to devote even a tiny space in their garden to some oddball plant that may or may not be useful to them." Though he doesn't have any intention of starting a seed company, Bonsall sometimes makes extra seed available for a small handling fee because he believes the seed should be distributed as widely as possible. "The most effective way to assure continuity of any cultivar," he insists, "is for a number of scattered individuals to be growing these kinds year after year, using some for food and swapping seed with others."

Still another localized approach to seed exchanging is in operation at the Conservancy Garden run by Meals for Millions in Tucson, Arizona. The goal of the program is to help Native Americans who live in the Southwest become more self-sufficient by providing them with crops that are highly adapted to conditions in the region. In many cases, these crops were developed by generations of Native American farmers who selected

Early Cluster cucumber. *A popular, early cucumber, producing its fruit in clusters near the root of the plant: hence the name. The plant is healthy, hardy, and vigorous; fruit short and thick. Its usual length is five inches and its diameter about two inches; skin prickly, green . . . flesh white, seedy, tender, and well flavored, but less crispy or brittle than that of other varieties . . . a good early garden sort.* FB

plants that grew well in the harsh desert climate. Gradually, they were abandoned in favor of "new and improved" varieties, which often did not perform as well as the traditional crops. Staff members at the Meals for Millions project set out in search of the old varieties and found that many were being preserved by elderly Native American gardeners. Among the heirlooms rediscovered by the project are several varieties of the tepary bean, whose deep roots allow it to utilize whatever moisture the desert has to offer; varieties of corn that put themselves on hold during drought and produce ears during the first rainfall; and melons that can survive in scorching summer heat.

All of these crops are grown in the Conservancy Garden, located in the Tucson Botanical Garden, where Mehina Drees, the garden's caretaker, uses traditional cultivation techniques. The Pueblo garden, for example, has a sand "mulch" that conserves moisture, and in the Sonoran garden, cornstalks support the tepary beans. Though the garden gives visitors a new appreciation for the traditional wisdom of Pueblo, Papago, and other Native American gardeners, its primary purpose is the propagation of seed that can be distributed to local people. "We believe seed banks are a back-up system," says Gary Nabhan, an ethnobotanist who directs the project. "The health of agriculture in a region depends on these things being grown where they are naturally adapted and in fields where they have evolved over centuries."

To give more gardeners access to these seeds, Nabhan established Native Seed/SEARCH, a nonprofit organization that searches out, preserves, and distributes native crops, particularly those from the Southwest. The organization has the world's largest collection of heirloom Native American vegetables and grains and makes special efforts to document their origins and cultural uses. Members receive a seasonal newsletter, but anyone can order seeds from a list of fifty rare, native varieties.

SINGLE-CROP SEED EXCHANGES

When seed exchanges are organized by region, members share the same growing conditions and are likely to have success with similar varieties. Some exchanges, however, unite members who have a common interest in a particular crop. The now defunct Wanigan Associates was devoted to heirloom beans; CORNS, an exchange run by Carl Barnes (a corn collector profiled in Chapter 2), recruits people who are willing to preserve old varieties of corn.

Fruit is the interest of members of the North American Fruit Explorers (NAFEX), which was founded in 1967 by a group of hobbyists. "Since we were all interested in the same thing, we started a round robin," recalls Robert Kurle, the organization's corresponding secretary. "As the group grew, it took about three years for the letter to go through all the round-robin groups; so we started a magazine."

The magazine, named *Pomona* after the Roman goddess of fruit, is filled with information about every aspect of fruit culture, from grafting and pruning through disease and insect control. The best articles are collected into occasional yearbooks that NAFEX sells. Subscribers can also borrow books from the organization's library. Members of NAFEX do more than read about fruit, however. Many seek out old orchards and propagate heirloom apple, peach, and other fruit varieties that were believed to be lost. Both old and new varieties are tested by members, who report on their performance in different regions of the country. Outstanding varieties are brought to the attention of nurseries, which are encouraged to make them available commercially. Varieties that cannot be purchased are exchanged by members through listings in *Pomona*.

Another organization that concentrates entirely on fruit is the Home Orchard Society. Unlike NAFEX, which draws its members from every state and several foreign countries, this group has a decidedly local flavor. The "home" orchard, located near the Bybee-Howell House in Portland, Oregon, consists of pioneer fruit trees planted by L. L. McGraw in the early 1970s. While tracking down varieties for that orchard, McGraw came upon a tree that has become a sort of symbol of the Society. The Bellflower apple tree, whose history has been traced back to 1848, stood on an estate that was supposed to be subdivided for homes. Home Orchard Society members persuaded the developer to spare the tree, and they visit the tree regularly to prune and care for it. When they are not saving old trees, Society members publish a quarterly newsletter filled with advice about raising fruit and questions about old varieties. Since members are, for the most part, located in the Northwest, they meet regularly for workshops and other events, such as a scion exchange each spring and a fruit show each fall.

Other Strategies for Seed Savers

Seed exchanges are a grassroots effort to keep old varieties alive; yet they do much more. By confirming the value of the seeds they are saving, they give their members a new sense of urgency about their work. The sense of urgency is not misplaced. Despite the sometimes heroic efforts of these organizations, varieties are still being lost. There is more to be done to preserve rare fruits and vegetables, and there are models pointing the way to how that might be accomplished.

For example, the Garden Club of America has initiated a nationwide search for worthwhile "species, cultivars, and hybrids of trees, shrubs, and groundcovers that are not generally available for garden and landscape use." The program began in part because Garden Club officials observed a sameness in American gardens. In addition to aesthetic monotony, the officials were concerned about the lack of genetic diversity. "The need for increased diversity of plant material in our horticul-

Green Curled lettuce. *The Green Curled strongly resembles the Endive-leaved {which} forms no head . . . When well grown, the plant measures ten inches in diameter and is one of the most beautiful of all the Lettuces. The exterior leaves are finely frilled and curled, and of a rich, golden-green color; the central leaves are smaller, but frilled and curled like those of the exterior. When in perfection, the plants have the form of a rosette and make an excellent garnish.* FB

tural work is crucial," says project advisor Charles Lewis of the
Morton Arboretum in Lisle, Illinois. "With the increasing environmental stresses around us today, we cannot afford to live
with a restricted array of plant material." The club is counting
on its members to identify little-known plants that have desirable characteristics and plans to publish a manual entitled *Plants
that Merit Attention*. Unfortunately, the Garden Club's effort reveals a familiar bias against utilitarian plants such as fruits and
vegetables. Nonetheless, it offers an example of what could be
done to publicize valuable heirloom varieties.

Another model is the Henry Doubleday Research Association, a British organization. Formed in 1954, the Association is
named after Henry Doubleday, a Quaker who introduced com-
frey to Great Britain in hopes of preventing another famine like
the one that afflicted Ireland in the 1840s. Today, the organization has 6,500 members, and many participate in a wide range
of experiments and educational programs related to organic
gardening. A major concern is the preservation of old varieties.
"Today our vegetables are vanishing like our wildlife," writes
Association director Laurence Hills. "We feel the future may be
hungrier than you think and we'll need the inherited qualities
and varieties of the past . . . We hope to bring back the Goyas
and Rembrandts of the kitchen garden for the enjoyment of
gardeners of taste and the plant breeders of the future."

The work of the Henry Doubleday Research Association
has been made more urgent by the Plant Breeders Rights Legislation of 1974, which made it a crime for citizens of Common
Market countries to sell any vegetable other than those on official lists of approved varieties. The law, which was intended to
help with enforcement of plant patents, had a devastating effect
on traditional varieties. Hills believes that countless varieties
were lost, though some were saved through exchanges organized by the Association. "It is legal to grow the old varieties,
and neighbors can give home-saved seed to each other," he ex-

plains. "But if a price per packet were to be printed alongside the historic vegetable varieties in our guide, we could be fined up to £400 for every single one of them."

Faced with such a tragic loss of centuries-old varieties, the Association worked for and finally won the establishment of a gene bank that preserves varieties culled from official lists. So far, the National Vegetable Gene Bank, a British government facility, has successfully stored nearly nine hundred named varieties and six hundred synonym varieties. The seeds in the bank are available only to breeders; so the Association maintains its own "library" of rare varieties that can be withdrawn and replenished by members.

Other Association programs that deserve imitation in the United States include the Seed Guardian program, in which accomplished gardeners "adopt" varieties that are in danger of extinction. "A seed guardian is expected to raise seed for distribution and to maintain the purity of the variety," explains Hills. "We supply them with information so the variety will not revert back and lose the very characteristic that made it worthwhile." In a second program, the Association has established four Vegetable Sanctuaries located near historic homes. A cross between a botanical garden and a vegetable museum, each sanctuary raises nothing but old varieties, such as the Marstock bean, which dates back to the twelfth century, and Brown Golding lettuce, whose leaves stay sweet even after the plant has gone to seed. Finally, the Association maintains files showing the availability of all fruit and vegetable varieties known in Great Britain and publishes a quarterly newsletter.

HEIRLOOM FEVER

The Henry Doubleday Research Association was spurred on by legislation that actually outlawed selling the old varieties. Though people like Kent Whealy fear that similar legislation in

Silver Skin onion. *Bulb of medium size, flattened, average specimens measuring three inches in diameter, and an inch and a half or two inches in thickness; neck small; skin silvery white. After the removal of the outer envelope, the upper part of the bulb is often veined and clouded with green, while the portion produced below ground is generally clear white. Flesh white, fine grained, sugary, and remarkably mild flavored. It forms its bulb early and regularly, ripens off well and is quite productive . . . It is a poor keeper and this is its most serious objection.* **FB**

this country may eventually cause similar problems, at the moment, America's heirloom varieties are in greater danger from the pressures of the marketplace than from government interference. "Each year hundreds of vegetable varieties are dropped from seed catalogues, not because they aren't delicious and unique, but because it is only profitable for large seed companies to stock the varieties that sell the most," says Whealy.

Since seed exchanges don't need to worry about profitability, they have emerged as an alternative to seed companies. Obviously, the seed companies will continue to satisfy the needs of most gardeners. It is more convenient to order seeds from a glossy catalogue than to read the tiny listings in the *Seed Savers Yearbook*. It is easier to reorder new seed each year than to go to the trouble of selecting, harvesting, cleaning, and storing your own. It is simpler to order a "one size fits all" variety than to experiment from year to year to find a locally adapted heirloom.

Still, a growing number of people seem to be willing to take the trouble. "Our goal is to give people the greatest possible access to these old varieties," says Kent Whealy. "The Seed Savers Exchange exists to follow up on opportunities rather than to dictate what should be done. Ideally, we will have layers of participation, and the Exchange will be a sort of clearinghouse tying everyone together."

That ideal becomes more and more of a reality as each issue of the *Seed Savers Yearbook* describes new projects started by gardeners who have caught heirloom fever. Local gardeners have organized seed exchanges in California, Virginia, and Missouri. A professor in Appalachia has established a "library" of locally adapted heirloom varieties. Prisoners in Connecticut are raising endangered vegetables in a special garden on prison grounds. A woman in North Carolina is writing a cookbook so gardeners will know how to prepare unusual old varieties. Gardeners all across the country are combing rural areas to find the crops of their ancestors. Organic gardeners in Canada are band-ing together to sponsor a heritage garden and an Adopt-a-Seed program.

Like all volunteer efforts, projects such as these are vulnerable to discouragement and loss of interest. Yet the proliferation of seed exchanges and seed banks suggests that heirloom varieties are finally being recognized as a heritage that must be grown to be preserved. It's not enough to blame the loss of old varieties on seed companies or to expect the government to take care of the problem. "The best way to keep these old varieties alive is to grow them," says Kent Whealy. And seed exchanges make it possible for gardeners to do just that.

4

The Big Business of Selling Seeds

SEED COMPANIES OFTEN SEEM TO BE THE VILLAINS in the story of heirloom fruits and vegetables. Most varieties become genuinely endangered when they lose the protection of the seed companies that once sold them. For many heirloom enthusiasts, the obvious conclusion is that seed companies could keep old varieties alive simply by carrying them in their catalogues. Most seed companies respond that they, like any other business, expect to prosper by bringing their customers products they want. "A variety is valuable if people want it," says Robert Falasca of the American Seed Trade Association. "The old varieties that are on the market are there because companies can sell them. Companies can't keep listing varieties for sentimental reasons."

That argument might be effective in other businesses. No one expects clothing companies to sell bustles, but seeds evoke special feelings in those who buy them. Each January, when a new crop of seed catalogues matures, gardeners turn to them eagerly. The pictures evoke the smell of moist earth, the feel of sunshine, and the taste of fresh everything. Most gardeners willingly experiment with new introductions, but they also expect to find their old favorites. For many, the pleasure of browsing through seed catalogues is marred by the absence of varieties that won their allegiance through season after season of outstanding performance. As one seed saver put it, "We well remember growing much better vegetables than from the hybrids we now have to purchase."

Most gardeners resign themselves to whatever is available in the catalogues; yet those stubborn enough to hunt for their favorites have discovered that there are now two kinds of seed companies in the United States. Large companies, such as Burpee and Harris, are highly visible. Started a century ago and family-owned for decades, these old-line companies have recently been purchased by large corporations—ITT in the case of Burpee and Celanese in the case of Harris. Being part of a conglomerate changes seed companies. The emphasis shifts from plants to profit. In keeping with the economies of scale practiced by big business, the companies sell fewer varieties, chiefly "exclusive" varieties that are heavily advertised. The new approach results in a vicious circle for heirlooms. Because they are not exclusive, they are less likely to be promoted; so fewer gardeners are aware of them. As a result, demand recedes, eventually justifying the company's decision to drop "unpopular" varieties.

Fortunately, a new breed of seed company is stepping in to catch these old varieties as they are dropped. Motivated by principle as well as by profit, the new companies often start with the assumption that old, open-pollinated varieties are, in many cases, better suited to the needs and growing conditions of gardeners. "We offer both standard, open-pollinated varieties and F-1 hybrids," says the catalogue for one of the new seed companies. "We feel that both types have a place in the homestead garden but do not, as plant breeders, feel that all F-1 hybrids are superior to all standard strains." Unlike the national seed companies, which want to sell a few all-purpose varieties, the new seed companies often seek out seeds that are adapted to the growing conditions of a particular region.

The line between the two types of seed companies is not hard and fast. Both want the business of home gardeners, and both sell what home gardeners demand. However, the emphasis of some companies is on newly bred "super crops," and the emphasis of others is on time-tested heirlooms. Discerning gardeners who understand the differences can enjoy the best of both worlds. On the one hand, by supporting small seed companies, they can assure that heirlooms of merit will continue to be available. On the other, they can selectively choose new varieties when they offer genuine advantages, such as disease resistance. Though gardeners may not think about it, each seed purchase is a vote of sorts, and knowing the issues makes those choices more informed.

THE TALES OF TWO BIG COMPANIES

Many heirloom gardeners feel betrayed by the changes in the large, established seed companies. Perhaps that's because family-run seed companies had a tradition of personal concern about gardeners. Their founders were gardeners, not businessmen. The story of the Joseph Harris Company is typical. The Harris family, who lived originally in Moreton Corbett, England, fell upon hard times in the 1840s. Joseph Harris emigrated to western New York, where he purchased land and nostalgically named it Moreton Farms. After years of raising unusually fine vegetables for himself, he decided to sell seed. His first catalogue was a charming blend of woodcuts, personal anecdotes, treatises on individual vegetables, and general advice about agriculture.

Harris was apologetic about his catalogue—"I fear it will be a poor one," he wrote in the preface—but certain about his standards. "I know what a disappointment it is to prepare and manure and plant a field and then have the crop fail from poor seed," he wrote. "So I will try hard to send out only good, fresh, reliable seed—just such seed as I sow or plant myself." Harris's seeds were apparently as good as his word. In the catalogue's second edition, he published three pages of letters from enthusiastic customers.

Today, a glance through the Harris catalogue shows that many of its most luscious vegetables are Harris exclusives, bred by the company's thirty-member research staff. The company prides itself on the classics it has developed, including the Moreton tomato, Pioneer carrot, and Market Prize cabbage, as well as its more recent disease-resistant introductions. In the 1982 catalogue, Joe Harris, former president of the company, praised these new varieties, noting that he'd seen "many an experienced gardener growing with two strikes against him because he has never made the switch to the newer and far better disease-resistant varieties that are now available."

Most large seed companies lure gardeners by promising varieties that are "newer and far better." Though we've become more jaded in recent years, Americans are still great believers in "progress," and many of us salivate on cue when offered something "new," "better," or "improved." But, like the deodorant whose container has been redesigned or the paper towel that comes in a new color, the changes in fruit and vegetable varieties are often superficial. Each year, between four and five hundred varieties are introduced, but most represent "minor modifications" according to the National Academy of Sciences. "The requirements for a new variety are novelty, uniformity, and stability," says Dr. L. J. Butler of the University of Wisconsin, who recently completed a U.S. Department of Agriculture study of the seed industry. "Novelty is the most important and can be obtained through a small morphological change. There are many new varieties, but I'm not sure that there's a change in the number of qualities available."

With so many new varieties making a debut each year, gardeners might expect that they would have more choices than ever before. Exactly the opposite is true. Because many of the new varieties are not significantly different from their predecessors, they never find a market and are dropped from subsequent catalogues. A few seed companies have expanded their lists with new hybrids and patented varieties, but most have streamlined their offerings to a few proven varieties that reappear in catalogue after catalogue. None of the seed companies offer the selection available a hundred years ago. For example, Burpee's catalogue may, at first glance, seem to include an embarrassment of riches; yet the 1888 catalogue listed half again as many varieties.

Burpee's history parallels that of Harris. Founded by W. Atlee Burpee in 1876, the company established an early reputation for innovation. Before the turn of the century, Burpee introduced Surehead cabbage, Iceberg lettuce, Golden Self-blanching celery, and Stringless green pod bean, four varieties that still hold a place in the company catalogue. Many early Burpee introductions were located by Burpee himself, who traveled widely to find out what was going on in the gardens of his customers. He found the Bush Lima bean growing in one of those gardens in Pennsylvania, and he acquired Golden Bantam from the estate of a farmer legendary for growing sweet, yellow roasting corn.

When W. Atlee Burpee died in 1915, he was succeeded by his son David, who was both a good gardener and a shrewd businessman. He was quick to appreciate the proprietary advantages of hybrids and introduced the first hybrid garden vegetables in 1945. When it became possible to patent varieties, Burpee was again first in line and in 1973 obtained the first plant patent, for Green Ice lettuce. Up until 1970, the company's aggressive marketing of new varieties was tempered by the instincts of its gardener owners, but in that year the company was

Burpee's Golden Self-blanching celery. *The best of all early "self-blanching" varieties . . . It is of dwarf, compact habit, with thick, solid, heavily ribbed stalks which blanch easily to a clear waxen yellow. The stalks are crisp and solid, free from stringiness and of most delicious flavor.* BP

purchased by General Foods, which, in 1979, sold Burpee to ITT.

THE PROFIT MOTIVE

Why does ITT—or any other multinational company—want to own a seed company? The unambiguous answer is profit. The *Global Seed Study*, published in 1978 by L. William Tewkes & Co., concludes, "The global seed trade is one of the fastest growing, most profitable industries in the food chain." Yet maximizing profit has meant changing the traditional ways of doing business, often by dropping traditional varieties. The pages of Burpee's catalogue, for example, are now peppered with "exclusives" and little patent symbols indicating that "unauthorized propagation is prohibited." The company has taught gardeners to depend upon it for anything new, from tomatoes that keep through the winter and cucumbers that grow on a bush to pumpkins with naked seeds and lettuce with heat resistance. Often, of course, "new and improved" means higher prices— the price of a packet of Burpee seeds frequently tops a dollar.

Seed companies and many scientists argue that newly bred varieties deserve premium prices because they offer so many advantages over the old, standard varieties. And, in many cases, they're right. Varieties that resist common diseases have freed gardeners from the thankless task of spraying. Varieties that take up less space make gardening possible in overcrowded communities. Varieties that ripen early or tolerate drought help gardeners overcome regional handicaps.

Yet the benefits that accrue to home gardeners are, for the most part, a bonus for breeders, whose first goal is to produce varieties that will satisfy the needs of commercial growers. There's good reason for this orientation. Plant breeding is expensive work, requiring in some cases years of preliminary crossing before a desirable new cultivar can be introduced.

Companies that invest in such research want to reap the largest possible return, and commercial growers buy more seeds than home gardeners. Harris, for example, sells three times as much seed to commercial growers as to home gardeners. "Large firms produce varieties primarily for the commercial vegetable grower," says one seedsman, "because that's where the larger acreage is and consequently the bigger, more profitable market."

Earlier in this century, there was less discrepancy between commercial growers and home gardeners. Market gardeners were often home gardeners turned pro. They used similar techniques and took their produce to the nearest city. Today, the commercial growers who stock the nation's supermarkets labor under circumstances vastly different from those of the home gardener. Vegetables are planted and harvested by machines. Many are shipped long distances or stored until they are needed.

These circumstances have given rise to new commercial specifications for fruits and vegetables, many inappropriate for home gardens. Commercial growers need varieties that will ripen on the same day so that harvesting machines can go through the field once; home gardeners would rather have varieties that ripen gradually so the produce will be available throughout the season. Commercial growers need vegetables with tough skins that will withstand rough handling; home gardeners dislike anything that stands between them and fresh flavor. Commercial growers are perfectly willing to use pesticides, fertilizers, and irrigation if they are justified by the market price; home gardeners would rather have varieties that do well with whatever nature makes available.

But the biggest and most passionately debated question is flavor. Do breeders neglect flavor in favor of other characteristics that make vegetables easier to grow, ship, and process? Gourmets and home gardeners say yes and point to the Delicious apple, Supermarket tomato, and Iceberg lettuce. All three

Early Blood Turnip-rooted beet. *Roots of this familiar variety are produced almost entirely within the earth, and measure from four to four and a half inches in depth, and four inches in diameter. Form turbinate, flattened, smooth, and symmetrical . . . Skin deep purplish-red. Flesh deep blood-red, sometimes circled and rayed with paler red; remarkably sweet and tender . . . succeeds well from Canada to the Gulf of Mexico . . . is more esteemed, and more generally cultivated for early use than any other variety.* FB are valued by commercial growers because they ship and store well enough to have them in markets year-round. Yet few who have tasted a lettuce like Buttercrunch, a tomato like Brandywine, or an apple like Mother would defend the flavor of the former three.

The complaints of gardeners aren't limited to apples, tomatoes, and lettuce. Many lament that corn is too sugary and beans have become bland. The point, perhaps, is that taste is individual. The tomato that one person proclaims superb may seem acidic to someone else. The corn that one gardener loves to sink his teeth into may seem coarse to his neighbor. Of course, Americans usually revel in their right to such differences. When the Declaration of Independence guaranteed the right to pursue happiness, it covered, presumably, raising any vegetable that satisfies an individual's taste. For many gardeners, that means older, open-pollinated varieties that were developed when the priorities of seed companies were the same as those of home gardeners.

Who Controls the Seeds?

So far, the problem isn't growing older vegetables. It's finding seed. During the past decade, the seed industry has undergone fundamental changes. "Most of our old-time seed companies that started 30–75 years ago are being gobbled up by multinational business giant companies," writes Archie Dessert, former owner of the Dessert Seed Company, in an open letter to his customers. "The strategy seems to be to reduce competition and survival chances for small seed companies which are, and were, producing open pollinated vegetables and cereal seeds." Shortly after that letter was sent, Dessert Seed Company was acquired by Atlantic Richfield.

The acquisition of family-owned seed companies by large conglomerates is, in some ways, a sign of our times. The trends

Cherry pepper. *Stem twelve to fifteen inches high, strong and branching; pod, or fruit, erect, nearly globular or cherry-form and, at maturity, of a deep, rich, glossy scarlet color. It is remarkable for its intense piquancy, exceeding in this respect nearly all the annual varieties.* FB

toward consolidation and nationalization are conspicuous in other industries and other aspects of our lives. National beer companies squeeze regional brewers out of business. Media conglomerates buy up family-owned publishing companies. Exposure to national television is diluting the richness of regional dialects. The pattern, in many areas, is unmistakably towards bigness and homogeneity.

The changes in the seed industry reflect that trend; yet they have disquieting overtones. Unlike many other commodities, seeds are fundamental to life. People may be able to live without television, beer, or even books, but they cannot live without seeds. Concentrating the distribution of seeds in fewer hands gives those hands enormous power. Indeed, some have suggested that multinational companies now eye food as covetously as they once eyed energy and see control of the seed industry as the first step in control of the food chain.

More immediately, consolidation in the seed industry has meant more homogeneity and less variety in what gardeners can buy. Companies once run by gardeners are now managed by businessmen who think of plant varieties as products that are more or less profitable. Larger companies need larger markets, and most set their sights on the commercial grower. Selling to home gardeners soon becomes a sideline because the seeds suited specifically to their needs are less profitable. Before long, those seeds disappear from catalogues, replaced by varieties that can also be sold to commercial growers. Gene Porter of Porter & Son, a seed-growing company, puts the matter bluntly, "Varieties not used by commercial growers (huge quantities) will be dropped for lack of demand."

The large seed companies, like large department stores, try to draw the public's attention to "exclusive" varieties. In the past, the only way to establish exclusive claim to a variety was to develop a hybrid. As a result, companies concentrated on crops that were easily hybridized, such as corn, tomatoes, cucurbits, and melons. With these crops, a company that created a new variety had "biological protection" because no one else knew the plant's parentage.

Though hybrids have been heavily promoted, there is debate about whether they are the best choice for home gardeners. At one end of the spectrum, Paul Ledig of the Petoseed Company notes "a definite increase in the demand for superior hybrid vegetable varieties and a decrease in the older, inferior open-pollinated varieties." At the other end of the spectrum is Archie Dessert, who boasted of never selling hybrids when he owned Dessert Seed Company. "We tested some," he says, "but usually found them unsatisfactory flavor-wise and from five to a hundred times as expensive to repurchase each year as compared to the cost of reproducing our open-pollinated varieties." David McCreary of Gurney Seed Company sees a trend somewhere between these two extremes. "Until four or five years ago, the demand was for more hybrids," he says. "Now that demand has leveled off, and most customers don't really care if the variety is a hybrid or not. They are more interested in how it performs."

PLANT-BREEDING LEGISLATION

The seed companies themselves have a renewed interest in open-pollinated varieties, thanks to the Plant Variety Protection Act, which gives such varieties the same exclusive protection that hybrids have naturally. Passed in 1970 and amended in 1979, the Plant Variety Protection Act was the American version of an idea that has gained prominence in every developed country. Simply stated, the act gives patentlike protection to anyone who develops a new variety. For eighteen years following patent registration, anyone who wants to sell the variety must be licensed by the patent owner and pay a royalty. At first glance, that seems reasonable enough since plant breeders, like playwrights and songwriters, should be entitled to a return on their time.

Yet plants are not like songs. To many people who regard plants as a natural gift like air and water, the very idea of owning varieties is objectionable. They worry that a breeder will latch onto a variety that has been evolving naturally for centuries, make a few cosmetic modifications, and then limit access to the variety with a patent. Others make the more pragmatic argument that living things are so complex that it is impossible to establish an enforceable claim. "No variety is absolutely uniform and fixed," writes a scientist in the U.S. Department of Agriculture yearbook devoted to seeds. "Although the plants from seeds of a variety may appear as alike as peas in a pod at the time of introduction, they are not at all alike genetically." The patent law requires breeders to identify specific characteristics that distinguish a new variety from those that already exist, but there are valid questions about whether varieties—particularly open-pollinated varieties—are stable enough to be owned. Plants are notorious for changing in response to their surroundings. Is a patented tomato the same when it's grown in Maine as when it's grown in New Mexico? Probably not.

The efforts to pin down plants have led, in some instances, to disastrous consequences. In Europe, Common Market governments decided that the only way to make order out of nature's chaos was to establish a list of legal varieties and prosecute anyone who sold unlisted varieties. In the process of drawing up lists, officials eliminated many variety names as synonyms even though the plants to which they referred had unique and useful characteristics. Laurence Hills, director of the Henry Doubleday Research Association and one of the most outspoken critics of the legislation, gives the example of the Up-to-date onion, which was dismissed as being identical to the Bedfordshire Champion. As Hills incredulously points out, the government's own researchers found that Up-to-date had the most resistance

Cushaw pumpkin. *A great favorite in the southern states but too tender for general cultivation in the Northern climates. In form, much resembling the winter crookneck squash, though growing to a very large size, frequently weighing seventy pounds; color light cream, sometimes slightly striped with green; flesh salmon colored. Very productive.* DM

to downy mildew and Bedfordshire Champion had the least. "English gardeners," Hills charges, "have lost not only synonyms but varieties that seed companies are no longer willing to handle because they don't sell 5,000 packets a year. It is better business selling something new, patented, and expensive than a cheap old kind that has sold on its merits since the 1900s." Better business, perhaps, but the genetic consequences of the European enforcement of plant patenting have been appalling. Dr. Erna Bennett of the United Nations Food and Agriculture Organization estimates that, by 1991, three-quarters of the vegetable varieties grown in Europe will be extinct.

The U.S. Department of Agriculture insists that such wholesale sacrifice of old varieties will not occur in this country, partly because the Plant Variety Protection Act is voluntary and partly because the burden for establishing a variety's uniqueness falls squarely on the breeder. Apparently, breeders have been up to the challenge since, as of November 1982, the Department had issued 1,044 plant protection certificates. Of that number, only 313 were for vegetables, including 108 pea, 105 bean, 44 lettuce, and 13 onion varieties.

The Department of Agriculture insists that these varieties must earn their status in the marketplace, competing against old and unpatented varieties. The law, they say, does nothing more than guarantee that a company that invests in variety research will be able to earn a return on its investment. Indeed, the promise of a big payoff does seem to have lured more companies into research. A 1976 survey by the Department of Agriculture revealed that research expenditures more than tripled between 1970, when the act was passed, and 1976. Representatives of individual seed companies confirm the change. Larry Hollar of Hollar and Company, a wholesale seed firm, reports that the act stimulated his company's breeding efforts because they are "able to use the profits from our PVP varieties to increase our research and development budget." Research money that would have gone into hybrids in the past is now being spent on open-pollinated varieties, according to David McCreary of Gurney Seed Company. "From our standpoint," he says, "this is better for gardeners, better for plant breeders, better for seed producers, and better for us."

As this comment suggests, the changes in the large, old-line seed companies are not uniform. Many have grown without abandoning old varieties that do well for home gardeners. The J. W. Jung Seed Company, for example, is seventy-five years old and still family-owned. "We attempt to maintain and reintroduce adapted and productive old-timers," says Jung. "When we do drop seeds from our catalogue, we send samples to the National Seed Storage Laboratory in Fort Collins, Colorado."

Other older companies have found that their best marketing strategy is to identify and satisfy local plant preferences. The Mayo Seed Company has been introducing bean varieties since it was founded in 1878. Because many Tennessee gardeners think the stringless beans have "had the flavor bred right out of them," according to Dan Mayo, the company carries old string varieties such as the Brown Bunch beans, Red Peanut beans, and Sulfur Bunch beans, all local heirlooms with a strong beany taste. "Research," notes Mayo, "is usually geared to the commercial grower." Mayo tries to compensate by seeking out old varieties that satisfy the tastes of Southern gardeners.

H. G. Hastings Company is another firm that has kept the needs of home gardeners uppermost. Elizabeth Whittle, education specialist for the company, has taken personal responsibility for sending samples of discontinued varieties to Kent Whealy's Seed Savers Exchange. She also notes that a customer survey conducted by the company turned up "*many* requests for old-timey seeds, old or unusual varieties, and for listings more clear about hybrids and open-pollinated seeds." Larger seed

Large Drumhead lettuce. *Heads remarkably large, somewhat flattened, compact; pale green without, and white at the center; crisp and tender, one of the finest summer varieties; seeds white.* DM

companies, she feels, "are interested in making money, not in the 'greater good' or even particularly in what the customer demands."

Of course, old and new seed companies insist that demand is the only determinant of what stays in their catalogues. "If people continue to purchase a variety, we continue to produce and sell it," says Charles Green of Rogers Brothers, a seed wholesaler in Idaho. Though seed companies can manipulate demand to a certain extent with slick advertising and promotion, eventually gardeners find varieties they like and stick with them. And more and more gardeners seem to be sticking with heirlooms. As Dick Meiners, owner of the Pine Tree Seed Company, observes, "There is a greatly increased awareness of the potential germplasm loss and thus demand for exclusively open-pollinated varieties among a percentage of our customers." He adds, however, that the percentage is very small—about 3 percent.

The New Breed of Seedspeople

Olive-Shaped Scarlet radish. *Bulb an inch and a half deep, three fourths of an inch in diameter, oblong, somewhat in the form of an olive, terminating in a very slim tap-root; skin fine scarlet; neck small; leaves not numerous, and of small size; flesh rose-colored, tender and excellent. Early and well adapted for forcing and for the general crop.* FB

Large companies cannot respond to the demands of such a small segment of the market. Like network television, they have to appeal to the broadest possible audience. Today, however, there are alternatives—small companies that are eager to attract gardeners who appreciate the older varieties. Many of the new-line seed companies are tiny and struggling, but most are imbued with a sense of mission. Like the larger companies, they want to offer their customers the best available varieties, but they believe that, in many cases, those varieties include the open-pollinated heirlooms being dropped by the larger companies. These smaller companies enjoy reverse economies of scale that make it possible for them to profitably offer varieties that sell a few hundred packets a year. Many grow their own seed; so they aren't locked into contracts with the big Western growers. And many are satisfied if their slice of the pie includes only gardeners in their region of the country. In some ways, the new seedspeople are reminiscent of legendary seedsmen such as W. Atlee Burpee and Joseph Harris. Like them, they started with little capital but lots of determination to sell customers quality seeds at a fair price.

William Ross, owner of G. Seeds, says that changes in the seed industry are directly responsible for turning his gardening hobby into a business. "The immediate side effect [of consolidation in the seed industry]," he says, "is that new businesses such as ours will arise to replace the old seed houses which have sold out." The *G* in his company name stands for "good," and for Ross, that includes many varieties dating back to the nineteenth century. Ross, however, is reluctant to use the term "heirlooms" because, he explains, "It's hard to know with certainty if these are the same varieties our great-grandparents grew." In some cases, the genetic make-up of the plant may have been changed through natural or human selection. In other instances, varieties travel under several common names, or one name refers to several varieties. Despite the difficulty of determining whether today's heirloom is the same as what was grown a hundred years ago, Ross is determined to save as many of these varieties as possible.

His catalogue lists only open-pollinated varieties, though he's not opposed to hybrids. "We think hybrids are an exciting idea," the catalogue states, "but our present focus is on preserving heirloom varieties while they are still around." Ross, who believes that the Plant Variety Protection Act will be an asset should his company decide to start breeding, is now acquiring as many heirloom varieties as he can and is eager to trade seeds with customers. His own collection of fifty tomatoes, thirty corns, ninety beans, and thirty squashes is partially represented in the catalogue. For example, the bean section includes Pre-Columbian varieties collected from Native Americans in the Southwest, such as the Hopi Mottled lima bean, a shelling bean called Montezuma Red, a Speckled Blue tepary, and Buckskin and Butterfly runner beans.

Despite his enthusiasm, Ross sees potential conflicts between the "bigs" and little companies like his own, and he worries that their size will give the larger companies financial and political clout. Ross fears, for example, that the large companies might wage "massive advertising wars—like the Miller vs. Budweiser campaign—which have the potential to warp the desires of home gardeners." He is also concerned that large companies might use their political clout to enact laws that would make it impossible for small seed dealers to survive. For example, he cites the fact that some states now charge an annual registration fee for each variety a company intends to sell in that state. "A national program of the same sort would put our company on difficult financial footing," he concludes.

Liberty Seed Company is another company that owes its existence to recent changes in the seed industry. As an employee of Harris Seed Company, William Watson witnessed firsthand the changes that occurred when Celanese purchased the company, and he didn't like what he saw. "Big companies shoot for the big market," he says simply. "The home gardener is a 'fallout' result of their breeding and marketing. The policy was distasteful enough for me to leave and form a customer-oriented company."

For Watson, "customer-oriented" means testing every variety to be sure it is suited to the growing conditions available in home gardens. Though his catalogue contains many hybrids, he claims to be "very careful about replacing the older varieties unless something is really better."

Some of the new seedspeople, such as J. L. Hudson of A World Seed Service, are opposed to hybrids on principle. "We will not sell F-1 hybrids," Hudson says flatly, and they aren't missed in the company's encyclopedic listing of several thousand plants, including perennial flowers, trees, herbs, vines, bulbs, succulents, alpine plants, palms, and other "useful plants." The seeds, which come from every continent, are listed under their botanical names, and information about the culture and use of varieties is provided. The comparatively small section on vegetables lists only open-pollinated varieties.

Hudson also worries that the Plant Variety Protection Act may make it possible for companies to patent and restrict distribution of "rediscovered" varieties, such as heirlooms that drop out of circulation for a while. As an example, he cites the Sugar Snap pea, which was hailed as a new vegetable when it was introduced in 1978 and is often cited as an example of the kind of breeding stimulated by plant patenting. Hudson notes that peas similar to the Sugar Snap pea were popular in France in the 1880s. "It's a fine variety," he says in a letter published in the *Seed Savers Yearbook*. "And I don't mean to belittle the effort that went into it . . . It just raises the question of whether a variety of corn that has been in existence for a thousand years in some remote valley could be patented because an American 'discovers' it."

Actually, many heirloom seed companies are started because their founders "discover" a single extraordinary vegetable variety that has been overlooked by other seed companies. Fern Hill Farm in New Jersey sells nothing but the Dr. Martin Pole lima bean. The history of the variety is obscure—no one is absolutely sure which of several Dr. Martins first developed the bean. The proprietors of Fern Hill, however, have no doubt about the "superior nutlike flavor" of this heritage variety, and their entire seed program is devoted to preserving its trueness to type. Taos Pueblo Native Seed Company is another company organized around a single heirloom variety. Taos Pueblo blue corn produces huge ears with deep blue kernels that make excellent cornmeal. The company hopes that, by building on the interest in blue corn, they can eventually offer other native varieties, such as squash, beans, pumpkins, and chilis.

Large Crooked Sugar pea. *A tall climbing variety . . . pods very large, whitish, entirely free from membrane, often twisted—whence the variety derives its name—sometimes from 4 to nearly 5 inches long . . . the size and fine appearance of its pods cause it to be always more sought after than any other kind, so that it is more extensively grown than any other variety of Edible-podded Peas, especially in the eastern parts of France and Switzerland. It is rather surprising to see the comparatively low estimation in which the Edible-podded Peas are held in the vicinity of Paris.* AV

Other companies specialize in several unusual varieties of a single vegetable. Horticultural Enterprises of Dallas, Texas, sells nothing but chili peppers. The company's "catalogue" is a poster listing more than forty peppers and showing their comparative shapes and sizes. Alston Seed Growers sells only a few varieties of open-pollinated corn, including Old Hickory King, African Zulu Maize, Old Red Field corn, and Pencil Cob corn. The Vermont Bean Seed Company started in the late 1970s by offering the "largest bean and pea selection available anywhere in the world." Though the company has since expanded to other vegetables, it still carries an unusually large selection of beans, including such rare varieties as Wren's Egg, Sulpher, Missouri Wonder, and Black Valentine.

REGIONAL SEED COMPANIES

Other small seed companies carve out a territory by offering varieties that are especially adapted to different regions of the country. For example, Plants of the Southwest specializes in native grasses, wildflowers, trees, and shrubs that do well in Arizona, New Mexico, and southern California. Its catalogue is packed with cultural information about unusual wild plants as well as articles on everything from techniques for capturing water to making novel dried arrangements. Though vegetables are not its primary interest, the company does offer a selection of Native American crops that are adapted to the conditions of the Southwest. It is one of the few sources for tepary beans, posole corn, and devil's claw, a Sonoran crop grown for its edible seeds as well as the long black fibers from the "claws" on the fruit.

Perhaps the most successful of the regional seed companies is Johnny's Selected Seeds, which was founded in the early 1970s when owner Rob Johnston noticed that no one was paying attention to crops that would grow in his native Maine. Today, his company's handsome catalogue is filled with short-season crops that thrive in cool weather. Though he is open to heirloom varieties, each must earn its place in his catalogue. "The older varieties in our catalogue have a uniqueness or usefulness right now," he explains. "To be offered to our customers, an heirloom has to have more than historical value."

Johnston has successfully combined an instinct about plants with a shrewd sense of business. He believes in open-pollinated varieties because he's grown them, and he's able to convince his customers about their advantages. Though his catalogue lists a few hybrids, his company doesn't breed them. "In the long run," Johnston writes in the catalogue, "it seems more valuable to enjoy the 'constant warmth' of well-maintained varieties than to depend on the short-lived 'fire' of the hybrids."

Though Johnston understands that many people don't want to bother saving seeds, he also finds that "many gardeners feel more secure knowing that they can or could save seed from open-pollinated varieties year after year." Johnston encourages those gardeners—he's written a useful manual about saving seeds—and is perfectly willing to swap seeds with gardeners who have a variety that deserves his attention.

Selling the Rare and Unusual

Seed swapping is also a feature of Redwood Seed Company, another veteran among alternative seed companies. Founded in 1971, Redwood is a cottage industry run by Craig and Sue Dreman. To encourage their customers to send in heirlooms, they offer $2.50 in credit for samples of any seed they don't have. Thanks to this policy, their own seed explorations, and exchanges with botanical gardens and research stations in this country and abroad, the Dremans have assembled an extraordinary catalogue listing hundreds of rare and unusual plants.

They collect seed from 1,800 native plants and grow or purchase seed for 500 varieties, nearly all heirlooms known in the nineteenth century. "We've tried the new and we've tried the old," says Dreman. "And the old are really good." As examples, he offers Early Autumn spinach, which has smooth leaves that don't get gritty like the crumpled varieties, and Large Red tomato, which is, as he puts it, "chock full of good genes." He encourages gardeners to save their own seed so they can produce varieties adapted to their own conditions. "Seeds," says Dreman, "are one of our last uncontrolled natural resources. Everybody can't have an oil well in their garden, but they can take a little personal share of the genetic resources that are still around."

Spreading genetic resources around is also the goal of Jan Blum, owner of Seeds Blum. The inspiration for her company came from an eighty-two-year-old neighbor who complained that all the good seeds were disappearing from the catalogues. "He passed along some of his treasured bean and corn seeds to us," she recalls, "and we found them in every way superior to any we had tried before." Blum's fascination with the old varieties led her to the Seed Savers Exchange, where Kent Whealy encouraged her dream of starting a seed company. "Lots of gardeners are interested in the old varieties, but they are hesitant about joining the Seed Savers Exchange because they aren't familiar with seed-saving techniques," Blum explains. "We wanted to make it easy—and fun—for gardeners to get involved with old varieties."

The Seeds Blum catalogue does include many intriguing and hard-to-find vegetables, such as purple broccoli and sea kale. Her list of tomato varieties includes Persimmon, Blushing, Early Rose, Potato-leaved, Angor, and Evergreen. Though offering these unusual varieties is Blum's goal, it has spawned a new set of problems. "Our initial goal as a seed company was to grow all our own seed," says Blum, "but it soon became apparent that there is more of a demand for our seed than we can ever

Large Red tomato. *Fruit sometimes smooth, often irregular, flattened, more or less ribbed; size large, but varied much by soil and cultivation—well grown specimens are from three to four inches in diameter, two inches and a half in depth, and weigh from eight to twelve ounces; skin smooth, glossy, and when ripe, of a fine red color; flesh pale red, or rose-color—the interior of the fruit being comparatively well-filled; flavor good. From the time of the introduction of the tomato to its general use in this country, the Large Red was almost the only kind cultivated or even commonly known.* FB

possibly grow without help. Without a very large operation, it would be nearly impossible to grow enough different varieties to offer a well-rounded selection to gardeners."

Faced with this situation, most seed companies would obtain seed from growers, specialized companies that multiply large quantities of seed and sell it, in turn, to the catalogue companies. Most seed growers are located in the arid West, where seed-borne diseases are less of a problem, and most are willing to multiply only seeds for which there is significant demand. Blum notes that when one seed supplier changed hands, it established a new minimum of five pounds of seed per order. "This stipulation doesn't faze the larger seed companies," she says, "but it virtually eliminates the smaller ones overnight."

To protect herself—and other small seed companies—from similar developments, Blum hopes to organize a network of small-scale growers who would custom-grow seed of heirloom varieties for small, alternative companies. "The efforts of alternative seed companies can easily go down the drain," she says, "unless there is a cooperative and unified effort made to create and support a consistent . . . source of seed free from the control by the powers that are shaping agribiz today."

The Nonprofit Motive

One of the forces that shapes agribusiness is the search for profit, and one organization that found a way around the profit problem is the Abundant Life Seed Foundation, founded by Forrest Shomer. Shomer originally started a seed company but quickly found that his goal was more to get seeds into circulation than to make money. So he turned the company into a nonprofit foundation. "A nonprofit foundation has no dividends, no stockholders, no investors," he says contentedly. "It belongs to

Early Rose potato. *Tubers oblong, rather flattened, often more pointed at the top than at the bottom . . . skin smooth and of a pink colour slightly tinged with salmon colour; flesh white. A very productive and early kind.* AV

itself." And its members. The Abundant Life Seed Foundation has seven hundred members who either contribute seed or pay $6 annual dues, as well as 4,000 subscribers who pay $2 per year to receive the annual catalogue and four newsletters.

The catalogue includes seeds for native and naturalized plants that grow in the Pacific Northwest. Some members collect native seed and contribute to a calendar that lists the seed-collecting time for 350 wild plants. "It reminds people that it's the third of August, so it's time to go out and get the hyssop seed," says Shomer. Foundation members and staff raise most of the seeds for beans, beets, chard, corn, kale, melons, mustard, parsnips, peas, spinach, squash, sunflowers, and turnips. Though they are hoping to locate growers for cucumbers, peppers, lettuce, pumpkins, radishes, onions, and tomatoes, seeds for those crops now come from commercial growers in the United States, Japan, England, France, and Italy. The home-grown seed is considered most desirable, so when it is in short supply, it is not sold in bulk. Instead, the catalogue notes, "it is put in single packets in order to spread it as widely as possible."

Spreading seed around is one of Shomer's goals. As he puts it, "It's important to keep the seeds moving because then they become part of the fabric of our lives and they mean something." Education is another priority. The Foundation conducts seminars, sponsors an apprenticeship program, and makes available an excellent selection of resource books, including MM. Vilmorin-Andrieux's *The Vegetable Garden* and a series of pamphlets from J. L. Webster that were out of print until Abundant Life took responsibility for reissuing them. According to Shomer, his organization simply imitates what plants do. "A plant gathers different elements from its environment and combines them in the seed," he explains. "When seed ripens, it gets distributed and starts another cycle. We emulate that process, using paper, the mail, and human cooperation."

Cooperation is also the key word for the Butterbrooke Farm Seed Coop, run by Tom and Judy Butterworth. The coop has two hundred members whose $5 annual dues entitles them to discounts on seeds sold to the public and access to heirloom varieties that are not available in sufficient quantities for public sale. "Multiplication of heirloom varieties is given first priority at Butterbrooke Farm," says Tom Butterworth. Some of the heirlooms the coop is preserving come from members, and others come from the Seed Savers Exchange. Either way, the staff multiplies the seeds and makes them available to members. One recent offering of seeds for coop members included White Snowball tomato, which has low acidity; the Pepper tomato, which looks much like a sweet pepper; Multiplier garlic; and Spinach-leaf Swiss chard, whose smooth leaf makes washing easier.

Butterbrooke's sales to the public consist of standard, open-pollinated varieties that do well in New England. There's no fancy catalogue—just a list of available seeds—but the simplicity is reflected in the price of twenty-five cents per packet. The Butterworths believe that such low prices will become more and more unusual as a result of consolidation in the seed industry. "Open-pollinated varieties have been and will continue to be dropped by larger seed houses as they substitute their more profitable hybrid varieties," says Tom Butterworth. "This forces gardeners to become more dependent on seed houses, which makes it possible for seed houses to raise prices."

FRUIT FOR HEIRLOOM ORCHARDS

Several nurseries have long made a profitable business out of supplying heirloom varieties to home fruit growers. One of the finest is Southmeadow Fruit Gardens, a Michigan nursery that recently merged with Grootendorst Nurseries. Southmeadow was founded by Robert Nitschke after an article about his home orchard set off an avalanche of mail from gardeners who wanted to know where to find his rare varieties. Ever since, Southmeadow has prided itself on finding and offering choice varieties for the connoisseur. "The requirements for profitable commercial orcharding and fruit marketing have drastically reduced the number of varieties available on the market," notes Nitschke. "Most of the choicest and most desirable varieties from the standpoint of intrinsic quality can only be obtained by growing them oneself."

To educate customers who might not be acquainted with the old varieties, Nitschke published a now famous catalogue that describes each fruit and its history. The catalogue, which makes fascinating reading, lists more than 150 apples, as well as pears, peaches, nectarines, plums, cherries, and grapes. Nitschke's descriptions blend poetry and experience. He praises Sweet Bough apple for its "honeyed sweetness which makes it pleasant to eat out of hand." Of Summer Rambo, he writes, "When in perfect ripeness, it is almost impossible to eat without abundant juice running down one's chin." Descriptions like these are often supplemented with historical notes. For example, Nitschke reveals that because of the small size and sweet scent of Lady apples, French women of the seventeenth century carried them in their pockets as a sachet. Nitschke also does not hesitate to recommend varieties that he feels have been neglected, such as the Mother apple, which has almost disappeared in its native America though it is "widely grown in English fruit gardens as one of the finest dessert apples."

Several other nurseries also specialize in old fruit varieties. Converse Nursery in Amherst, New Hampshire, offers nearly two hundred varieties of rare apples grafted on semidwarf rootstock. Herman L. Suter in St. Helena, California, sells scionwood from nearly fifty apples and is willing to swap scions for

Thanksgiving Hardy plum. *Very productive, good quality and long keeper. It will keep for weeks after picking, like an apple. Further experience with this valuable plum leads us to think that we have not claimed enough for it. Notice that Thanksgiving plum is not only a variety of superior merit in many other respects, but that it is hardy makes this one of the most valuable varieties of the age.* GR

varieties he doesn't have. Lawson's Nursery in Ball Ground, Georgia, offers rare apple and pear varieties including Sops of Wine apple and Old June Sugar pear. Worley Nursery in York Springs, Pennsylvania, offers fifty old-time apple varieties in addition to the standard commercial varieties.

CHALLENGES FOR THE NEW SEED COMPANIES

The success of these nurseries with heirloom fruits suggests that there is room for seed companies that want to sell heirloom varieties. At the same time, there are cautionary tales of well-intentioned entrepreneurs who started selling heirloom seeds and couldn't make a go of it. In the 1940s, for example, Billy Hepler, a biologist, began selling old bean varieties from his extensive personal collection. When he died, his son sold the Hepler Seed Company to Farmer Seeds, and within a few years, all the old varieties had been lost or discontinued.

A more recent casualty is Self-Sufficient Seeds. Started in 1981, the company existed for three years under the leadership of Richard Grazzini, a plant breeder who was inspired to start a seed company by the Seed Savers Exchange. Grazzini's vision was ambitious. To find varieties that would perform well in home gardens, he organized a system of trial gardens to evaluate the performance of more than a thousand vegetable varieties, many of them heirlooms. Unfortunately, the sales of his fledgling company did not keep pace with his dreams. "I still believe that people want good, reliable varieties—both old and new," he said shortly after the company folded in 1983. "We just made the mistake of many new businesses and tried to do too much too fast."

Selling old varieties successfully presents a chicken-and-egg problem. On the one hand, gardeners must want the old varieties enough to buy them. On the other hand, they can't even try many heirlooms unless someone sells them. At the moment, there seems to be just enough consumer interest to persuade small and venturesome seed companies to test the market. A survey of seed companies found a surprising number who planned to expand their selection of heirloom varieties. Internode, a California company, praised old varieties for having "more flavor" and expects to make a large selection available within a couple of years. Curtis Seed, a South Dakota company that has suspended its sales for the time being, plans to return with a catalogue that will feature "old-time" varieties. Greenleaf, a Massachusetts seed company that grew from its owner's large garden, sells only open-pollinated varieties because owner Robert Wagner feels it is "a real disaster that many interesting old varieties of vegetables are disappearing right in front of us."

The small, new seed companies have their work cut out for them. Starting any new business is a challenge. Some owners have had to take a second job to nurse small companies through difficult times. In addition, these companies must find growers willing to bother with small quantities of seed and customers discerning enough to seek them out.

In the end, gardeners will decide whether there will be two kinds of seed companies in this country or only one. Thanks to their sales to commercial growers, the large companies will prosper with or without home gardeners. The small companies will survive only if enough home gardeners became curious about old varieties and committed to their availability. Buying from the alternative seed companies may take extra effort. These firms can't grab the gardener's attention with splashy ads or blanket the country with colorful catalogues. Yet gardeners who order even a part of their seeds from the small companies will be keeping their own options open.

There are, after all, no villains among the seed companies. Each simply sells what it believes gardeners will buy. Some companies are convinced that gardeners will be happiest with "new and improved"; others are just as certain that "tried and true" works best in the backyard. Which side is right? Only gardeners can decide. At the very least, the existence of small, alternative seed companies allows gardeners to make the choice for themselves.

5
Living History

HOW IS A FIJI ISLAND TOMATO LIKE A high-buttoned shoe? For some people, both are antiques that should be preserved and respected for what they tell us about our past, regardless of their usefulness in the present. These people would no more plant a Flat Dutch cabbage in their gardens than they would ride to work in a horse and carriage or cook on a cast-iron cookstove. They expect, however, that someone will see to it that the cookstove, carriage, and cabbage survive for posterity. Cookstoves and carriages have always been preserved by historical museums, and now some people are suggesting that museums should also take responsibility for heirloom cabbages, apples, and other fruits and vegetables.

Certainly old vegetable and fruit varieties reveal as much about the lives of people in the past as the tools they used or the clothes they wore. And some heirloom varieties do resemble museum pieces because they have been superseded by new varieties, better suited to contemporary needs and preferences. Yet heirloom plants differ from historical artifacts in one important respect—they are alive. Other museum pieces are static. Once they have been protected from obvious problems, such as moisture and insects, most artifacts will keep for decades. Plants are much less stable. Under the ordinary storage conditions available to museums, seeds will survive only a few years. And, if they are grown, varieties are susceptible to "damage" through cross-pollination. Though most museums have experts who know how to preserve fabric, wood, and other materials, few have gardeners who know how to grow true seed.

YOU-ARE-THERE MUSEUMS

Despite these problems, many museums are making tentative efforts to include old fruit and vegetable varieties in their collections. Their interest grows less from the concern that these vegetables are disappearing and more from the changing nature of American museums. Before 1960, most historical museums were little more than dusty collections of artifacts kept at arm's length from the public by velvet ropes and glass cases. In the 1960s, a small group of historians began to call for museums that were less sterile and more participatory. The new generation of museums takes its cue from Williamsburg, which, with a fifty-year grant from the Rockefeller Foundation, brought the past to life by arranging artifacts in appropriate settings and adding costumed interpreters to carry out everyday tasks typical of the period. "Living museums," as they came to be called, are designed to create a time-warp experience for their visitors. Authentic buildings, tools, and furniture become props for a stage on which the past can be reenacted.

For most of the living-history villages and farms that sprang up in the 1960s and 1970s, gardens and fields were an afterthought. Virtually all depicted life before the turn of the century, when 90 percent of all Americans raised their own food; yet most museums put their initial efforts into creating authentic buildings and interiors. Outdoors, interpreters might have

Early Dwarf Flat Dutch cabbage. *A most excellent second early variety. Heads medium size, some flat on the top; grows low on the stump and is of good flavor. Popular in the Southern states having become acclimated.* DM

used horse-drawn plows and antique tools, but the plants were straight from the twentieth century. The results of these policies were often attractive but anachronistic. Williamsburg, for example, has included tomatoes in its kitchen gardens, even though colonists would have been horrified at the idea of eating such a close relative of deadly nightshade.

Gradually, curators at living museums began to realize that even minor lapses in accuracy undermine the "you are there" effect. "Authenticity intensifies the experience at a living historical farm," explains Terry Sharrer, editor of the *Association of Living Historical Farms and Museums* [*ALHFAM*] *Bulletin*. "We really want people to believe for a moment that they are in another time. If the interpreter is wearing a digital watch, the illusion is shattered." The idea that hybrid corn could be an equally jarring anachronism was at first foreign to historians, but many museums now acknowledge that heirloom plants are simply one more detail that must be correct if a museum is to recreate the past for its visitors.

With the quest for authenticity as their motivation, museums have the potential to play an important role in the preservation of heirloom varieties. "Living historical farms could be . . . living conservation sites," says Edward Hawes, director of the Clayville Rural Life Center and Museum in Illinois. "Simply through regrowing old varieties with properties of genetic diversity, they will do a great service."

Are museums performing the "great service" of preserving heirloom varieties? To find out, a questionnaire was sent to 120 historic homes, farms, and museums. More than sixty institutions responded, and almost half had made some effort to include historically appropriate varieties in their orchards or gardens. A few were successfully preserving an even broader range of plants that were valued during the time period represented by the museum. "We have plants in our park that were historically important to Louisiana life ways but that are neither fruits

Common Yellow Field pumpkin. *Fruit rounded, usually a little more deep than broad, flattened at the ends, and rather regularly, and more or less prominently, ribbed. Its size is much affected by soil, season, and the purity of the seed. Color rich, orange-yellow; skin, or rind, if the fruit is well matured, rather dense and hard; flesh . . . of a yellow color, generally coarse-grained and often stringy, but sometimes of fine texture, dry and of good quality. The cultivation of the Common Yellow field pumpkin in this country is almost co-eval with its settlement . . . not only extensively employed as a material for pies, but much used as a vegetable, in the form of the squash, at the table.* FB

nor vegetables in the common sense," says Charles Brassieur, curator of the Acadian House Museum in St. Martinville, Louisiana. "Plants were grown to smell good, to clean out chimneys, to make brooms, mattresses, hats, and chair bottoms." Other institutions, such as Hancock Shaker Village in Pittsfield, Massachusetts, reported extensive herb collections, including many rare varieties that were indispensable in the past but are rarely grown today.

The gardens that concentrate on herbs and other "useful plants" are often based on research in early herbals, which usually describe species of plants but not varieties. Museums that have applied the same approach to fruits and vegetables tend to have generic orchards and gardens—they plant pumpkins, for example, without worrying about the variety. The question, of course, is whether the pumpkin variety is one that would even be recognized by a gardener from the past. In many cases that question is not addressed until someone on the museum staff "discovers" heirloom varieties. For example, Pennsbury Manor in Morrisville, Pennsylvania, has had extensive gardens since 1942 but made little effort to plant heirloom varieties until a new staff member with an interest in heirlooms developed a five-year program to "incorporate many more authentic flowers, vegetables, and field crops."

More Questions than Answers

Though many living-history museums would like to have heirloom gardens, the number of surveys that came back with more questions than answers suggests that museum staff members know relatively little about how to find and authenticate, much less propagate, heirloom varieties. The Association of Living Historical Farms and Museums has tried, in recent years, to circulate information about exemplary programs, but many heirloom gardens and orchards that could serve as models remain unknown. Those that do become known are often copied by other institutions that have neither the resources nor the inclination to do their own research.

Many museums are struggling to master a single aspect of heirloom gardening. Some manage to gather variety names by interviewing older local residents or by assigning student interns to cull names from old agricultural journals, but then are stumped about where to find seed for the named varieties. Other institutions have solicited old varieties from local gardeners or other museums but cannot verify that they belong to the place and time the museum represents. Few of the survey respondents had a firm grasp of even the most basic techniques for growing and preserving true seed. Finally, most of the museums work within tight budgets and are inevitably concerned about how all exhibits, including heirloom gardens, can be made appealing to the public that supports them.

These findings suggest that some museums still need to be convinced that heirloom gardens are a good idea, and others need information about how to research and maintain such gardens. Fortunately, innovative and successful programs at a few museums offer persuasive proof of what can be done and practical models for how to do it. Programs like those described in this chapter suggest that museums can play at least four significant roles in the preservation of heirloom varieties. First, museums often have staff members whose historical training enables them to determine which varieties are genuine heirlooms as well as where and when they were grown. Second, because of their unique role as custodians of local history, museums can solicit regional seeds and information about rare varieties that might otherwise be lost. Third, some museums are willing to commit themselves to preserving heirloom varieties with the same seriousness that they devote to saving butter churns and blacksmith tools. And, finally, by growing a few old varieties, museums can kindle public interest in heirlooms and their preservation.

A Focus on Heirlooms

Few museums spread the word about heirlooms as well as the Genesee Country Museum in Mumford, New York. Each fall, visitors gather in this recreated nineteenth-century village for a harvest festival. The focus is on food, and honors go to those who have baked the tastiest pies, put up the best preserves, and grown the finest vegetables. Exemplary specimens are often those most likely to last through the winter ahead. Judges scrutinize bins of dried legumes such as flashy Speckled Cranberry beans and creamy green Alaska peas. The corn has been dried too, and people often gather to gawk at the unusual black variety from Mexico. There is a large exhibit of plump root vegetables—Hollow Crown parsnips, Purple-top Strap-leaved turnips, Early Horn carrots, and Winter Keeper beets. But it is the squashes that always steal the show; displays are likely to include a summer crookneck with its pebbled golden skin, a White Bush Scallop impersonating a fleshy flower, and a wrinkled Green Hubbard looking ancient and venerable. All these vegetables are living artifacts, which, at the Genesee Country Museum, receive the same respect and attention as antique tools and kitchen implements.

Like other living-history museums, the Genesee Country Museum began by assembling a collection of buildings—in this case, more than forty—ranging from a primitive log cabin to an elegant Victorian townhouse. To attract visitors, the museum also hired costumed interpreters to demonstrate nineteenth-century skills such as shoemaking and cooking over an open hearth. Lynne Belluscio, the museum's head interpreter, made

Purple-top Strap-leaved turnip. *Bulb flat, smooth, and regular in form, produced almost entirely above ground . . . skin above clear, bright purple—below, pure white, often finely clouded or shaded at the union of the colors, flesh clear white, firm, solid, sugary, mild, and remarkably well-flavored; size medium . . . This variety is unquestionably one of the best flat turnips, either for the field or garden. It is early, hardy, thrives in almost any description of soil.* FB

a special effort to locate authentic nineteenth-century recipes to be prepared in the village's kitchens, but found she couldn't create authentic meals with the vegetables being grown in the museum gardens. The gardener kept planting tomatoes, beans, and sweet corn while her recipes called for peas that could be dried, corn that made good meal, and "turneps—an excellent and very healthy vegetable." To find out more about appropriate vegetables, Belluscio began studying the *Genesee Farmer*, a progressive agricultural publication that had begun printing seed lists in 1831.

She also enlisted the help of Robert Becker, a vegetable specialist at the New York State Agricultural Station, who had compiled lists of nineteenth-century varieties by studying seed lists, invoices, and catalogues. Becker has since become a sort of guru for living historical museums in search of old varieties. In his professional life, he introduces newly bred beans and cabbages to upstate New York farmers, but privately he is fascinated by the old varieties. His curiosity was sparked by his father, a book collector, who gave him several nineteenth-century horticultural volumes when he was in college.

For twenty years Becker collected and studied nineteenth-century sources as a hobby, but his interest came out of the closet in 1976, when the New York State Agricultural Station asked him to plant an heirloom garden for the Bicentennial. Since then Becker has accumulated a modest collection of heirloom varieties, including White Flat Dutch turnips, Early Bassano beets, Prince Albert and Champion of England peas, and Cowhorn, Early Rose, Snowflake, and Triumph potatoes. He has also culled lists of nineteenth-century varieties from his extensive library and, in many cases, located contemporary sources for them. Published in the *ALHFAM Bulletin*, these lists have proved invaluable to living historical museums that have wanted to start heirloom gardens.

Snowflake potato. *Tuber oval, always flattened, and quite remarkable for its neat symmetrical shape; skin pale yellow or grayish white, sometimes smooth but usually wrinkled; flesh white, very floury, and light in texture . . . This is one of the best American varieties.* AV

The Search for Authentic Heirlooms

Lynne Belluscio at the Genesee Country Museum already had a "want list," and some of the varieties on it simply couldn't be found in American seed catalogues. That didn't surprise Becker or Belluscio. "Many of these vegetables are not disease-resistant, don't produce high yields, and don't have particularly fine flavor," observes Belluscio. "So a museum is really the only place to grow them." To find the old varieties, she turned to Joseph Harris, then president of the century-old Harris Seed Company. Harris located seeds for twenty-six old varieties, sometimes by going to wholesale growers and foreign seed firms.

At first glance, the heirloom garden at the Genesee Country Museum doesn't reveal this effort. The differences between nineteenth- and twentieth-century varieties are subtle, and Belluscio eagerly points them out to visitors. For one thing, nineteenth-century gardeners were interested primarily in vegetables that would keep over the long winter. "In the early 1800s, people didn't have a varied vegetable diet," says Belluscio. "They paid little attention to fresh vegetables and concentrated on vegetables that could be pickled, dried, or preserved in root cellars." Though some beans and corn were eaten fresh, most varieties were chosen because they dried well. Similarly, nineteenth-century gardeners were partial to a large beet called Winter Keeper, which looks ungainly but stores well in a root cellar. "The garden also reflects changes in America's tastes," says Belluscio. "Our cooks don't really like to use turnips—they'd rather substitute potatoes—but nineteenth-century cooks preferred the taste of turnips."

To make visitors more aware of the heritage gardens, the museum decided to distribute seeds from the old varieties to interested gardeners. Those who grow the vegetables are invited to bring their produce to the harvest festival held each fall. The seeds have been received with enthusiasm, and hundreds of

Champion of England pea. *Universally admitted to be one of the richest and best flavored peas grown, and very productive. Height four or five feet; seed whitish-green and much shrivelled. We consider this equal in quality to any in cultivation, either for the amateur or the market gardener.* DM

packets are distributed each year. Roger Kline, a vegetable specialist at Cornell University who helped arrange the distribution, explains the response as a search quite literally for roots. "The heirloom garden makes the past accessible," he observes. "It's not just a description or a text but a living plot of history growing in the yard." The seeds have also made gardeners aware, often for the first time, of the changes in vegetables and the fact that old varieties, like antique kitchen implements, are heirlooms that should be preserved.

The Genesee Country Museum's collection of seeds has also caught the attention of other museums, which have used it to sidestep original research into authentic local varieties. Several of the institutions surveyed for this book reported that they order the Genesee Country Museum heirlooms each year just as they would order from any other seed supplier. The advantage to the museums is clear. Founded with high hopes and low budgets, many are overwhelmed by the task of recreating the minutiae of the past. "Research for living historical farms demands an attention to detail seldom encountered in other kinds of historical work," writes John Schlebecker in *The Living Historical Farms Handbook*. "If a general historian cannot find all the details on some aspect of life in the past, he can often write around the subject or even ignore it. The historian for a farm, however, must somehow or other find out such details as the kind of fences, plants, animals and equipment the original farmer had used."

RESEARCHING LINCOLN'S CROPS

Historical research can be particularly exasperating when it concerns plants and animals, which are constantly evolving. Historians can make educated guesses about appropriate tools and buildings from surviving physical specimens, but plants leave few physical clues. Some researchers try to work backward from contemporary varieties, a process rather like trying to reconstruct a log cabin by looking at a subdivision split-level. Others try to work from historical sources, but there, too, information is sparse. The problems faced by the staff of Old Sturbridge Village in Massachusetts when they tried to expand the Pliny Freeman Farm are typical. "Everyone knew there had to be a garden next to the house," recalls John Schlebecker. "What no one knew and what was very difficult to find out was what crops were usually planted in that garden."

Some living historical farms and museums are fortunate enough to have someone who will do the extensive research on appropriate crops. For example, the Lincoln Boyhood National Memorial in Lincoln City, Indiana, solicited the help of Henry Waltmann, a Purdue University historian. His 143-page monograph, "Pioneer Farming in Indiana," describes the crops that were probably grown by Abraham Lincoln's father between 1816 and 1830. In the early pages of the monograph, Waltmann notes the inevitable dangers of drawing conclusions about old varieties. "An inquiry of this nature has many inherent difficulties," he notes. "Not the least of these are the scarcity, vagueness and inconsistency of primary historical records. Frontiersmen of the early 1800's rarely kept permanent records of the specific names or botanical traits of their crops."

Despite that disclaimer, the Waltmann study is a model of the detective work that living historical farms must do to determine who grew what, where, and when. Separate sections address field crops, including corn; cash crops; orchard crops; and intertillage crops such as beans, pumpkins, and turnips. In each case, Waltmann sifted through letters, diaries, agricultural journals, and other documents to come up with educated guesses about what Thomas Lincoln might have grown. For some crops he recommends specific varieties, such as Rawle's Janet apple, Old Connecticut pumpkin, and White Globe turnip. In other cases he pieces together a description of an unnamed crop. He recommends, for example, that the Lincoln City farm plant a yellow gourd seed corn—"preferably a cross between Virginia Gourd Seed and Large Flint . . . which should be capable of attaining a height of at least twelve feet and bearing thick ears with at least 16–24 rows of yellowish kernels." Waltmann's recommendations have, for the most part, been followed at the Lincoln Boyhood National Memorial, where visitors can see Yellow Gourd corn, Mammouth pumpkins, White Globe turnips, and other crops much like those young Abraham Lincoln must have known.

RESTORING JEFFERSON'S GARDENS

The gardens at Monticello have also been scrupulously researched, thanks in large part to Thomas Jefferson's own *Garden Book*. This journal, which details garden activities between 1809 and 1825, was the basis for the extensive restorations of the gardens that began in 1979. While archeologists excavated the grounds to determine precisely where fences had been located and trees had been planted, curator Peter Hatch researched the 250 vegetable and 150 fruit varieties mentioned by Jefferson. "Jefferson demonstrates a remarkable horticultural sophistication in his choice of varieties," notes Hatch, "whether the choicest fruits of the Old World, such as English cherries, French pears, or Dutch cabbages, or the new, often untested American varieties, such as salsify from the Western mountains, giant cucumbers from Ohio, peppers from Mexico, or the countless apple and peach seedlings that were to be so successful."

Many of the varieties described by Jefferson have disappeared; Hatch estimates that only 15 percent of the vegetable varieties and 45 percent of the fruit varieties can be retrieved. Finding the varieties is further complicated by the fact that Jefferson named varieties but didn't describe them. In addition, he

Long Red pepper. *Fruit brilliant coral-red, generally pendulous, sometimes erect, conical, often curved towards the end, nearly four inches in length, and from an inch to an inch and a half in diameter; skin or flesh, quite thin, and exceedingly piquant. Stalk two feet high; foliage of medium size, blistered and wrinkled.* FB

used his gardens to test new varieties—some acquired from friends and named after them, some sent from overseas. "Jefferson may have grown as many as forty different varieties of beans," explains Hatch. "Three or four would become the standard of excellence and the others would be discarded."

Today, the layout of the gardens matches that described by Jefferson in 1812, and heirloom fruit trees have been planted in the eight-acre orchard. The vegetable garden follows Jefferson's plan of grouping plants according to the part that was eaten—fruit, roots, or leaves. For the moment, most of the varieties are, in Hatch's words, "the grandchildren of old varieties still offered by seed houses." Hatch intends to acquire old varieties gradually since the garden, as he puts it, is a "long-term commitment."

RESEARCH PROBLEMS

Few historic sites are fortunate enough to have documentation as elaborate as Jefferson's *Garden Book* or a researcher as dedicated as Henry Waltmann. Many museums opt for an approach similar to that taken by the Clayville Rural Life Center and Museum in Pleasant Plains, Illinois. The centerpiece at this museum is a 150-year-old stagecoach stop, where, research indicates, the presiding family would have had a large kitchen garden. To find out what would have been grown in the garden, the museum staff relied on two sources—*The Young Gardener's Assistant*, a book published in 1836, and "On Practical Gardening in Illinois," an essay published in 1857 by the Illinois Agricultural Society. According to Edward Hawes, the museum's director, the first step was to make lists of all the vegetable varieties mentioned by the two sources. Next, the staff examined contemporary seed catalogues from Henry Field, Gurney Seed Company, and Shumway. Any variety that appeared on both the seed list and in a catalogue went into the garden.

Though the Clayville approach produces authentic gardens, it preserves the heirlooms that need it least because they have survived commercially. Museums could play a more significant preservation—and educational—role if they sought out varieties that have been dropped by seed companies. For example, in the essay "On Practical Gardening" used as a research source by the Clayville staff, the author mentions three varieties of sweet corn—Smith's Early White, Red Cob Sweet, and Mammoth Sweet. Instead of looking for those heirlooms, Clayville settled for Country Gentleman, a nineteenth-century variety that is still widely sold by seed companies. The test, of course, will be whether museums such as Clayville accept responsibility for gathering and preserving seed from old varieties even if they are discontinued by the seed companies.

Another problem with the Clayville approach is that variety names change, so that what is called Egyptian beet in a twentieth-century catalogue may bear little resemblance to the Egyptian beet grown in the nineteenth, much less the eighteenth, century. Staff members at the Claude Moore Colonial Farm at Turkey Run, in McLean, Virginia, have tried to circumvent that problem with a different research approach. To find crops typical of the eighteenth-century period the farm represents, staff members comb almanacs, herbals, period gardening manuals, cookbooks, and eighteenth-century advertisements. Their goal is to find descriptions of fruit and vegetable varieties rather than variety names. Staff members then study contemporary catalogues to find vegetables that match the descriptions. "We look for seeds that produce proper-looking vegetables," explains one staff member.

Unfortunately, the Turkey Run approach to heirlooms also results in the preservation of varieties that are still being sold by seed companies. In fairness, it must be acknowledged that museums like Clayville and Turkey Run have valid reasons for depending on purchased seed. Most living historical museums are

Mammoth Sweet corn. *This variety produces the largest ears of any sort with which we are acquainted, a single ear sometimes weighing two or three pounds. The quality is excellent— sweet, tender and delicious. For family use, it cannot be excelled.* DM

run by historians who have little training in horticulture. "I am a self-taught gardener," says Clarissa Dillon of the Colonial Pennsylvania Plantation. "My historical interest is the uses of plants in the eighteenth century, not the plants themselves." Though Dillon is teaching herself the techniques for seed saving, many institutions are not able to hire staff members who are trained in the methods for plant variety preservation.

One solution to this problem might be the use of community volunteers. For example, the Heckler Plains Farmstead in Harleysville, Pennsylvania, has an elaborate garden that is planned and tended by several volunteer organizations. Unlike other museums that expect to attract tourists, Heckler Plains Farmstead serves the local citizens with monthly meetings at which historic skills are demonstrated. "We do not believe history should be taught exclusively from textbooks," says one museum publication. "At the center of all our efforts is respect for a community's collective wisdom, kept alive by an oral tradition." Collective wisdom is evident in the garden, for which research was done by amateur historians and whose rarer plants were donated by local collectors. The garden is the special project of a local 4H group and the volunteer Herb Committee that meets once a month. Because of the interests of its members, herbs dominate the Heckler garden; yet it takes little imagination to see how a volunteer group of this kind could take responsibility for locating and growing old fruit and vegetable varieties.

TRACKING DOWN HEIRLOOM SEEDS

Museums also settle for commercial varieties because they don't know where else to find seeds. Some museum gardeners have joined seed exchanges, and some have sent specific requests to the National Seed Storage Laboratory in Fort Collins, Colorado. Few, however, take advantage of uniquely local resources such as land grant universities and local collectors.

One exception to that rule is the George Washington Birthplace National Monument, which has had an heirloom garden since 1932. The garden includes crops that young George Washington might have known on his father's Tidewater tobacco plantation around 1740. The vegetables are, for the most part, old varieties that are still being offered in seed catalogues—"It's remarkable to me how many varieties have come right down from colonial times," says gardener Barry Whitman—but several field crops were acquired from universities. "I recommend starting with a state agricultural school," says Whitman. "They'll either have what you want or they'll refer you. And you just follow the chain until you get to the source." By following a chain of referrals, Whitman obtained Christa fiber flax from the University of Minnesota, Purple straw wheat from the Small Grains Collection in Beltsville, Maryland, and Venezuelan tobacco from Duke University. "It can be a slow and convoluted process," says Whitman, "but it works."

Approaching local collectors is often quicker and more productive. When the Pioneer Farm in Austin, Texas, decided in 1982 that it wanted to have "locally adapted plant varieties" in its gardens, director John Peterson turned to three local collectors, who contributed seeds from old and sometimes rare varieties. The garden now reflects the interests of those collectors, with rare grape varieties such as Dogridge and Marguerite from the Munson grape collection managed by Dr. Roy Renfro. In the fields, old bean varieties, including Willow Leaf Pole lima and Frosty Pole bean from Robert Daubert, climb contentedly on the stalks of Gourd Seed corn from R. C. Mauldin, a seed certifier who is concerned about the disappearance of old varieties and tries to keep a few selected ones going. Having been entrusted with seeds from the old varieties, the farm has started its own seed-saving program so that the varieties will be available year after year.

Another innovative approach to seed acquisition was

Surprise muskmelon. *Said to be the finest-flavored melon grown; resembles the Nutmeg; flesh deep-salmon color, and very thick.* PW

adopted by the New Hampshire Farm Museum in Wilton, N.H., during the mid-1970s, when staff members solicited seeds from local gardeners who would never have called themselves collectors. The founders of the New Hampshire Farm Museum felt that the agricultural heritage of their state could best be preserved if it were understood as the collective heritage of individuals. With that philosophy, it was natural for the museum to turn to the community to find out about crops that might have been grown in New Hampshire in the early nineteenth century. Museum staff members coaxed old varieties out of the community by spreading the word that the museum was establishing an heirloom seed bank. Staff members tried to document the authenticity of donated varieties through family records such as ledgers or journals.

The program was remarkably successful. Among others, the museum obtained samples of Cowhorn potatoes, Rhode Island White Cap corn, and various beans, including New Hampshire Red Flint, Lowe's Champion, Trout, and Yellow Eye. One exceptional find was a box of still-viable seeds from a seed company that had been in business in the 1870s. For a while, the old varieties were distributed to local gardeners, who agreed to return replenished seed.

The New Hampshire Farm Museum's seed-saving program demonstrates that, as custodians of local history, living-history farms are in a unique position to obtain old varieties that have been passed down from generation to generation by local families. Unfortunately, it also reveals the dangers in such programs. In 1978, because of financial difficulties, the museum changed directors and curtailed its programs. As a result, the heirloom seeds were stored while other programs took precedence. Although the new director has good intentions of reactivating the program, the seeds have already waited beyond their usual shelf life. The moral is that museums that want to include heirloom varieties in their collections must treat them as the precious and vulnerable artifacts they are by storing them properly and growing them out regularly.

A Model Program at the
National Colonial Farm

Fortunately, there are living historical museums that have committed themselves to protecting as well as acquiring rare heirloom varieties. One of these programs is ably managed by Dr. David Percy at the National Colonial Farm in Accokeek, Maryland.

Established in 1958 to preserve the view from Mount Vernon, the National Colonial Farm has always regarded scientific and agricultural research as "a vital part of the program." One of the farm's first efforts was the restoration of a grove of American chestnuts, a climax tree in the mid-eighteenth century that has since been decimated by disease. More recently, the farm has begun an ambitious twenty-year program to identify, procure, and preserve varieties like those that would have been grown on the modest Tidewater Plantation in about 1750.

So far the staff has added two or three varieties each year, though they expect to accelerate the pace of acquisition so that the farm will be maintaining more than a hundred varieties at the end of twenty years. To determine which varieties should be grown, staff members study original documents, particularly diaries from planters such as George Washington, Thomas Jefferson, Landon Carter, and John Beale Bordley. Every decision to introduce a variety as an heirloom must be supported by two sources. To locate old varieties, Dr. Percy depends on a list of almost seventy seed companies. "You'd be surprised what they have sitting on the back shelf," he smiles. Percy has also found that some old varieties are still available in Africa, which was colonized at about the same time as Virginia by settlers who brought along similar seeds.

One of the varieties being preserved at Accokeek is Virginia Gourd Seed corn, which was the chief corn cultivated south of Pennsylvania until 1820. Grown for people, not animals, the corn was eaten green on the cob. Thanks to its unusually high starch content, it makes particularly nourishing cornmeal or hominy. Another variety being preserved at Accokeek is Red May wheat, which represented 4 percent of the U.S. wheat crop in 1940. Today, it has virtually disappeared, and the farm had to obtain its supplies from the Small Grains Collection in Beltsville, Maryland. Other varieties in the Accokeek collection include the Danvers White carrot, West Indian gherkin, Champion of England pea, and several old bean varieties. Dr. Percy acknowledges that his varieties are probably not identical to those grown in the 1700s. "We can't produce conditions identical to the eighteenth century," he concedes. "Evolution occurs; varieties disappear. But the old varieties that still exist are survivors. In the 1700s, they were subjected to extreme conditions—insects, disease, and weather—yet they were productive."

The National Colonial Farm's primary purpose is to illustrate agricultural practices from the eighteenth century. "I'd like to think," says Dr. Percy, "that if you could pluck someone from the eighteenth century, that person would walk through our fields and say, 'That's Virginia Gourd Seed corn.'" To strengthen the eighteenth-century illusion, the farm also practices cultural techniques common to the period. Tobacco leaves are used as mulch because they discourage insects. Corn, beans, and pumpkins are planted together because the corn provides a natural trellis for the beans and the pumpkins quickly cover the ground to keep down weeds.

Despite its allegiance to the past, the National Colonial Farm could also be a model for the future. Dr. Percy likes to speculate that "if each of the established living historical farms cultivated a hundred varieties common to its period and geographical area, more than 15,000 old varieties would be pre-served in cultivation." Yet even Percy admits that most living historical farms don't have the resources or capabilities to pursue such programs. As a result, Accokeek, like the Genesee Country Museum, has been a coattail program, sharing seeds with other less ambitious institutions. The farm also shares its research in a series of reports covering such topics as the "Origin and evolution of *Zea mays*."

Regardless of whether or not other institutions can match Accokeek's research, perhaps they can emulate its commitment. Once a variety has been accepted into the Accokeek collection, it is replenished every two years by researchers who are careful to screen seed parents to be sure they are true to type. "This is a long-range project," says Dr. Percy. "We intend to stay in the old-seed business. What's the point of collecting these seeds if we don't plan to perpetuate them?"

The Need for Long-term Commitment

Dr. Percy's question is not rhetorical. Many institutions have started heirloom gardens, often at the urging of an enthusiastic staff member, only to abandon the project when the staff member moved on to another institution or another interest. At Old World Wisconsin, in Eagle, Wisconsin, Jim Johnson, an expert on old varieties, volunteered to plan and plant different heirloom gardens for several of the homes in the living historical village. At the time, staff members responded enthusiastically. "We wanted to avoid cutesy, sanitized history where there's no manure in the barnyard," says one museum staff member. "We wanted everything to be authentic, right down to vintage plants."

Working from written and oral records, Johnson created four vegetable gardens, often using rare vegetable varieties from his own collections. One of the most elaborate included vege-

White Spine cucumber. *One of the best sorts for the table; and is greatly prized by market-men on account of its color, which is never changed to yellow, though kept long after being plucked . . . plants grow from six to ten feet in length; and . . . are of a healthy, luxurious habit. The fruit is of full medium size . . . skin deep green, prickles white, flesh white, tender, crispy and of remarkably fine flavor. As the fruit ripens, the skin gradually becomes paler and when fully ripe is nearly white; by which peculiarity, in connection with its white spines, the variety is always readily distinguished.* FB

tables that would have been grown by a Pomeranian farmer in 1860, such as the Gigantea cabbage, White Spine cucumber, White Marrow Fat bean, and Blue Victor potato. When Johnson, who was not an employee of the museum, left, the gardens collapsed. Museum staff members stopped saving seed from the old varieties and gradually replaced them with contemporary varieties. Had antique furniture been lost and replaced with contemporary "equivalents," the staff and the public would have been outraged; yet the loss of fine old garden vegetables was treated casually. "We're evaluating the whole situation," says one staff member. "Gardens are very elusive. The best we can hope for is a composite that approximates what would have been grown."

Old Apples at Old Sturbridge Village

Museums that are unable to make the commitment required by seed-bearing vegetables may be better off caring for heirloom orchards, which, once planted, can survive benign neglect for many years. At Old Sturbridge Village, one of the largest and most active living-history museums, the vegetable gardens are filled with old varieties that are still available from seed companies. The museum's commitment to keeping old plants alive appears in the orchard, which is managed jointly with the Worcester County Horticultural Society. The Society started the orchard in the 1930s, when Stearns L. Davenport made a list of sixty varieties that had become rare even then. It took Davenport thirty years to locate them all, and by then he was too old to maintain the collection.

In 1970, Old Sturbridge Village agreed to relocate the collection to five acres of land near the village, and all the trees were grafted onto dwarf rootstock to simplify their care. The Preservation Orchard contributes to the historical flavor of Old Sturbridge Village and is as much a treat for apple connoisseurs

In the temperate regions, the apple is not only the most valuable fruit, but it is of more importance than all others. Other kinds are more luscious and delicate, but these qualities render them transient, while the apple endures and may be had in excellence throughout the year . . . We have had fruit from a tree in Plymouth 200 years old . . . with its blossoms of white, tinged with red, or with beautiful fruit, the apple is an ornamental tree, and some with fine forms and rich dark green foliage, are always so in the gay season. AFB

as a visit to the Tuileries would be for fans of Impressionism. Each tree is represented by a single specimen; visitors can stroll up and down the wide aisles remarking on the deep crimson color of Sops of Wine, the aroma of Grimes Golden, and the history of High Top Sweet, which was a favorite in the Plymouth Colony.

INTERPRETING HEIRLOOMS AT THE OLIVER H. KELLEY FARM

Teaching history is, of course, the purpose of living historical museums, and many don't bother to plant old varieties because they believe the differences between old and new crops are too subtle to be appreciated by the public. Indeed, surveys show that museum visitors like crafts demonstrations and have minimal interest in crops. "Interpreting crop varieties is not easy," admits Tom Woods of the Oliver H. Kelley Farm in Elk River, Minnesota. "But it is not an impossible task, and visitors can begin to understand that our corn, wheat, potatoes, and tomatoes are different today, just as our houses and furniture are different." Educating the public about old varieties is one of the most valuable roles museums can play, and the newly organized Oliver H. Kelley Farm has an exemplary program.

The farm focuses on Oliver Kelley, a "book farmer" who was interested in finding new crops that would grow well in Minnesota. He wrote articles on agricultural research, arranged for seed exchanges, promoted agricultural fairs, and organized a county farming society that became a model for the Grange. Today, the farm staff holds a seed swap in the spring at which they offer the public seed from heirloom crops grown on the farm, including Black Norway oats, Early Horn carrots, and Yellow Eye beans. All the varieties were selected because they were mentioned by Kelley or his contemporaries as crops grown

King Philip corn. *Ears ten to twelve inches in length, uniformly eight-rowed when the variety is pure or unmixed; kernel copper red, rather large, somewhat broader than deep, smooth and glossy; cob small, pinkish-white; stalk six feet in height, producing one or two ears, about two feet and a half from the ground . . . in warm seasons, it is sometimes fully ripened in ninety days from the time of planting . . . Very productive, and recommended as one of the best field sorts now in cultivation. Said to have originated on one of the islands in Lake Winnipiseogee, N.H.* FB

between 1850 and 1876. In the fall, gardeners are encouraged to bring heirloom vegetables to an agricultural fair.

The seed exchange and agricultural fair are intended to whet the public's interest in heirloom varieties. Yet Woods also weaves the stories of old varieties into the history of the site. For example, one of the most prominent crops on the farm is Improved King Philip corn, a brown-kerneled corn that was very popular in the mid-1850s. When visitors comment on its different appearance, Woods steps in to tell them that Improved King Philip was the first dent corn to be grown successfully so far north. Before it was introduced, farmers had grown flint corn, which is not as productive. Improved King Philip resulted from a cross between King Philip (a flint corn) and a dent corn. Its growing season was short enough for Minnesota, and its dramatically improved yields made it possible for Northern farmers to raise livestock for market for the first time.

Woods believes that information like this is both interesting to the public and central to the purposes of living historical farms. "To interpret the significance of agriculture's role in society, you have to talk about crops," he says. "Authentic plants tell as much, if not more, about agricultural history as an antique plow." In fact, he argues, museums that plant inappropriate varieties can pass on inaccurate historical images. He notes, for example, that the wheat grown in the nineteenth century had much longer stems than contemporary varieties. To the knowledgeable eye, the shorter wheat looks as out of place in a nineteenth-century field as a garbage disposal would in a nineteenth-century kitchen. Furthermore, the twentieth-century wheat cannot be harvested in the nineteenth-century manner because the stems are too short for making shocks or tying bundles. Though Woods is the first to admit that heirloom varieties are expensive and time-consuming, he believes agricultural museums have no choice but to seek out and preserve authentic fruits, vegetables, and field crops.

Breeding the Old

Museum curators appear to be allies of heirloom gardeners; yet the historian's preoccupation with authenticity does not always lead to the preservation of existing heirlooms. For example, in the interests of historic accuracy, some museums have considered "back-breeding," a deliberate effort to recreate what was grown a century ago by breeding for undesirable characteristics. "Back-breeding is what the Indians did in reverse," says Terry Sharrer of the *ALHFAM Bulletin*. "The Indians wanted larger and larger food crops. Living historical farms select for smaller and smaller. The goal of back-breeding is to select the scrawniest animals and rangiest seeds for next year."

So far, the most successful back-breeding efforts have been with animals. Theorizing that the unique genetic characteristics of old breeds are scrambled in their modern descendants, two German zoologists decided to breed an auroch, a wild ancestor of cattle that became extinct about 350 years ago. The scientists located cattle that had characteristics associated with aurochs and crossed them to produce two auroch lookalikes. When bred, the pair produced more new-wave aurochs.

Historians have suggested that similar efforts be made with plants—back-breeding carrots, for example, to produce yellow varieties. Peter Hatch, curator at Monticello, speculates that "in theory, the continual sowing of hybrids should result in a regression to a more primitive variety similar to what Jefferson may have had, though there is no scientific substantiation for such a process." Indeed, most plant scientists throw up their hands in horror at the thought that time, skill, and money should be spent breeding deliberately inferior vegetables in the name of historic accuracy. Willing as they may be to save existing varieties, they think it profligate to expend resources reconstituting extinct varieties when the world needs new varieties that are more productive, more disease-resistant, and more nutritious.

Early Scarlet Turnip-rooted radish. *Bulb spherical—measuring in its greatest perfection an inch in diameter; skin fine, deep scarlet; flesh white, sometimes stained with red; leaves large and numerous. The variety is early and deserves more general cultivation, not only on account of its rich color, but for the crisp and tender properties of its flesh. It is much esteemed in England.* DM

Historians are predictably nonplused by the argument that new is better, but most are intimidated by the cost of plant breeding.

Perhaps that cost will help living-history farms see that their needs for authentic fruit and vegetable varieties can be satisfied with heirloom varieties that already exist and are in need of protection. Kent Whealy has offered the use of his Growers Network to find old varieties that will be appropriate for particular periods and places. "Some of the varieties in the Seed Savers Exchange have been kept by the same family in the same area for one hundred and fifty years," says Whealy. "Certainly these local heirlooms would be more appropriate than the older commercial varieties, which may now be only distant cousins of the materials museums are seeking." In return, Whealy hopes museums will make a commitment to preserve and "showcase" the old varieties.

Few museums have demonstrated the ability to keep old varieties alive, but more and more seem willing to try. Whealy's organization has received requests for old varieties from dozens of living-history sites, including many small, community-based historic farms and homes. The Association of Living History Farms and Museums has initiated a Breeds and Seeds program to help members locate and exchange rare old varieties. Older historic homes, such as Mount Vernon and the Hermitage, are considering heirloom fruit and vegetable varieties for the first time. And, perhaps most important, new museums seem to be including appropriate fruit and vegetable varieties in their plans from the beginning. The Blue Ridge Institute, for example, started searching for Hotspur peas and other heirloom vegetables as soon as they began work on the restoration of an 1800 German-American farm in Virginia. In Ohio, a twelfth-century Indian Village recently excavated and restored by the Dayton Museum of Natural History is surrounded by gardens that include Iroquois Flour corn, Tamaroa Flint corn, and Genuine Cornfield beans.

All of these developments suggest that living-history museums may soon play an important role in the preservation of heirloom fruit and vegetable varieties. Though the commitment to heirloom varieties can come only from the museums themselves, gardeners can help such programs become established by contributing expertise and, perhaps, seeds from heirloom varieties. The museums can, in turn, share both knowledge and seeds through interpretive programs and seed exchanges. "The potential for historic sites to maintain selected seed stocks is great," says Andy Baker, the gardener at Old Sturbridge Village. "The potential for public education is phenomenal."

6

The Seed as a Ward of the State

GARDENERS WHO HEAR THAT THE UNITED STATES GOVERNMENT
is saving seeds from rare fruit and vegetable varieties have one
of two reactions—relief that the government is "taking care of
it" or pessimism because bureaucrats always botch the job.
Those responses reveal more about the political philosophies of
the speakers than about the national seed-storage program. The
United States has one of the world's best systems for storing
seeds. And it is not good enough.

The U.S. program is called the National Plant Germplasm
System because it focuses on plant materials as raw materials to
be used by plant breeders. Simply stated, the goals of the system
are to identify, collect, store, and distribute seeds and other plant
materials that can be used to improve the food and forage crops
grown in the United States. Because of this orientation, varieties
that are stored in the system are not freely available to ordinary
gardeners and farmers. Furthermore, the system discriminates
against old American varieties, which make up only a fraction
of the collection.

The U.S. Department of Agriculture downplays American

heirlooms by pointing out that "of the fifteen crops that stand between mankind and starvation, not one is native to the United States." There's no disputing the natural history. Though Americans have been brought up to believe that our nation is rich in resources of every kind, when it comes to plant diversity, we are, relatively speaking, a have-not nation. Of the world's estimated 300,000 flowering plants, only 30,000 are native to North America. Of thirty major food crops, none originate on this continent. These facts have skewed the government's priorities on plant collection. Nearly all the plants in the germplasm system come from "centers of origin" that are invariably foreign.

It would be absurd to deny the value of the government's collections. Foreign plant materials, particularly "land races" and "wild relatives" of our food crops, have legitimate value as breeding material. Through patient crossing and back-crossing, their characteristics can be incorporated into contemporary varieties. Often, wild relatives are tough, weedlike varieties that resist environmental stresses such as disease and drought; land races are crops that have been cultivated by native people for centuries and have a high degree of genetic variation. Land races and wild relatives are found mostly in the region where a species originates. Because so few food crops originated in this country, we have no choice but to collect foreign plant materials if we hope to preserve the valuable genetic characteristics of these primitive types.

However, in the drive to accumulate foreign plant resources, the National Plant Germplasm System has largely ignored genetic resources at our own doorstep. Precisely because this country was so poor in food crops, immigrants had to depend upon plants and seeds brought from their native lands. Thousands of years ago, Native Americans brought squash, corn, beans, potatoes, and tomatoes when they emigrated from South to North America, and European settlers did the same

Custard squash. *Plant healthy and of vigorous habit, often twenty feet and upwards in length; fruit oblong, gathered in deep folds, or wrinkles, at the stem, near which it is the smallest, abruptly shortened at the opposite extremity, prominently marked by large, rounded, lengthwise elevations, and corresponding deep furrows or depressions; skin or shell cream-white; flesh pale yellow, not remarkable for solidity or fineness of texture, but well-flavored . . . It is one of the hardiest and most productive of all varieties.* FB

thing. Columbus brought lettuce and cucumbers when he landed in the West Indies, and Cartier planted cabbage and turnips in Canada.

This informal method of introducing new plants has continued throughout our nation's history. Each wave of immigrants brought along seeds, sometimes because they were essential to a national cuisine and sometimes because they were a tangible reminder of the country left behind. Either way, many of these immigrant fruits and vegetables flourished to become today's heirlooms. In a recent issue of the *Seed Savers Yearbook*, some members wrote of their search for seeds brought decades ago from Germany and Italy, and other members offered to share varieties given to them by new neighbors from Cambodia and Cuba.

Thanks to this casual system of plant introduction, the gardens of the United States have become the repositories for some of the best fruit and vegetable varieties in the world. Yet many of these old varieties are not represented in the National Plant Germplasm System. The government made an initial effort to collect "obsolete" varieties from seed companies in the 1960s, but now it depends largely upon the companies to voluntarily supply samples of varieties that are being discontinued. A survey of seed companies suggests that only a small percentage participate in the seed-storage program. As a result, fine heirloom varieties are disappearing quite literally in our own backyard.

THE GOVERNMENT'S INTEREST IN PLANT INTRODUCTION

The bias against domestic varieties has its roots tangled in the history of plant collection. Governments have been trying to procure, if not preserve, new plants ever since 1500 B.C., when Queen Hatshepsut of Egypt sent explorers to bring back the incense tree. Even then, governments justified their existence by serving the public good, and enlightened rulers realized that few things are as good for the public as the introduction of a valuable new plant. No less a public figure than Thomas Jefferson put the matter succinctly when he wrote in his *Garden Book*, "The greatest service which can be rendered to any country is to add a useful plant to its culture."

Jefferson was one of several eighteenth-century leaders who realized that the United States needed an aggressive campaign to import edible and economic plants. He collected plants on all his diplomatic missions for the fledgling nation and once risked the death penalty by smuggling rice seeds out of Italy. His *Garden Book*, kept from 1776 to 1824, records hundreds of plants gathered from around the world for trial at Monticello. Benjamin Franklin was also an avid collector. When he served as the nation's first European ambassador, he sent back many plants, including soybeans and rhubarb.

Jefferson and Franklin acted as private citizens, but the government was close on their heels. In 1819, Secretary of the Treasury William Crawford made an official effort to collect plants by enlisting the help of foreign diplomats and U.S. Navy personnel in "the introduction of useful plants . . . an object of great importance to every civilized state." Unfortunately, the rhetoric about the value of plants was not backed up with funds; so the results of those early expeditions were erratic.

Money for plant introduction wasn't allocated until 1839. By that time, responsibility for importing new plants and seeds had shifted to the Patent Office under the dubious logic that newly discovered plants were little different from human inventions. The Patent Office strategy for establishing new plants was to obtain seeds and distribute small quantities to as many people as possible. Knowing that the annual appropriation of $1,000 was too little to accomplish this goal, a resourceful commissioner named Oliver Ellsworth persuaded sympathetic congressmen to use their postal frank to distribute the seeds. The political benefits of handing out free seeds were immediately obvious, and by 1847 Americans were being treated to 60,000 packets a year, courtesy of their congressmen.

Politics being what it is, the pork-barrel possibilities of seed distribution soon took precedence over plant introduction. By 1862, when Congress established the Department of Agriculture, nearly a million packages of seed were being distributed each year. Among other things, free seed eroded the self-reliant habit of saving seed and gave rise to the idea that home-grown seed was inferior. Ironically, the vegetable seeds being distributed by the government were of uncertain value. The Department of Agriculture paid greatest attention to market crops such as sorghum, cotton, and wheat, and vegetable seeds were often gleaned from undistinguished varieties.

By the end of the nineteenth century, seed companies were complaining that the Department of Agriculture was undermining their business by distributing common seeds, and scientists were objecting that the unusual varieties were not going to people qualified to test them. By 1893 the situation had deteriorated so badly that Agricultural Commissioner Sterling Morton charged that seeds being given away were inferior varieties that had been dumped in the United States by foreign governments and seed companies. Congress, however, had become attached to the idea of giving away free seeds and distributed a record nineteen million packets in 1897.

A SYSTEMATIC APPROACH TO PLANT INTRODUCTION

While Congress was giving away seeds of doubtful worth, American plant explorers were combing the planet for new plants of genuine value. Such legendary plant explorers as Niels Hansen, David Fairchild, and Seaman Knapp sought out unusual plants in wild and remote corners of the earth. Despite the effort that went into their collection, the new plants were often

Carolina watermelon. *Fruit of large size, and of an oblong form, usually somewhat swollen towards the blossom end; skin deep green, variegated with pale green or white; flesh deep red, not fine grained, but crisp, sweet, and of fair quality; fruit frequently hollow at the centre.* FB

lost through careless handling when they arrived in the United States. In 1898, the Department of Agriculture decided to curb such losses by establishing a Plant Introduction Office with responsibility for collecting, cataloguing, testing, and distributing valuable new plants. A cabbage from Russia was the first entry in the new system and was duly designated Plant Introduction #1. Today, more than 465,000 plant introduction numbers have been assigned, and each acquisition is described in annual plant inventory publications.

The plant introduction system was an important advance because it systematized all known information about a new plant, making it more likely that breeders and farmers would exploit its valuable features. The system's glaring weakness, however, was the total lack of any provision for preserving seeds once they were introduced. At the time, scientists had not yet mastered the principles, much less the techniques, of plant breeding; so plants that had no immediate and obvious economic value were neglected or even discarded.

Mason cabbage. *In shape . . . nearly hemispherical; the head standing well out from among the leaves, growing on a small and short stalk. Under good cultivation, the heads will average nine inches in diameter and seven inches in depth. It is characterized for its sweetness and for its reliability for forming a solid head.* FB

As plant genetics came of age, scientists began to realize that even apparently worthless plants might include valuable genes for, perhaps, stronger stems, larger fruits, or disease resistance. When scientists looked for older plant introductions whose descriptions included useful characteristics, they found, to their dismay, that many had vanished. By the 1940s, 90 percent of all soybean and 98 percent of all clover introductions had simply disappeared.

Recognizing the seriousness of the problem, the National Research Council recommended construction of a national repository for seeds in 1944. Two years later, the Research and Marketing Act established a cooperative plant introduction program in which the federal government agreed to procure foreign plant material and the states took responsibility for evaluating its usefulness at their agricultural research stations. To simplify distribution of plant materials, four regional plant introduction stations were established. The first, built in 1948 in Ames, Iowa, served states in the Midwest. Within five years, Western, Northeast, and Southern stations had been built in Pullman, Washington; Geneva, New York; and Experiment, Georgia. Finally, in 1956, Congress authorized $450,000 for construction of a central seed-storage facility in Fort Collins, Colorado.

LESSONS OF THE CORN BLIGHT

During the 1960s, the National Seed Storage Laboratory and the plant introduction (PI) stations limped along, chronically underfunded but doing their best to serve the ever more sophisticated needs of plant breeders. Plant exploration ground to a halt even as scientists were expressing alarm over the rapid destruction of land races and wild relatives of domestic plants in developing countries. No one paid much attention to their warnings—until the corn blight.

In 1970, a now infamous fungus destroyed 15 percent of the corn crop in the United States and up to 50 percent in some states. The disease, which had previously been confined to the Deep South, spread when, according a *New York Times* report, "a vicious mutant variety appeared." Of course, like every other living creature, disease organisms are constantly mutating—and that means the possibility of potentially "vicious" forms. The corn crop was vulnerable to the new disease because nearly all the varieties being grown by American farmers had descended from a single parent.

That parent strain, called Texas (T) cytoplasm, excited breeders because it had genes that rendered the male part of the plant sterile. As a result, seed growers didn't have to detassel their corn and could produce hybrid seed more efficiently. Enthusiastic breeders promptly incorporated the new genes into

all their corn varieties, never realizing that they were also breeding in susceptibility to the "vicious mutant" disease.

The corn blight was shocking evidence that the "genetic
vulnerability" scientists had been talking about was real and potentially devastating. Fortunately, seed companies still had leftover reserves of seed from plants without the sterile cytoplasm.
They quickly increased their supplies, and within a year the
blight was under control. The epidemic, however, brought the
problem of germplasm preservation out of the laboratory and
into farmers' fields and congressional conference rooms. In
1972, the National Academy of Sciences issued a report confirming that genetic uniformity had been the villain in the corn
blight and warning that other crops were equally vulnerable.
"This disturbing uniformity is not due to chance alone," the report noted. "The forces that produced it are powerful and they
are varied. They pose a severe dilemma . . . How can society
have the uniformity it demands without the hazards of epidemics?"

Clearly, one answer was an improved system of germplasm
preservation; so early in the 1970s, the Department of Agriculture devised an elaborate blueprint for a new National Plant
Germplasm System (NPGS). For its main components, the Department dusted off the PI stations established in the 1940s and
the National Seed Storage Laboratory built in the 1950s. The
system also included a few contemporary touches, such as a
computerized Germplasm Resources Information Network
and a support system of advisory groups. The goal was a coor-
dinated system that would clarify and oversee germplasm preservation in this country.

THE ROLE OF PLANT INTRODUCTION STATIONS

Today, NPGS has an estimated 500,000 germplasm samples in
storage. At first glance that figure might look more than ade-

quate; yet the system suffers from a variety of problems that make the preservation of plant materials uncertain at best. For one thing, the new system perpetuates the old bias against domestic varieties. Most materials enter the system through the Plant Introduction Office, whose historic function is to process materials from foreign countries. About 20 percent of the plant material that comes through the Plant Introduction Office is acquired through foreign plant explorations. The rest is donated by foreign governments, usually in response to requests from scientists and plant breeders. After any neccessary quarantine, the Plant Introduction Office identifies, catalogues, and distributes plant materials to the appropriate PI station. (See Appendix VI for a list of PI stations and their crop responsibilities.)

Each of the four PI stations has responsibility for germplasm related to crops that are important in its region. When a PI station receives new seeds, its first obligation is to grow them out. This task, in itself, can be overwhelming since the system absorbs 7,000 to 15,000 plant introductions each year. In 1981 alone, the Southern PI station had to grow out more than 8,000 accessions.

Not all the seeds can be grown successfully, but scientists make careful notes about each introduction. They look for unique and useful characteristics and make special efforts to determine whether the plant is resistant to diseases and insects that are troublesome in the region. All information about the plant is published in a catalogue of available new materials that goes to plant breeders. To draw attention to promising new materials, government researchers may undertake preliminary crossing. The "improved" germplasm is then released to private breeders, who further refine it until it is ready to be released as a named cultivar.

Thousands of varieties have been developed this way, but two examples will illustrate the process. In the early 1930s, scientists drew attention to PI #79532, a wild Peruvian tomato

Yellow onion. *One of the oldest varieties, and as a market onion, probably better known and more generally cultivated in this country than any other sort. The true Yellow Onion has a flattened form and a small neck. Its size is rather above medium . . . Skin yellowish-brown or copperyellow—becoming somewhat deeper by age, or if exposed long to the sun. Flesh white, finegrained, mild, sugary and well flavored. It keeps well and is very prolific . . . for the vegetable garden, it may be considered a standard sort.* FB with resistance to fusarium wilt. Today, fusarium wilt has been virtually eradicated because new varieties carry resistance derived from the genes of PI #79532. In 1948, plant explorer E. M. Meader collected a cucumber in Korea that was labeled PI #220860. When researchers at the Northeast PI station grew out the plant, they found that most of the plants had only female flowers. This "gynoecious" trait made plants more productive because female flowers produce the fruit. PI #220860 was shown to breeders in 1954, and they quickly incorporated the trait into many of their new introductions.

The PI stations must also multiply seed and make it available to any plant breeder who wants it. The process of growing out seed requires special precautions. Varieties must be grown in an environment similar to that in which they developed or their genetic make-up will be subtly altered. Pollination must be controlled, sometimes through time-consuming hand pollination or caging plants with bees and other pollinating insects. Disease is another problem, and PI stations make every effort to eradicate seed-borne diseases by growing susceptible plants in sterile greenhouse conditions and roguing out infected plants.

Once seeds have been replenished, each PI station preserves them in what is called a "working collection." Bona fide scientists can obtain free samples, and some stations also share seeds with individual collectors or museums with heirloom gardens. When seed supplies get low, the PI station is supposed to replenish them. As a fail-safe against crop failure or some other accident, every variety in the PI working collection is also supposed to be stored at the National Seed Storage Laboratory.

THE NATIONAL SEED STORAGE LABORATORY

Colorado was selected as the site for the National Seed Storage Laboratory because of its low humidity, a factor that makes it possible to store seeds under ideal conditions with a minimum expenditure of energy. Critics have since objected that the site on the Colorado State University campus is not disaster-proof, and officials do concede that future facilities should be built underground. For now, the Laboratory is housed in an unimposing building whose chief defenses against catastrophe are concrete walls ten inches thick; inside, it resembles any academic office, with cluttered desks and the inevitable computer in the corner. However, despite its low-key appearance, the Laboratory is the Fort Knox of germplasm.

During its first quarter-century, the Laboratory has become accustomed to shoestring budgets; yet its storage vaults are virtually filled with 180,000 different types of seeds. (Appendix VI includes a partial list of vegetables stored by the NSSL.) The seeds come not only from PI stations but also from seed companies, which are expected to deposit current and obsolete varieties; plant breeders, who are supposed to store breeding materials; and, occasionally, private collectors, including home gardeners. Seeds acquired by the Laboratory are catalogued, cleaned, weighed, and tested for germination.

After being dried in a 38°C oven to an optimum moisture content of 4 to 7 percent, the seeds are sealed into moisture-proof containers. For years, the Laboratory used metal cans, but now, in an effort to conserve space, they have switched to flexible laminated bags. The bags of seed are heat-sealed and stored in vaults where the temperature is maintained at −10° to −20°C. A back-up generator is available to maintain those conditions should the power fail.

The conditions at the Laboratory should keep most seeds viable for thirty years, but seeds are tested for germination every five years. Some seeds from wild varieties never have a germination rate much better than 50 percent, but in general, the Laboratory grows out a variety to obtain more seed when the germination rate falls to 60 percent. In the past, the Laboratory replenished its own seed, but that task will now be turned over

Best of All Dwarf bean. *A very popular variety in the south, and, as its name indicates, one of the best and most valuable green-podded beans for market or family use. The pods are about six inches long, very fleshy, succulent, stringless and of good quality. Early and prolific.* NBG

to the regional PI stations, which are already growing out seeds from varieties distributed by the Plant Introduction Office. A number of seed companies have also agreed to replenish seed for crops for which they have breeding programs.

No matter who does it, growing out seeds is a costly operation; so scientists are experimenting to find conditions that will keep seeds alive longer. Among other things, they have found promise in cryogenics—storing seeds at temperatures so low that life processes, including deterioration, almost come to a stop. "You can store seeds for a thousand years in liquid nitrogen," enthuses one researcher. For now, the new techniques remain experimental, partly because of cost but also because their effects on the genetic structure of seeds are undetermined.

Unlike the working collections of the PI stations, the collection at the National Seed Storage Laboratory is considered a source of last resort. Even plant breeders must exhaust all other possible sources before obtaining seed from the Laboratory. If seed is unavailable elsewhere, the Laboratory supplies a sample of 15 to 200 seeds, which the breeder must increase. "Citizens-at-large are provided with seed from the National Seed Storage Laboratory only in unusual situations," explains Dr. Eric Roos, a plant physiologist at the Laboratory. "Private requests for this rare and irreplaceable resource are handled on an individual basis."

Rather than requesting samples from the Laboratory, some heirloom gardeners make it their goal to increase a rare variety until they have a seed sample large enough to be accepted by the Laboratory. The Laboratory prefers a sample of 10,000 seeds—equivalent to five pounds of beans, for example—because frequent germination testing depletes the seed supply. "We're glad to cooperate with people who are saving heirloom varieties," says Dr. Louis Bass, director of the Laboratory. "We can't supply seeds, though we often try to suggest another source when someone requests an heirloom variety. If someone wants to contribute an old variety, that person should write to us so we can check our computer to see if it's already in the collection." If the Laboratory does want a sample, the donor will be asked to supply as much detailed information as is known, including the botanical name, a description of the plant, and a list of scientific references to the variety.

All of that information is recorded in a computerized information system called the Germplasm Resources Information Network (GRIN). As the third component in the National Plant Germplasm System, this newly installed information system should, for the first time, give those concerned with germplasm a realistic idea of what has been stored and when it needs to be replenished. Scientists who use the system can obtain accurate information about varieties that meet certain criteria. A breeder, for example, could obtain a print-out listing all the beans with resistance to anthracnose, a common bean disease. Obviously, GRIN can help breeders make better use of materials already in the germplasm collection, but it should also reveal gaps that can give direction to future collection efforts.

The fourth and final component in the germplasm preservation system is a network of advisory bodies. The National Plant Germplasm Resources Board advises the Secretary of Agriculture on germplasm policy. The National Plant Germplasm Committee includes experts outside the government and coordinates the efforts of federal, state, and private programs. And thirteen Crop Advisory Committees give advice about specific plants.

KEEPING TRACK OF GERMPLASM RESOURCES

On paper, the National Plant Germplasm System sounds plausible. In its favorite metaphor, the Department of Agriculture describes the working collections as checking accounts—"there to be drawn upon as needed but not overdrawn"—and the base collection as a savings account—"to be used only when the checking account runs out." In practice, the system is more like a large family in which everyone has a checkbook and no one knows just what's in the bank.

Part of the confusion arises because so many satellite collections exist on the periphery of the NPGS. Though the Department of Agriculture considers these "branch banks" part of the system, many do not operate under federal authority; so there is no standardization of procedures or priorities. Even the collections that are federally managed do not always agree on what needs to be done. For example, the Small Grains Collection, which contains 90,000 varieties of wheat, barley, and other cereal grains, only recently got around to sending samples of the items in its collection to the National Seed Storage Laboratory. Similarly, the Soil Conservation Service, which maintains a collection of 16,000 plants that have conservation value, has virtually no connection with the larger germplasm system.

Other federal repositories have been established to store materials that are excluded from the National Seed Storage Laboratory because they can't be reliably propagated from seed. In the future, it may be possible to preserve the genes of such plants by freezing small quantities of tissue, but for now they must be preserved as tubers, vines, and even entire trees. One such center is the Interregional Potato Introduction Station at Sturgeon Bay, Wisconsin, which has been collecting potato germplasm since 1950 and has 4,000 varieties. More recently, the Department of Agriculture proposed a system of eleven clonal repositories that would keep reserves of berries, nut trees, and other fruits. Six of the repositories are already in operation, but the fate of the others is uncertain because of budget cutbacks. (All existing and proposed federal repositories are listed in Appendix VI.)

Still other collections have been established and maintained without the help of the federal government. The Department of Agriculture admits it doesn't have a complete inventory of these

Mercer potato. *An old and familiar variety; at one period almost everywhere known, and generally acknowledged as the best of all varieties . . . but within a few years past, it has not only greatly deteriorated in quality and productiveness but has been peculiarly liable to disease. When well grown, the tubers are of good size, rather long, a little flattened, and comparatively smooth; eyes slightly sunk; color white, with blotches of purple . . . flesh, when cooked, often stained with pale purple . . . Quality good; dry, mealy and well-flavored.* FB

collections but estimates that there are about thirty. Most are operated by seed companies and universities that feel their plant breeders will have quicker and easier access to breeding materials if they maintain their own collections. Still other scientists have established genetic stock collections that are often used for basic genetic research because they include plants with readily identifiable genes controlling specific traits.

Collections outside the jurisdiction of the Department of Agriculture are of special concern to the government. Often they are amassed by a single, dedicated individual, commonly called a curator. When a curator dies or is transferred to another project, the collection may be abandoned. A U.S. General Accounting Office (GAO) report issued in 1981 noted that many curators consider research and plant breeding their primary goals. For them, the germplasm collection is simply a means to those goals, not an end in itself.

On the surface, having so many collections may seem as sensible as keeping your eggs in many baskets. In practice, the lack of any central organization makes the system unwieldy and, in some instances, unworkable. The same GAO report to Congress noted that "the organization of the plant germplasm system is almost impossible to decipher." This complexity leads, on the one hand, to costly duplication and, on the other, to equally costly complacency because material is presumed to be in another collection. As the GAO report put it, "Germplasm that was thought to be in storage and, in reality, was not in storage could affect many aspects of germplasm maintenance. Germplasm that needs to be collected would not be collected, germplasm thought to be available for research would not be available."

FILLING GAPS IN SEED COLLECTIONS

Lack of a central authority also makes it more difficult to identify gaps in the existing germplasm collections. Such gaps often remain invisible until plant breeders run up against a problem that cannot be solved with available germplasm, such as glume blotch in Eastern wheat. Many scientists fear that we are losing our last opportunity to collect plant materials to combat glume blotch and other problems. They point out that the increased use of hybrids and development in the Third World are causing the rapid loss of plant materials—some estimate that one species becomes extinct each hour.

Because time and resources for plant collection are limited, many scientists want the Department of Agriculture to identify vulnerabilities in major crops. The GAO report to Congress argued that intelligent plant exploration must start with such fundamental questions as "How much germplasm is needed? How vulnerable are existing resources? and What needs to be collected?" Those questions are now being studied by a newly formed Plant Exploration Office, which is creating computer maps that show where plants have been collected and where they remain unsampled. Though it will take several years for the project to be completed, it will give the best picture yet of what needs to be collected in foreign countries.

Urgent as foreign collections are, they will seriously overtax the existing plant germplasm preservation system. For one thing, plant exploration requires scientists who are adventurous enough to go to the remote places where wild relatives are found and knowledgeable enough to collect samples that reflect the genetic diversity of land races. Since this country has neglected plant exploration for the last twenty years, people with this expertise are difficult to find.

Yet even if there were a sufficient number of plant explorers, collecting only a fraction of what needs to be saved would short-circuit the germplasm preservation system. Even now, the Plant Introduction Office can't manage all the materials that pass through its hands. In 1979, only 5,500 of the 34,000 foreign acquisitions were entered into the system.

Land races and wild relatives of crops may have tremendous long-term value, but in the short run they create problems for breeders. "Many breeders hesitate to use wild and primitive types," explains Dr. Desmond Dolan, director of the Northeast PI station, "because they bring in many wild traits and it is difficult to breed back to a good commercial type." With a wild relative, a breeder may want only 10 percent of the plant's genes. The other 90 percent will be undesirable and will have to be bred out of successive generations.

The NPGS and American Heirlooms

With American heirlooms the percentages are reversed. These varieties already have many characteristics that satisfy American tastes and growing conditions—that's why they survived to become heirlooms. Most have fallen out of favor because of relatively minor problems; so they are much more promising raw material for breeders. A report by the National Plant Germplasm Task Force noted that when heirloom varieties are represented in germplasm collections, they are among the "most heavily used" because breeders do not have to do as much backcrossing to produce a usable variety.

Despite these facts, the National Plant Germplasm System does not make much of an effort to identify, collect, store, and distribute heirloom varieties. Because of an outmoded preoccupation with foreign germplasm, domestic heirlooms are neglected. For example, in 1982 the public paid for scientists to look for lettuce in Turkey and Greece, potatoes in Central America, caneberries in England, peanuts in China, and lychees in Sumatra. There were no funds for explorers to seek out beans in Appalachia or corn in New Mexico, even though such expeditions would, presumably, be less expensive and offer more immediate returns for plant breeders.

Fortunately, a few officials within the NPGS have taken it

Improved Long Blood beet. *Diameter, which is retained for more than half its length, is from four to five inches. It is seldom symmetrical . . . though it has but few straggling side roots, it is generally more or less bent and distorted. Flesh dark blood-red, sweet, tender and fine-grained while the root is young and small, but liable to be tough and fibrous when full grown . . . A popular winter sort.* FB

upon themselves to seek out old domestic varieties. Willis Skrdla, director of the Midwest PI station, reports that his station attempts "to collect and maintain as many old varieties as possible, including open-pollinated materials and varieties used by Indian tribes." Other PI station directors agree in principle that "there is tremendous merit in preserving older domestic varieties," but most also concur with Dr. Desmond Dolan, who notes that his station "has enough to do just to keep track of plant introductions." Ironically, these introductions often include varieties which have been domesticated in foreign countries.

Because the system is biased against American heirlooms from the outset, concerted efforts are not made to evaluate old American varieties and catalogue their desirable traits. That omission is obvious in two reports on valuable germplasm introduced by the Northeast PI station between 1965 and 1979. The reports describe valuable characteristics found in beans from India, Mexico, France, Turkey, British Cameroons, El Salvador, Chile, Honduras, Peru, Colombia, Syria, Venezuela, Hungary, and China. Of the fifty-seven bean accessions described, only one domestic plant is mentioned, Dunkle's Half Runner, a West Virginia bean resistant to common bean mosaic.

The casual disregard for American heirlooms is distressing to any gardener who has had an old variety outperform a recent introduction in his or her garden. Now, a few scientists also are beginning to protest the imbalance in favor of foreign varieties. A report by the National Germplasm Task Force noted that "the lack of a systematic procedure for incorporating domestic material into the National Plant Germplasm System is a serious problem." Still, in the recent reorganization of the system, no new provision has been made for locating and preserving American heirlooms. Without minimizing the need for foreign plant collections, it seems absurd to have such elaborate mechanisms for collecting plants halfway around the world while ignoring valuable heirlooms that are quite literally in our own backyards.

THE STORAGE CRISIS

No matter where they come from, acquired seeds must be stored. Here, too, the NPGS has its problems. Though researchers have made advances in prolonging the life of seeds, existing storage facilities do not reflect them. Many of the working collections are held in makeshift facilities such as refrigerators without humidity controls. The collection that has been most criticized is the Small Grains Collection in Beltsville, Maryland, whose facilities were called "totally inadequate" by a government task force in 1970. The task force found that the space was too small for the collection, the environmental control equipment was barely operable, and the funds for maintaining the collection were insufficient. In a separate report, the General Accounting Office concluded that poor conditions had already damaged the Small Grains Collection. When GAO staffers requested 457 random samples of seed, they found that 15 percent of the total collection and up to 45 percent of individual grains were simply unavailable. In some cases, seeds were no longer viable; in others, the supply was so low that samples could not be made available. Though the Department of Agriculture has developed a proposal for a new Small Grains Facility, Congress has not authorized its construction.

Unfortunately, similar conditions exist throughout the system. In most collections there is minimal control over the moisture content of seeds, one of the key determinants of viability. Experts estimate that under the conditions typical throughout the system, seeds will survive for about five years. In 1981, more than 71 percent of the accessions in the working collections had reached that age.

Of course, the working collections are supposed to be

Sand vetch. *In 1897 we procured from Europe a large amount of the seed of this grand, good forage plant . . . So glorious were the results that we were in receipt of thousands of testimonial letters in its praise . . . makes the very best hay imaginable, the equal of clover.* HWB

"checking accounts," backed up by the "savings account" at the National Seed Storage Laboratory. Unfortunately, the savings account idea works better as a metaphor than a reality. Of the 252,000 seed samples in the working collections, only 129,000 are backed up by storage in the National Seed Storage collection. Although the Laboratory can request seeds from various facilities, it cannot require contributions from collections that are not controlled by the federal government. Even collections that are under government control may not be adequately represented. In 1980 only 5,466 of the total 22,000 seed samples at the Midwest PI station were represented in the National Seed Storage Laboratory.

The obvious solution is to have all the working collections send samples of all their seeds to the National Seed Storage Laboratory. Yet that would simply add to the Laboratory's backlog of uncatalogued seeds. When the deterioration of the Small Grains Collection was recognized, samples of 70,000 seed lots were promptly sent to the Laboratory, where many are still sitting in unopened cartons. Though the Laboratory is struggling against the backlog, thousands of accessions are still waiting to be catalogued and stored.

If the National Seed Storage Laboratory were up-to-date, it would simply have run out of room. The facility has space for an estimated 180,000 cans or 200,000 envelopes for seed storage. As of early 1983, the facility had stored 180,000 varieties and had thousands of varieties awaiting storage. Dr. Louis Bass, the Laboratory's director, hopes to double the available storage space, but that seems, at best, a stopgap.

Keeping Seed Collections Alive

Even the best storage facilities cannot keep seeds alive forever. Although scientists are experimenting with techniques that might keep seeds viable for a century, most seeds degenerate after ten to twenty years. They must be tested regularly because deterioration is usually rapid once it begins. The National Seed Storage Laboratory has sophisticated facilities for germination testing, but many other collections have primitive equipment and are behind on testing their seeds. As a result, when they do get around to testing a particular seed, it may already be dead. The National Seed Storage Laboratory reports receiving seed samples with a germination rate of less than 5 percent.

The solution is to replenish seeds that are losing viability by growing them out. Most collections, however, are also behind on their grow-out schedules, in part because the process is so expensive. The General Accounting Office found that "some accessions are in danger of being lost by being repeatedly omitted in grow-out plantings." Also, grow-out procedures can alter the genetic make-up of the stored germplasm. If the crop is grown in an environment different from the one in which it was collected, genetic changes will occur. If the seed crop is harvested early, plants with genes for later maturation will be lost. If only thirty plants are grown, a characteristic that shows up only once in every hundred plants may be lost. "Every time you handle the germplasm—sampling it, sending it out, regrowing it—the composition of the population can be altered," says Dr. Eric Roos of the National Seed Storage Laboratory. "The ultimate solution is to do the best job of storing so that the seed doesn't have to be regrown frequently."

But long-term storage also poses problems. The entire germplasm preservation system is based on the assumption that seeds can be reliably preserved in storage; yet that assumption is currently being challenged by scientists. The goal of storage is to preserve the genetic characteristics of a particular plant, but storage itself may cause genetic changes. "Mutations, including chromosomal aberrations, occur with increasing frequency as the seed deteriorates," says one scientist. Holding a seed sample until its germination rate hits 50 percent contributes to such

Large Squash pepper. *Large and thick; flat, tomato-shaped; fruit compressed, more or less ribbed; skin smooth and glossy; flesh mild, and pleasant to the taste, although possessing more pungency than many other sorts; very productive, and the best variety for pickling alone.* DM

mutations and eliminates seeds with genes that, for one reason or another, make them short-lived.

In other words, the very process of storage changes the genes that storage is supposed to protect. Dr. Roos demonstrated this fact by mixing a special sample of beans that included eight varieties to represent eight different types of genetic material. When the experiment started, each bean was represented in the same quantity. Within five years, two varieties had virtually disappeared, and within fifteen years, two varieties dominated the sample.

Scientists also worry that seeds stored for a long time are insulated from environmental changes that would stimulate beneficial adaptations if the seeds were being grown more often. "The plant's evolution is effectively frozen," says one scientist. "But in the meantime, various threats to which it is subject in the natural environment continue to evolve, producing new forms of attack to which the host plant will not have coevolved adequate defenses."

In other words, scientists are worried if the seeds change and worried if they don't change. Their twin concerns have led many to conclude that seed storage is at best a partial solution. "It is now recognized worldwide by germplasm specialists that simply storing seeds in vaults is not enough to meet the goal of preserving genetic variability," concludes a publication from the National Seed Storage Laboratory. Some scientists are even more emphatic. "Seed banks may help plant breeders today," says Dr. Hugh Iltis of the University of Wisconsin, "but preserving varieties for more than 1,000 years? Forget it."

GERMPLASM PRESERVATION AS A SURVIVAL ISSUE

It is clear that even the best storage system needs the back-up of gardeners and farmers who will simply grow the useful varieties and save their seed. In the foreign centers of genetic diversity, international groups are trying to save land races and wild relatives by setting up "preserves" similar to those that have been established to protect endangered animals. The problems are enormous, and the results are uncertain. In this country, the government could preserve a vast reservoir of genetic diversity simply by encouraging gardeners to raise traditional varieties in addition to recent introductions. It could authorize land grant universities to collect regionally adapted varieties. It could support nonprofit organizations such as Kent Whealy's Seed Savers Exchange. All of these measures would cost less in a year than a minute's operation of the Pentagon; yet they would go a long way toward safeguarding the nation's future. As Dr. David Percy of the National Colonial Farm in Accokeek, Maryland, puts it, "Stockpiling old varieties makes a hell of a lot more sense than stockpiling nuclear weapons."

Money, of course, is always the measure of how seriously a government takes a problem, and money has been at the root of many of the problems in the National Plant Germplasm System. In 1983, Department of Agriculture officials were jubilant about a proposed germplasm budget of $13,102,000, which represented a $3.8 million increase in a year in which other departments had been pruned. Though the total did compare well with the budget of $7.1 million for 1980, the hard truth is that after adjustments for inflation, the budget was less than it had been in 1967. "The resources available just aren't up to what needs to be done," says Dr. Bass. "It's not as glamorous as putting a man on the moon or sending a spaceship to Mars. Yet it's absolutely essential for ultimate survival."

Perhaps if Americans viewed germplasm preservation as a "survival issue," Congress would be deluged with mail when it came time to budget money for the National Seed Storage Laboratory and other components in the National Plant Germplasm System. "Nobody is against germplasm preservation," says Dr. Bass, "but it gets lost when it's lumped together with

Early Drumhead cabbage. *An intermediate variety of the size of Early York and a little later. The head is round, flattened at the top, firm and well formed, tender in texture and well-flavored. It is a good sort for the garden as it heads well, occupies but little space in cultivation and comes to the table immediately after the early sorts.* **DM**

other things. We're trying to keep it visible." Perhaps the best way to make the system visible is to make it easier to use, something that is happening in relation to plant breeders. In 1979, breeders requested and received 304,863 seed samples, a figure that may sound impressive at first. Unfortunately, many of the samples were sent in response to requests for "all" the seeds in a particular category so breeders could screen them for a specific characteristic. In the future, the computerized GRIN system should enable scientists to enter the results of such screening projects so that other scientists can be more selective. As the system becomes more useful to them, scientists will undoubtedly form a more vocal constituency.

Farmers, home gardeners, and consumers could form another constituency. Though private citizens cannot use the germplasm preservation system directly, they do benefit from its existence. Nearly every improvement in fruits, vegetables, and grains is made possible because someone collects plant materials, tests them for valuable characteristics, and stores them for the day they can be used. Breeding plants that resist disease has proven far less expensive than using pesticides; yet disease resistance is just the beginning. Using germplasm resources already stored in the National Plant Germplasm System, plant breeders may be able to produce foods that are more productive, more nutritious, and more economical.

Of course, seed banks can be established by private companies. The Asgrow Seed Company maintains a collection of pea varieties; Campbell Soup collects tomato genes. However, seeds held by private companies become a private resource, and a variety that has evolved over centuries shouldn't belong to individuals any more than clean air and pure water. The only way to assure that seeds from rare varieties will be available to anyone who has the skills to use them is to maintain public seed-storage facilities.

In short, the National Plant Germplasm System is an

American resource that, like the Grand Canyon and the California redwoods, needs protection from political whim. The thirty million gardeners in the country could form a powerful lobby, as vocal in defending the NPGS as senior citizens are in defending Social Security. Gardeners, as a group, need to see that germplasm preservation gets its fair share in competition with other programs and that it gets that share year after year after year.

At the same time, those who are concerned about American heirlooms cannot help being dismayed by a number of national germplasm policies. First, domestic heirlooms are not adequately represented in the system; so they are more vulnerable to loss and less likely to receive attention from plant breeders. Second, varieties that do get into the system cannot be retrieved by home gardeners. They become wards of the state, locked away until some plant breeder notices their useful characteristics. Since breeders are usually looking for characteristics that suit commercial growers, varieties that are ideal for home gardeners could be effectively buried in the seed bank.

The only recourse is for gardeners to grow the old varieties that matter to them. Though the National Plant Germplasm System may provide a reassuring backstop to the efforts of home gardeners, it is only that. Only gardeners can keep alive heirloom varieties that have not yet been stored in the system. And, even after storage, only gardeners can keep heirloom varieties in circulation. The best place to store these backyard resources continues to be our own backyards.

PART THREE

How To
Find and Grow Heirlooms

7
Old Seed Search and Research

THE BEST WAY TO KEEP HEIRLOOM FRUIT AND vegetable varieties alive is for gardeners to adopt and grow them. Important as seed companies, seed museums, and seed banks may be, all need the back-up of committed gardeners who will plant, tend, and save the seed from old varieties year after year. This doesn't mean jettisoning every new variety in favor of one that is old. Gardeners can blend old and new, evaluating each variety on its merits until they find the crops that thrive in their gardens and satisfy their tastes. The important point is that no variety should be adopted simply because it is new or excluded only because it is old.

Some gardeners, disturbed by the idea that old varieties are becoming extinct, may be moved to grow them out of pity for their plight. Unfortunately, pity is usually a short-lived motivation. If heirlooms are to survive, gardeners must seek out varieties they can care about for other reasons. Sometimes an heirloom takes on meaning because it has historical associations. Like other "antiques," heirloom fruits and vegetables can make us feel closer to those who have gardened before us. Other heirlooms appeal because they are unusual or challenging. Gardeners who like to pamper exotic plants often find that they get similar satisfactions from coaxing an old apple tree to bear fruit or maintaining the purity of an old variety of corn.

Yet most gardeners who stick with heirloom varieties grow them for the most basic reason of all—they like the way they grow and the way they taste. Sometimes an heirloom wins a gardener's heart because it performs well in an environment where other varieties have failed. More often, an heirloom corresponds to a very personal sense of what a "real" bean—or tomato or apple—should taste like. Whatever the reason, gardeners who have found "their" heirlooms are often fiercely loyal. For them, heirloom varieties are more than this year's gardening fad. Some gardeners have spent years searching for lost varieties and, once they find them, expect to grow them for the rest of their lives.

Many gardeners are eager to have heirlooms of their own but don't know how to find them. Some start by looking for a specific named variety—Whippoorwill cowpeas, which were particularly delicious; Blue Goose beans, which didn't turn brown when cooked; or White Sprout potatoes, which had tubers so long people carried them like firewood. Others begin, not with a name, but with the exceptional characteristic of an old variety—a red-and-black-seeded pole lima remembered from a 1930s childhood, or a sharp-hulled popcorn that produced red kernels one year and white the next.

Whippoorwill cowpea.
A very early maturing variety of upright or bush growth . . . The seed is light brown, speckled darker brown, of the same coloring as the eggs of the Whippoorwill. BP

START WITH THE SEED COMPANIES

Those who are seeking specific old varieties should first comb as many seed catalogues as possible to see whether the varieties are still being sold commercially. Though the tendency is toward fewer heirlooms, all companies carry a few, and some companies, particularly those listed in Appendix II, offer a solid selection. Seed companies have also been known to resurrect old varieties if demand is great enough. For example, a recent catalogue from the Park Seed Company proudly reintroduced Mountaineer White Half Runner, also called Old Dutch Half Runner, a bean that was brought to South Carolina a hundred years ago.

Ordering and studying a hundred seed catalogues is a daunting task; so start with regional seed companies since they are most likely to offer heirlooms suited to your local soil and climate. An even quicker way to find out whether an old variety is still being sold is to consult the *Vegetable Variety Inventory* compiled by Kent Whealy of the Seed Savers Exchange. This computerized inventory is a tremendous time-saver for gardeners, who can, for the first time, look up an old variety and find out which of 150 seed companies is selling it. The inventory can also help gardeners identify "endangered" vegetables in need of protection since Whealy plans to flag varieties that are being carried by fewer than three seed companies. To find out the cost of the inventory, which will be updated annually, send a self-addressed, stamped envelope to Vegetable Variety Inventory, Seed Savers Exchange, 203 Rural Avenue, Decorah, Iowa 52101.

What Whealy has done for vegetables, the federal government has done for fruit and nut trees. *The North American and European Fruit and Tree Nut Germplasm Resources Inventory*, published by the U.S. Department of Agriculture, lists sources for more than a thousand apples, as well as pears, cherries, plums, and exotic fruits such as mangoes. Sources range from individual collectors to foreign experiment stations, and many varieties have coded descriptions. The inventory makes it easy for a gardener in search of a specific variety but is nothing short of exhausting for a gardener who is undecided. Though copies of the 730-page inventory can be purchased from the U.S. Government Printing Office (Washington, DC 20401), the inventory should also be available in agricultural libraries.

Those who would rather have someone else do the research can contact Plant Finders of America, a service organized by Richard Fox, who feels that gardeners need a central source from which they can find out whether and where a specific plant is available commercially. Fox has contacts with more than four hundred companies around the world, and his ultimate goal is to have all available plant sources on file so that he can locate "any plant in cultivation." To participate, the gardener pays $5 per plant and fills out a form giving the common and scientific name of the plant as well as a full description. Plant Finders promises to respond within thirty days and refunds the initial fee if the plant cannot be located. Forms are available from Plant Finders of America, 106 Fayette Circle, Fort Wright, KY 41044.

Those fortunate enough to find an old variety through a seed company should not count exclusively on the company as a source of seed. Because companies drop varieties so frequently, it is important to master the techniques for seed saving described in Chapter 9. Then, whether you order or save your own, reserve some seed each year. Otherwise, a variety that means a great deal to you may be lost again on the day a seed-company executive decides it is no longer profitable enough to remain in the catalogue.

GETTING SEEDS FROM OTHER GARDENERS

Of course, many old varieties are simply not available through seed companies. If the variety sought is one of the many deemed obsolete by the seed industry, the search will require more detective work. The best way to locate an heirloom vegetable variety is through the Seed Savers Exchange. In the *Seed Savers Yearbook*, members (defined as people who have seeds available for exchange) list heirlooms they hope to find. A person who has no seed to exchange can be included in a special Plant Finder Service listing if he or she sends the name of the "lost" variety, a description, and the last date and place where it was known to be grown.

Though Exchange members swap seeds for postage, non-members must pay $1 for each variety obtained through the Exchange. They are also expected to multiply the seed and offer it for exchange in future issues of the yearbook. Taking a listing in the yearbook puts a gardener in touch with hundreds of other gardeners who are concerned about old varieties, and each issue includes success stories from people who have found lost varieties. "I'm often amazed at what our members can come up with," says Whealy. "Some gardeners have located varieties they have been trying to find for fifty years."

Other seed and plant exchanges can be helpful in locating rare varieties. If possible, consult an exchange that specializes in the crops that interest you, such as CORNS for old corn varieties, North American Fruit Explorers for fruit, or KUSA Research Foundation for old grain varieties. Addresses for these and other seed exchanges are listed in Appendix I. Those lucky enough to have a regional exchange should contact it so that the sought-after variety can be mentioned in newsletters and at exchange meetings.

Collectors often advertise when they are looking for something specific, and some heirloom gardeners have found lost varieties by placing classifieds in gardening magazines or by taking small ads in local newspapers. Give the name of the variety and also describe it in case it is being raised under another name. Offer to exchange seeds with respondents. A gardener who is especially keen on finding a particular heirloom might even offer a small reward to attract attention.

In some rural communities, a gardener in search of an old variety is news. Don't be shy about contacting the editor of the local paper to talk about your interest in heirlooms, especially if your garden already includes a few old varieties. Kent Whealy is convinced that, in isolated rural areas, stories in weekly news-

Long Red Altringham carrot. *Similar in form to the Long Orange, but of a bright red color, growing with the top an inch or two above ground. Flesh bright and lively, crisp and breaking in its texture; the heart, in proportion to the size of root, smaller than other varieties; a very fine sort.* DM

papers are one of the best ways to contact other gardeners who might be saving seed for the variety you want.

Working with the Seed Banks

Though fellow gardeners are the most common source for heirlooms, some gardeners have obtained old varieties from seed companies, scientists, and even seed banks, such as the National Seed Storage Laboratory in Fort Collins, Colorado. Some seed companies save samples of seeds that no longer sell well enough to be listed in their catalogues. A particularly winning letter might pry loose a few. Better yet, try visiting local seed suppliers. One museum with an heirloom garden struck gold in a Springfield, Illinois, hardware store, where a never-throw-it-away owner had jars of nineteenth-century varieties sitting beside twentieth-century hybrids on the stockroom shelves.

Scientists and plant breeders are an uncertain source of old varieties if only because so many are justifiably impatient with backyard amateurs who ask time-consuming questions or want samples of rare plant materials. Getting one "Do you have any old varieties?" letter is enough to sour most breeders on the idea of working with heirloom gardeners. A gardener who has reason to believe a scientist may have a sought-after old variety should do plenty of homework first so that he or she can supply the variety's name, common synonyms, and a good description of its special characteristics.

Often, the scientists most likely to respond are those at state land grant universities. Every state has one, and because they are supported by public funds, staff members may feel more of an obligation to respond to public inquiries. The cooperative extension agent in your county should know—or be able to find out—the names of plant breeders specializing in particular crops. Sometimes breeders maintain small private collections and will share with serious amateurs.

Vegetable Marrow squash. *Plant twelve feet and upwards in length; fruit nine inches long, and of an elliptic shape . . . surface slightly uneven, but irregular, longitudinal, obtuse ribs, which terminate in a projecting apex at the extremity of the fruit. When mature, it is of a uniform pale yellow or straw color. The skin, or shell, is very hard when the fruit is perfectly ripened; flesh white, tender, and succulent, even till the seeds are ripe. It may be used in every stage of its growth.* FB

Other times, requests will be referred to the regional plant introduction station. These stations exist to supply plant materials to professional breeders and researchers, but they, too, will sometimes send small quantities of seed to individuals who make specific requests. Since a regional station may have thousands of stored varieties, staff members take an understandably dim view of letters asking for "a list of all the tomatoes in your collection." On the other hand, the holdings at the PI stations are computer-filed; so a request for one or two named varieties should be relatively easy to process. At the very least, the station should be able to tell you whether a variety is being protected by the National Plant Germplasm System and where it is stored.

Sometimes, the only known sample of a variety is stored at the National Seed Storage Laboratory in Fort Collins, Colorado. Though the Laboratory is sympathetic to the concerns of heirloom gardeners, its primary task is long-term storage of seeds. "Our supplies are not sufficient to supply anything but breeding material," explains Dr. Louis Bass, the facility director. "Even then, we can give only very small samples, which the breeder must increase." Because the facility is underfunded and understaffed, corresponding with individuals in search of a few varieties drains energy and resources that could be better spent cataloguing and caring for the germplasm collection.

On the other hand, varieties that exist only in the seed-storage facility would be better protected if they were also being grown by gardeners with the skills to save pure seed each year. In that way, dedicated heirloom gardeners could actually supplement the efforts of the National Seed Storage Laboratory— if they treat the collection as the vital national resource that it is. Though the facility is not obliged to work with heirloom gardeners, it has been willing to cooperate with those who meet the following self-imposed guidelines. First, gardeners should approach the Laboratory only after exhausting every other possible source of seed. Second, those who request seeds should be "master gardeners" with extensive seed-saving experience. Finally, those who actually receive seed should be prepared to make a lifelong commitment to keeping the variety alive.

Family and Community Heirlooms

Gardeners who do not have a specific named variety to seek out need not abandon the idea of growing heirloom varieties. Instead, they can search for varieties that have personal or geographical significance. Heirlooms, of course, are usually passed from generation to generation; so some gardeners start by shaking the family tree to find great-aunts and second cousins once removed who may be saving seeds. One heirloom gardener reports that when he became interested in heirloom varieties, he visited his grandmother. Sure enough, there on the basement shelf was a musty box of seeds, left by his grandfather and untouched since he had died. Of course, seeds neglected after a gardener dies lose viability; so it is better for the seeds—and more meaningful for the people—to acquire seeds while elderly relatives are still alive. Older gardeners are often delighted to find someone else who appreciates their favorite old varieties and will probably be glad to share the family and horticultural lore that goes along with them.

Appealing as it may sound, raising family heirlooms is not always possible. The gardener who wants to grow an heirloom bean from the family's Minnesota homestead may find that it just doesn't do well in southern California. Uprooted gardeners must depend on "geographical relatives," local gardeners who have been growing the same varieties so long that they are perfectly adapted to the environmental idiosyncrasies of the region.

To locate gardeners who are saving such varieties, think back to gardens that have attracted attention. Perhaps one is the neighborhood standard by which progress in other gardens is measured or another has more than the usual number of bean rows. Pay particular attention to older gardeners, many of whom acquired the habit of saving seed in less affluent times and simply persisted in it. If possible, visit ethnic sections of the community, since people who identify with the traditions of their home country may also be saving its seeds. Visit the county fair and talk to gardeners who display exceptional produce. Contact the local cooperative extension agent for a list of master gardeners who are willing to share expertise and, perhaps, seeds. Ask if the local Garden Club knows of members who are keeping rare or unusual fruits and vegetables. In other words, use the same imagination and persistence that would be needed to locate anything rare and elusive.

The effort to uncover varieties that are indigenous to local communities is one of the most valuable contributions an heirloom gardener can make. "The best way for gardeners to help us," says Kent Whealy of the Seed Savers Exchange, "is to become small-scale explorers within their own areas. Such localized botanists could be invaluable in building up small collections of vegetables native to their various regions." Heirloom gardeners who seek out and take responsibility for propagating and sharing seeds are quite literally rescuing these old varieties from extinction.

Perhaps the best evidence that heirlooms are there for the finding is the success of gardeners such as Jim Johnson, a Wisconsin collector who has accumulated more than four hundred varieties. Though Johnson has taken advantage of the correspondence columns in magazines such as *Family Food Garden*, most of his collection has come from word-of-mouth contacts with individuals. "There's a surprising number of things out there that people don't know about," he says. "It's hard to track them down, but once you meet a few people who are interested in heirlooms, one thing leads to another. It gets to be a kind of game in a way. You're constantly looking around the corner to find something you've never heard of."

Gherkin cucumber. *A very small, oval-shaped, prickly variety, having somewhat the appearance of a burr. It is grown exclusively for pickling; is the smallest of all the varieties, and should always be pickled when young and tender. Seed is slow to germinate.* DM

Johnson's collection includes plenty of varieties that most gardeners don't know about, including green radishes, purple carrots, and beans that have been traced to King Tut's tomb. "My garden looks like a circus," he says cheerfully. Johnson enjoys novelties, but he also saves a lot of standard workhorse varieties, though he doesn't recommend all of them to home gardeners. "Many old varieties are not commercially available because they aren't that great," he says. "A lot aren't worth a gardener's time."

At the same time, Johnson firmly believes that all heirloom varieties should be saved for their breeding possibilities. "I have at least twenty white beans," he says. "If you hold the seeds in your hand, they all look like white beans, but each has its own merit and is worthy of being saved for its genetic potential." Because of this conviction, Johnson is now trying to arrange for his unique varieties to be stored in the National Seed Storage Laboratory. When he obtained a print-out of the Laboratory's collection and found that "much of what I have, they don't have," he decided to grow the required 10,000 seeds for each of his unique varieties, even though, as he is the first to acknowledge, it will be "quite a bit of work."

To be sure he's saving what he thinks he's saving, Johnson does extensive research on the varieties he locates. "Some people find a variety with an old name and let it go at that. But to be sure the variety is a genuine heirloom, you have to seek out old descriptions," he says, adding that he uses about forty books in his own research. Some of what Johnson has learned about old vegetable varieties is included in his *Heirloom Vegetable Guide*, which describes and names sources for hundreds of vegetable varieties that are still commercially available. A comparable booklet on fruit is in production and should soon be available. For details on the availability of both guides, write to Jim Johnson, 7705 Normandy, Oconomowoc, WI 53066.

THE STORIES BEHIND THE PLANTS

Though some gardeners feel their research is finished once they find an old variety, many share Johnson's fascination with the stories behind the plants. Some investigate a variety's past because they want to know how old it is or to verify that it is properly named. Others are simply curious about the history of a variety good enough to have survived so many years.

Whatever the motivation, the best place to start learning about an old variety is its source. Some gardeners keep records, and others may simply remember the history of the variety in question. Try to trace the history of the seed as far back as possible, making notes about names, dates, and places where the variety was grown. If the stories about a variety are particularly colorful, borrow a trick from oral historians and tape-record the conversation. One way or another, be sure to find out whatever information the person has about the idiosyncrasies of the variety as well as his or her reason for having saved it so long.

Based as it is on memory, oral history is often dubious, and heirloom gardeners may want to confirm what they've heard with written records. Written history can also be highly personal. Start with Grandpa's gardening diary or sift through old letters to find references to what was growing in the garden that year. Check the attic to see whether someone saved old seed packets or made a scrapbook from advertising cards handed out by seed companies.

Though it may be fascinating for other reasons, sorting through family letters, diaries, and household journals probably won't yield a lot of information about gardening. A more productive approach is to study old horticultural texts, though they, too, can be frustrating for the gardener in search of variety names and descriptions. The oldest books that include references to American plants are accounts of travel in the New

World and seventeenth-century herbals. Though original copies of such texts are costly collectibles, two of the most famous herbals have been reissued in facsimile. *The Herbal or General History of Plants*, published by John Gerard in 1633, includes descriptions of 2,850 plants with 2,705 illustrations. *Culpeper's Complete Herbal* also provides fascinating insights into what plants were considered useful in the seventeenth century.

Herbals and other seventeenth-century sources make intriguing reading, but they are of scant help to gardeners trying to confirm the identity of a variety. For the most part, herbals focus on species with little discrimination among varieties. Fortunately for heirloom gardeners, full varietal descriptions became a standard feature in gardening books during the nineteenth century. A succession of talented seedsmen, including Thomas Bridgeman, Robert Buist, Fearing Burr, Jr., and Peter Henderson wrote about vegetables and recommended their favorite varieties. Fruits received even better coverage from authors such as A. J. Downing, Charles Hovey, John J. Thomas, and S. A. Beach. For an annotated listing of books by these and other authors, see Appendix IV.

Agricultural Libraries

For most heirloom gardeners, the problem is finding old and, in some cases, rare volumes. Older local libraries may have gardening books from the early twentieth century, but few will have the more valuable nineteenth-century works. Occasionally, an heirloom researcher will stumble upon a historical library with an extensive horticultural section—the library of the New York Historical Association in Cooperstown is an excellent example—but results are more likely in libraries of colleges or universities with an established agricultural or horticultural program. "So many old books were printed on gardening," says Jim Johnson, "and those libraries have them. You might have to go

White Paris Cos lettuce. *A variety largely grown for the London and Paris Markets. The heads are long, upright, with oblong leaves. It is very hardy, of large size, and long in running to seed, tender, brittle and mild flavored.* DM

to an upper balcony or a faraway corner of the basement, but they've got them."

In most states, the best agricultural libraries are located at land grant universities. Established by an Act of Congress in 1862, these universities conduct research to improve agriculture in their respective states. Usually they are located in state capitals, but they may have interlibrary loan arrangements with local libraries.

Land grant universities are often co-located with state agricultural experiment stations, which are, in themselves, extraordinary sources of information about old varieties. Founded in the 1880s to supervise crop improvements, these stations usually publish annual reports containing descriptions of crops being tested and of "standard" varieties against which they are compared. Some of the most comprehensive reports have been published by the New York State Agricultural Station, which, unlike other agricultural stations, is located on its own campus in Geneva, New York. In 1882 and 1883, the station's annual reports described all varieties of beans known at the time. In subsequent years, the station commented on varieties of corn (1884), peas (1884), lettuce (1885), and cabbage (1886). In 1887, Geneva scientists outdid themselves with varietal descriptions for beets, carrots, radishes, turnips, onions, celery, celeriac, spinach, cucumbers, squashes, eggplants, and tomatoes.

Much of this material was prepared by the station's director, Peter L. Sturtevant, and was subsequently compiled by U. P. Hedrick into a volume called *Sturtevant's Notes on Edible Plants*. This classic volume, reissued by Dover in 1972, contains most of what nineteenth-century scientists knew about 2,897 edible plants. The entries on common fruits and vegetables summarize what Sturtevant, a voracious reader, had learned by studying hundreds of volumes, ranging from ancients such as Pliny to nineteenth-century plant explorers and scientists. In each case, he traces the history of the plant and cites sources to justify every conclusion. Though Sturtevant includes only the most general varietal descriptions, he notes where more extensive descriptions can be found, thereby saving the researcher the time of sifting through other references.

The New York State Agricultural Station was also responsible for *The Vegetables of New York*, a series of four monographs cataloguing varieties known in the 1930s. The volumes have sumptuous color plates and extraordinarily detailed descriptions of bean, pea, cucurbit, and corn varieties. The Depression called a halt to the project before other volumes in the series were completed, but the four that exist are a superb source of information for heirloom gardeners. Publishing varietal descriptions is one of the basic functions of state agricultural stations. Though most other states did not produce such elaborate reports, the observations of state scientists are most helpful to gardeners in search of regionally adapted varieties.

Heirloom gardeners can also benefit by studying other regional materials, such as reports by state agricultural or horticultural societies. The availability and quality of such materials vary tremendously from state to state. For example, in Michigan, Agricultural Society reports date back to 1870, in Illinois to 1856, in California to 1852, and in Massachusetts to 1794. In some cases, historians have sifted through these primary sources to write agricultural histories of their states. These books usually concentrate on field crops and livestock, but heirloom gardeners may find short chapters on the history of fruits and vegetables in the state.

The libraries at land grant universities usually have comprehensive collections of books, periodicals, and monographs covering agriculture in the state. Another source of information is a series of bibliographies prepared by the Agricultural History Center of the University of California. Among other subjects, the bibliographies cover the history of agriculture in California, the Pacific Northwest, the Southern states, the

Mountain states, the Midwest, the Great Plains, and Iowa. Copies can be obtained by writing to the Agricultural History Center at the University of California, Davis, CA 20250.

Agricultural libraries should also have complete sets of the yearbooks issued annually by the U.S. Department of Agriculture since it was established in 1862. Gardeners familiar with the contemporary yearbooks, each of which concentrates on a single, trendy topic such as "Cutting Energy Costs" or "Living on a Few Acres," will be surprised to find that early volumes are yearbooks in the true sense. Each summarizes the year's events in agriculture, including research, agriculture statistics, and crop descriptions. For example, the 1862 yearbook includes illustrated descriptions of "leading popular varieties of apple and pear."

Another function of the Department of Agriculture was to distribute seeds for new and useful plants to farmers and scientists; so after 1886, the yearbooks include state-by-state performance reports on varieties. These reports are helpful in tracing the introduction of varieties, as well as for identifying heirlooms that should do well in a particular region. Volumes of particular interest to heirloom gardeners include the 1899 yearbook, which contains an essay on the progress of plant breeding in the United States, and the 1925 yearbook, which has extensive notes on fruit and vegetable production. Early volumes of the yearbook have also been indexed. Those issued between 1837 and 1893 were indexed in 1896 and published as *USDA Bulletin #1*. *Bulletin #7* covers 1894–1900, *#9* covers 1901–1905, and *#10* covers 1906–1910.

Old Horticultural Periodicals and Books

Horticultural periodicals are yet another source of information about old varieties. Land grant universities often have back issues, particularly of regional publications such as the *New En-*

Green Citron melon. *Fruit nearly round but flattened slightly at the ends—deeply and very regularly ribbed; size medium or rather small—average specimens measuring six inches in diameter, and five inches and a half in depth; skin green and thickly netted—when fully mature, the green becomes more soft and mellow, or of a yellowish shade; flesh green, quite thick, very juicy, and of the richest and most sugary flavor. It is an abundant bearer, quite hardy and remarkably uniform in its quality. It is deservedly the most popular as a market sort; and for cultivation for family use, everything considered, has few superiors.* FB

gland Farmer (1822–1846), the Genesee Farmer (1831–1839), the Ohio Cultivator (1845–1850), and the Western Farmer and Gardener (1839–1845). Other popular periodicals include The Horticulturalist, which was founded by A. J. Downing, a nurseryman who became one of the century's most prolific garden writers; American Gardener's Magazine, which, in an expansive style befitting the nineteenth century, changed its name to The Magazine of Horticulture, Botany and All Useful Discoveries and Improvements in Rural Affairs; and the Gardener's Monthly, published in Philadelphia between 1859 and 1888.

To locate a library that has these or other nineteenth-century horticultural magazines, consult the Union List of Serials, a standard reference work found in large libraries. The Union List catalogues periodicals held by major libraries throughout the country; in some regions, local libraries have cooperated to produce a regional catalogue of periodical holdings. Be forewarned, however, that gardeners who hope to find horticultural information in these journals must be dedicated browsers since, for the most part, they are not indexed. The Agricultural Index, published by H. H. Wilson, did not appear on the scene until 1916. After that date, it is comparatively easy to locate articles that compare varieties or unravel the history of a particular crop.

Satisfying as it may be to spend entire afternoons in the stacks of a great library, most heirloom gardeners eventually find that they want to have a few reference works at home. Those who do not want to become book as well as seed collectors should take advantage of nineteenth-century classics that have been reprinted in modern editions. By far the best of these is The Vegetable Garden, written by the French nurserymen Vilmorin-Andrieux in 1885. The book, including its handsome drawings and painstaking descriptions, has been reissued by Ten Speed Press, P.O. Box 7123, Berkeley, CA 94707. Though the book concentrates on varieties grown in Europe, it is valuable to American collectors because, first, so many heirlooms were brought to this country by European immigrants and, second, the authors make regular references to varieties being grown in America.

McMahon's American Gardener is a nineteenth-century book that has been reissued by Funk & Wagnalls. Bernard McMahon, one of this country's first nurserymen, corresponded with Thomas Jefferson and nearly every other horticulturist of note in his day. His book is organized according to the popular calendar format, prodding gardeners with notes about what should be done each month. Varietal information is buried in the voluminous instructions for tending the orchard, vineyard, flowerbed, and kitchen garden. Nonetheless, McMahon is a valuable source of information, sometimes revealing as much by what he omits—for example, mentions of sweet corn, which didn't become popular until mid-century—as by what he includes.

Most of the valuable old horticultural books have not been reissued. Gardeners who have their hearts set on a specific reference book will find the quickest satisfaction by working through a rare book dealer who specializes in horticultural works. Several publish catalogues devoted entirely to fruit and vegetable books. One recent catalogue from Elizabeth Woodburn of Booknoll Farm in Hopewell, New Jersey, listed 352 books on fruit and 209 on vegetables. Not every item was old, but the list included hard-to-find classics such as *The Fruits of America*, by Charles Hovey; *The Fruits and Fruit Trees of America*, by A. J. Downing; *The Family Kitchen Gardener*, by Robert Buist; and a complete set of *The Vegetables of New York*. Other rare book dealers specializing in horticultural texts are listed in Appendix V. In addition, names can often be found in the classified sections of horticultural magazines or in the directory of members published by the Antiquarian Booksellers Associa-

tion of America (50 Rockefeller Plaza, New York, NY 10020).
To obtain a copy of the directory, send a self-addressed envelope
with fifty-four cents postage.

Of course, gardeners can do their own sleuthing for old horticulture books. As any devotee of auctions or flea markets
knows, cartons of old books and papers are often sold for preposterously low prices. Few garden books have been targeted by
collectors, so bargains are often available to those who keep their
eyes open. An alternative for those who prefer to spend their
spare time gardening rather than antiquing is to ask a local antiques dealer to keep an eye out for old gardening books and
alert you to what he or she finds.

Old Seed Catalogues

Lists and catalogues from seed companies are another valuable
source of information about old varieties. Fruit and vegetable
varieties sold in Europe between 1400 and 1900 are well documented in three books by John Harvey. *Early Garden Catalogues*
includes facsimiles of some of the earliest seed lists in Europe;
Early Horticultural Catalogues is a checklist of all catalogues issued by English and Irish nurseries and seed companies before
1850; and *Early Nurseryman* is a history of the seed trade from
the Middle Ages through the nineteenth century. These books
were published in Great Britain and are difficult to find in this
country, though good agricultural libraries have them and book
dealer Elizabeth Woodburn sells copies.

In the United States, shipping lists are the earliest sources of
information about fruit and vegetable varieties. A few companies started selling seeds early in the eighteenth century, but
most of their stock was imported from England. Seed dealers
didn't bother to promote varieties—they simply printed circulars listing seeds they had available. David Landreth is credited
with founding the first commercial seed company, which wasn't

Strasburg onion. *Most
generally cultivated in
Great Britain. Its form
varies from flat to globular or oval; bulb large,
three inches wide, and
full two inches in depth;
outside coating brown, of
firm texture. Divested of
this, the color is reddish-
brown, tinged with
green. Flavor mild and
pleasant. It is a very
hardy sort, succeeds in
cold localities, and
keeps well.* FB

much more than an import house, in Philadelphia in 1784. Other companies soon followed Landreth's lead. Though many of the earliest firms concentrated on ornamentals and exotic plants instead of the more plebian fruits and vegetables, there were exceptions, notably Grant Thorburn, who started selling seeds in 1805 and later published *The Gentleman's and Gardener's Kalendar*.

Meantime, the Shakers, who had practical as well as religious proclivities, began raising seed for garden vegetables. Around 1800, a Shaker named Ebenezer Alden invented a "printing box" for printing seed packages. This was the first time seeds had been packaged in envelopes, and the innovation revolutionized the trade. At first the Shakers sold only seed that they raised themselves, but by 1819 the demand was so great that, after a debate about the ethics of the move, they began selling seed raised by others.

The Shakers also became increasingly scientific and began conducting "trials" of the vegetables whose seeds they sold. Finally, in 1836, when they were distributing 150,000 seed packets a year, they published a manual to help their customers select and grow the right vegetables. Written by a man named Crossman, *The Gardener's Manual* sold for six cents at the time; today, the surviving copies of the 16,000 that were printed are valuable collector's items. There were obvious advantages to having a catalogue with variety descriptions, and soon other companies began producing them too.

Seed catalogues came into their own during the latter half of the nineteenth century. Seed companies outdid themselves with lovingly detailed engravings and extravagant descriptions. From the heirloom gardener's point of view, some of the best nineteenth-century catalogues were published by Peter Henderson of New York, Henry Dreer of Philadelphia, D. M. Ferry of Detroit, W. Atlee Burpee of Philadelphia, and James Gregory of Marblehead, Massachusetts. Twentieth-century catalogues are also of interest, particularly when they come from companies that specialized in older varieties, such as the Hepler Seed Company, which carried old beans collected by Billy Hepler, or the Will Seed Company, which specialized in seeds collected from the Arikara tribe of South Dakota.

Old seed catalogues now excite a lively interest in collectors; so they are often available from book dealers, though prices are high. Several libraries have amassed collections of old catalogues, and some of them are listed in Appendix V. Unfortunately, many of the collections are inadequately catalogued, and their curators are understandably reluctant to permit gardeners to browse through materials that are so easily damaged. The Council of Botanical and Horticultural Libraries is trying to improve access to these materials by encouraging its members to identify what they have. The Council depends on volunteers to research what is available; so their surveys are complete for some states and not for others. Eventually, the Council hopes to have a system of regional repositories for seed catalogues and other materials of interest to heirloom gardeners. For information about contacting member libraries in specific regions, see Appendix V.

For those who have no inclination to track down dusty old catalogues, two other resources are helpful. *A Nineteenth Century Garden*, by Charles van Ravenswaay, includes a useful section on the significance of seed catalogues, as well as reproductions of pages from early catalogues. Also, Burpee has reissued its 1888 catalogue, and copies are available from the company.

Finally, some collectors are eager to obtain master lists of American varieties to guide their collection efforts. Lists of variety names that have been used in the past have been compiled by the American Seed Trade Association as an aid to breeders who are naming new cultivars. The lists include dates of introduction whenever they are known, as well as the names of companies or organizations responsible for developing the varieties.

The lists vary in quality. Some compilers, apparently impatient with the task, treat many heirloom names as synonyms for a single important variety. Others had the patience to track down the heirloom varieties individually. Though the lists have limited value because they do not describe varieties, they are available from the American Seed Trade Association, Suite 964, 1030 Fifteenth St. NW, Washington, DC 20006.

ADVICE FROM EXPERIENCED RESEARCHERS

Research into old varieties can be tedious; yet Jim Johnson found that it became easier and more rewarding as he became familiar with old sources. He recommends that gardeners who aren't particularly comfortable with large libraries start with less scholarly sources, such as premium lists from state and county fairs. These lists, which describe varieties that can be entered in fair competitions, may be found in local libraries or may be kept by members of local fair committees. He also recommends consulting old cookbooks, since, as he puts it, "if they ate it, they grew it."

The purpose of research is to confirm the identity of heirloom varieties; so gardeners must first make careful observations of what is growing in their gardens and then match those notes and, perhaps, photographs with the descriptions and drawings in old texts. Though this may seem hopelessly difficult at first, Johnson has been pleasantly surprised by how well the old descriptions fit the plants he's growing. "Most plants haven't really changed that much," he says. "Many descriptions match up very nicely, so you can really be sure you have what they describe."

Robert Becker, an heirloom expert who has been studying old horticultural texts for more than twenty years, agrees that descriptions and not variety names are what gardeners must use in identifying older varieties. "Identical names may have been

Summer Crookneck squash. *The richest and best sort for summer; very early and productive. It is small, crooked neck, covered with warty excrescences, the more the better; color bright yellow, shell very hard when ripe. It is used only when young and tender, which may be known by the pressure of the thumb nail through the skin.* DM

applied to two dissimilar varieties," he explains, "and a modern, recently developed variety may bear the same name as an older, completely unrelated one." He notes, for example, that commercial seed companies now sell two distinct varieties under the name Acorn squash—one is an heirloom that matches nineteenth-century descriptions and drawings, and the other is not.

The problem is compounded by heirloom gardeners who apply family names to their varieties and by careless collectors who mix up names when planting, storing, or exchanging seed. Such errors may lead to confusion even at the National Seed Storage Laboratory, which accepts the names supplied by donors because it doesn't have sufficient staff to verify them. Becker discovered the problem when he requested a sample of Jenny Lind, a melon that was very popular at the end of the nineteenth century. "What I got doesn't match the description by Fearing Burr," he says. "It's an old green melon, but beyond that I don't know what it is."

The only solution, says Becker, is for gardeners to get in the habit of making careful observations of the plants they grow and then comparing them with written descriptions. Even then, there's room for error. "Seeds are living organisms; so it's impossible to obtain viable seeds that are a hundred or two hundred years old," he explains. "It is probably also impossible to grow a plant of an old variety from a recently produced seed that is genetically identical to its ancestor. Living organisms constantly evolve—both from natural selection and from selection by seed savers." As an example, Becker cites a sample of Jacob's Cattle bean that researchers had obtained as part of a breeding program. Beans are relatively stable because they are self-pollinating; yet when researchers grew eight seeds, they got eight variations. Some seeds were brown and white, some were black and white, and some were solid brown. "It was like the Guernsey, Holstein, and Jersey of Jacob's Cattle beans," says Becker. "All these variations were new and undescribed."

Jenny Lind melon. *The earliest of the green-fleshed kinds, and one of the sweetest and most delicious sorts in cultivation. Small size, slightly ribbed; skin thickly netted and thin. Highly recommended for early market or home garden use.* DM

Becker appreciates heirloom varieties as a historian, not a gardener. Though he is keeping a few heirloom varieties, his family garden is filled with new varieties because he thinks they are superior to the old. He is concerned about the old varieties mostly for their genetic potential, and he regrets the material that was lost before the National Seed Storage Laboratory was established. "Only two or three really old onion, carrot, and beet varieties have survived," he says. "Old pea varieties have almost disappeared, and no really old turnip or muskmelon varieties seem to be available." Becker would like to see museums play a larger role in preserving old varieties; so he helped establish the heirloom gardens at the Genesee Country Museum. He has also prepared several papers on old varieties, including a booklet called *The Heirloom Vegetable Garden*, which is available from the Distribution Center, 7 Research Park, Cornell University, Ithaca, NY 14850.

Though he doesn't think old varieties should replace new varieties in home gardens, Becker finds that studying heirlooms is an ideal hobby. "In the past few years," he says, "there has been a growing interest in historical research . . . It seems only natural that an interest would develop in old vegetable varieties." Jim Johnson agrees. "Interest is growing rapidly in this area," he says, "and it's about time. So much diversity has already disappeared, so many things won't be available next year."

Obviously, heirloom gardeners don't have to be historians. The key to keeping old varieties alive is growing them, not researching them. At the same time, gardeners who take the trouble to seek out heirloom fruit and vegetable varieties might as well learn something about their history. For one thing, knowing about a variety's past may make growing it more meaningful. Gardeners who know they are planting the same crop as Thomas Jefferson or Great-Aunt Sophie add a new dimension to their gardening. Just as important, verifying the identity of old varieties guarantees that gardeners will spend their time preserving genuine heirlooms instead of imposters with the same name. Few gardeners will become as adept at research as Jim Johnson or Robert Becker; few will consult all the sources described in this chapter. Yet those who do take the time to search out old varieties and research their history will rediscover their roots in the fullest sense of the word.

8

Old But Good

OF THE WORLD'S 80,000 EDIBLE PLANTS, HUMANS use only a few for food. Scientists estimate that prehistoric people ate about 1,500 wild plants, ancient societies cultivated at least 500 major vegetables, and the modern world depends on about 30 plants for 95 percent of its nutrition.

Many scientists think it would be to our advantage to diversify our diets by cultivating a wider range of species. Several years ago, the National Science Foundation released a list of fifty-four little known but nutritious plants that deserved more attention. A few, such as amaranth and the winged bean, have since received publicity if not acceptance. But others, such as the pigeon pea, the ground nut, and a citrus called pummelo, have been virtually ignored. As the manufacturers of potato chips know, most people are reluctant to alter their eating habits even when they know the change would do them good.

Given that fact of human nature, it makes sense to take the best possible care of the fruit and vegetable species upon which most of us depend. This chapter traces the history of some of those crops. A description of all the heirloom varieties in any one of these categories would be a book in its own right; so the historical sketches that follow are necessarily incomplete. They are meant to tantalize gardeners with a glimpse of what is available and to inspire them to undertake their own search and research for heirloom varieties they can call their own.

Beans (Phaseolus vulgaris)

Beans are, without question, the most widely collected of all heirloom vegetables. Several collectors are keeping more than four hundred named varieties, and the listing of varieties available through the Seed Savers Exchange takes up more than two pages of single-spaced type. There are good reasons for the popularity of the humble bean. First, beans don't cross-pollinate much; so several varieties can be kept pure, even in a small garden. Second, the genetic variations in beans are often dramatically visible in the beautiful, many-colored seeds. Third, because hybrid beans are so difficult to produce—each hand-pollinated flower yields only a few seeds—most companies carry open-pollinated varieties, and many of the old varieties are still being sold. Finally, beans are a delicious and versatile food.

They are also an ancient food—Ezekiel mentions them in the Bible. Their scientific name was bestowed on them in 39 B.C. by Calumella, who observed that the seed looked like *phaseolus*, a "small boat." Beans were so common in the ancient world that they were often used as counters in elections—a white bean meant a yes vote; a dark one meant no. Actually, the beans known to the ancients were the broad beans, *Vica faba*, which are still appreciated in Europe but have never been particularly popular in this country. The beans of the New World were first noted by Columbus himself, who observed that Native Americans were growing "faba and faxone very different from those in Spain."

The indigenous cultures had, in fact, been cultivating beans for centuries. Beans found in Peruvian caves have been estimated by carbon dating to be 5,000 years old. One indication of the importance of beans in Aztec culture is the fact that Aztec rulers in Mexico expected their subjects to pay a collective tribute of 5,000 tons of beans each year. Eventually, the beans native to the Americas were classified into four groups—the lima bean (*P. lunatus*); the tepary bean (*P. acutofolius*), which grows only in the arid Southwest; the runner bean (*P. coccineus*), which produces long vines and, in some cases, showy flowers; and the common, or kidney, bean (*P. vulgaris*).

The common bean was most quickly accepted in Europe, where the French, dissatisfied with its plebian name, rechristened it the "French bean," or *haricot*. Today, most American collectors specialize in common beans, though that fact is often obscured by the many folk terms that refer to beans. *Green beans*, or *string beans*, are simply young beans that are eaten when the pods are tender and the beans immature. *Shell beans* have ripened one stage further so that the pods are thin and rubbery but the beans are still not fully mature. In the shell stage, the beans are taken out of the pods and then cooked. Beans that are tastiest at this stage are also called horticultural beans, shell beans, or cranberry beans in different regions of the country. Finally, beans are that left on the vine even longer become *dry beans* and can be stored for future use in soup, baked beans, cassoulet, and many other dishes.

Some of today's heirloom beans are undoubtedly descendants of beans grown by Native Americans, but it is difficult to trace their ancestry because the tribes did not keep written records. Nevertheless, bean collector John Withee is convinced that Hopi is a Native American heirloom from the Southwest, and many experts argue that Mohawk was grown by East Coast tribes before 1800. Other beans made the circuitous route from the New World to the Old and were reintroduced by early colonists. For example, Refugee, or Thousand-to-One, was rein-

White Runner bean. *Stems very vigorous-growing, climbing, attaining a height of nearly ten feet in a few weeks; flowers white, in numerous long-stalked clusters; pods broad, very flat, seldom containing more than three or four seeds each; seeds white, full, very large, kidney-shaped, sometimes 1 inch long, ³/₅ inch broad, and ²/₅ inch thick.* AV

troduced by French Huguenots around 1820, and Wren's Egg probably came from England at about the same time.

The first written information about bean varieties began to appear at the end of the eighteenth century. In 1797, Samuel Deane's *The New England Farmer* recommended several old varieties, including Caseknife, whose "half grown, green pods . . . were excellent food," and Cranberry, "so named because it resembled that berry in shape and color." Lazy Wife is another old variety that was supposed to have been brought to Pennsylvania by German settlers before 1810 and remained popular throughout the century. The 1888 Burpee catalogue apologizes for the name, "which seems rather discourteous to us," but suggests that it comes from the variety's "immense productiveness, making it very easy to gather a dish, and from the ease with which they are cooked."

Many other heirloom beans merit mention. Soldier beans, for example, have a dark-colored "figure" that resembles a man in uniform at the hilum of the seed. Jacob's Cattle beans are also called Dalmatian or Coach Dog beans because the white seeds are splashed with maroon. Black Turtle Soup bean, another very old variety, is popular in the South, where it is the basis for black bean soup. All of these varieties were dried for shelling since that was the most efficient way to preserve the crop in the early nineteenth century.

Though green beans were not readily stored, a few very old varieties have survived. In 1866, Fearing Burr, Jr., described Valentine as unexcelled "in the tender and succulent character of the pods in the green state." Burr was also partial to the Nonpareil bean for its "mildness and delicacy of flavor" and the Fejee bean, which he pronounced "decidedly one of the best."

Despite this praise, green beans did not achieve their fullest popularity until Calvin N. Keeney began tinkering with them. Keeney was one of many gardener-breeders who "created" new varieties by being alert to unusual crosses that appeared natu-

Case Knife bean. *A very vigorous growing kind nearly 10 feet in height. Stem thick and green; leaves very large, deep green, crimped; flowers large, white, fading to nankeen yellow, and forming long clusters. Pods straight, sometimes undulating on the sides, ten inches to one foot long, containing eight or nine seeds each . . . The seed or bean, when used fresh from the pod, is one of the best; it is also very good when dried. This is certainly one of the best varieties; the only objection to it is that it requires very long stakes when growing.* AV

rally in their gardens. "It is a curious fact," noted Keeney, "that most new varieties of beans are accidents rather than the result of hand pollination. Nature, by using bees, seems to do a better job of it than man." In *The Beans of New York*, Keeney is credited with introducing Pencil Pod Black Wax, Brittle Wax, Fordhook Favorite, and many other varieties; yet his greatest accomplishment was a stringless green bean. He sold the seed to Burpee, which introduced the variety as Burpee's Stringless Pod in 1894. Stringless Pod and its progeny hastened the demise of many of the old string varieties.

Though many beans have disappeared, some nineteenth-century "discoveries" have proved remarkably durable. The Henderson Bush Lima bean was, according to legend, first noticed by a pedestrian out for a stroll in Virginia. The variety, which was unique for its size and early maturity, eventually found its way to the Henderson Seed Company, where it was given the company name. As that story suggests, originality in names wasn't a strong suit for the firm. In 1896, the company asked its customers to help name a productive new green bean, and an Ohio gardener won five dollars with the name Bountiful. The Bountiful bean, which remained popular through the 1930s, fell out of favor for several decades. Fortunately, an astute seed saver must have kept a supply, for the bean has recently made a comeback in the catalogues of a few seed companies.

In some cases, the revival of an heirloom name doesn't mean the variety itself has been preserved. Kentucky Wonder, a staple in catalogues and supermarkets today, received rave reviews in an 1864 issue of *Country Gentleman*. Yet Kent Whealy of the Seed Savers Exchange is convinced that the new variety is nothing like the old, which kept its green color when cooked young and had bright brown seeds when it matured.

Often, the purest heirlooms have been kept by families. The catalogue for John Withee's collection lists dozens of these heirlooms, including Brown King, grown for a hundred years by a

Henderson Bush Lima bean. *Valuable variety on account of its earliness and wonderful productiveness, continuing to grow and set pods until stopped by frost. Rich, buttery Limas—the true flavor (even better). Pods short, flat and contain three to five Beans, which are of delicious quality.* HWB

Michigan family; Goose Pole, from a Tennessee gardener; Handed Down, an Arkansas heirloom; Kentucky Pioneer, a "treasure" from West Virginia; and Mountain, a real old-timer from West Virginia. Withee is also intrigued by beans that bear the same name but don't resemble each other. His collection includes several beans called Wild Goose. All, it seems, had been found in the crops of wild geese shot in the fall. Another name that recurs regularly is Ice or Icicle bean. Having seen so many different beans with that name, Kent Whealy has concluded that the name is almost generic for any bean with a white pod.

Since World War II, heirloom beans have come under great pressure from new varieties. As a recent publication from Asgrow Seed Growers puts it, "The common bean . . . has been almost entirely redesigned by plant breeders over the past twenty-eight years." Breeders have concentrated on white-seeded varieties because colored seeds discolor the liquid in canned beans. They have worked to produce beans that mature all at once so they can be mechanically harvested. Some varieties have even been bred so that they won't split when heated on the steam tables used in cafeterias.

Meanwhile, many old varieties have been lost. John Withee has looked in vain for Jewett, a pea bean that was known as the "fastest bean in New Hampshire." Kent Whealy's list of lost varieties includes the Sword bean, which had huge pods and red seeds; the Blue Queen, which had a purple pod; and the Stove-wood bean, which had enormous seeds four inches across. Though these varieties may not have survived, information about them has, sometimes in the oral histories of families but often in sourcebooks that deal exclusively with beans. The oldest and most difficult to locate is *Garden Beans, a Monograph*, published by George von Martin in 1860. Another source is *American Varieties of Garden Beans*, published in 1907 by the U.S. Bureau of Plant Industries. Finally, *The Beans of New York*, published in 1931 by the New York State Agricultural Station,

Improved Refugee bean. *Not an early variety, but very hardy and productive. Pods thick-fleshed and tender, and of good quality as snaps. It is a favorite main crop bean and one of the best for late planting, and for use as a pickling sort for which it is grown extensively.* NBG

includes color plates and exhaustive descriptions of beans known in the 1930s.

Peas (Pisum sativum)

Though peas are as easy to keep pure as beans, they are not nearly as popular a collectible because so many of the old varieties have been lost. Cultivated for so long that their origins are uncertain, peas have been discovered in the ruins of Troy and in the tombs of Egypt. However, the peas grown centuries ago were quite different from those in modern gardens. Their vines grew to be as long as eight feet, and their seeds were small, dark, smooth, and starchy, rather like the split peas used today in soup. These characteristics suited early gardeners, who wanted to shell, dry, and store their peas against hard times.

Before the seventeenth century, the only peas eaten fresh were sugar, or edible-podded, varieties that were known as early as 1536. The idea of eating ordinary peas fresh didn't catch on until the end of the seventeenth century, when the Dutch introduced a pea called *petit pois* in France. A passion for fresh peas swept the French court and eventually all of Europe. "The subject of peas continues to absorb all others," wrote one lady of the French court. "The anxiety to eat them, the pleasures of having eaten them and the desire to eat them again are the three great matters which have been discussed by our princes for four days past."

Peas were among the first crops imported to the New World. Columbus is reported to have planted some in Santo Domingo in 1492, and Native Americans promptly adopted them as a new crop. Thomas Jefferson considered peas his favorite vegetable, and his *Garden Book* mentions more than fifty varieties, including Charlton, Hotspur, and Marrowfat. Nearly all the varieties about which Jefferson raved have disappeared because of dramatic changes in peas that occurred during the

Large White Marrowfat pea. *An American variety, cultivated more extensively for the summer crop than all the others. About five feet high, of strong growth. Pods large, round, rough, light colored and well filled; seed large, round and yellow or white, according to the soil in which they are grown. This variety is so well known that it is needless to speak of its good qualities. It is excellent for summer use, and undoubtedly the greatest bearer in field or garden.* DM

nineteenth century. For one thing, breeders made the plants
more compact. Though semidwarf varieties had been available
since 1700, true dwarfs appeared in the 1800s. They were preferred by gardeners because they eliminated the arduous task of
"brushing" the vines by supporting them with twiggy branches.

An even more important change followed the discovery of
wrinkle-seeded peas, a mutant variety whose seed had a higher
sugar content. The new varieties, called Rouncivals in early gardening books, were first improved by an Englishman named
Thomas Knight. Knight's Marrow peas, introduced in the late
1780s, quickly gained acceptance among gardeners, though
naturally there were dissenters who preferred the old varieties.
The French nurserymen Vilmorin-Andrieux complained that
the wrinkle-seeded peas didn't germinate as well as the smooth
but added, "They are now nearly as numerous as the others."
This was an understatement since their book *The Vegetable Garden* included descriptions for 149 wrinkle-seeded varieties. Burpee included far fewer varieties in its 1888 catalogue but still felt
obliged to use a star to alert customers to the wrinkle-seeded varieties, which represented about half the selections.

Meanwhile, the sweeter flavor of the wrinkle-seeded peas
provoked passionate debate about how they should be cooked.
Many nineteenth-century cookbooks recommended boiling
peas with mint, an English habit that may have evolved as a way
of masking the starchy taste of smooth-seeded varieties. The
"American mode," which worked fine with the sweeter, wrinkle-seeded varieties, called for boiling the peas in plain water
until tender. One of the fiercest advocates of the new method
was Mary Henderson, whose *Practical Dinner Giving*, published
in 1882, dismissed the British method with this scathing comment: "This cooking of pease with mint is a good way of utterly
destroying the delicious natural flavor of the pea."

The proliferation of new pea varieties, many bearing chau-
vinistic English names such as Prince Albert and Champion of

Knight's Tall Green
Wrinkled Marrow pea.
*A tall-growing variety,
but having a compara-
tively slender stem . . .
pods at least 3 inches or
more in length, rather
narrow, but blunt at the
end, each containing
seven or eight medium-
sized peas . . . which,
when ripe, become wrin-
kled and of a slightly
bluish-green colour.* AV

England, was confusing both to scientists and garden writers. Most nineteenth-century writers took a stab at classifying peas, but the most painstaking effort was made by the authors of *The Peas of New York*, published in 1928 by the New York State Agricultural Station. The ninety-three varieties described in that volume were divided into fourteen categories, and an examination of those categories reveals something about the diversity that has been lost. The authors, who apparently still had samples of extra-early peas such as Prince Albert and Hotspur, Jefferson's favorite, condemned them as "rather tasteless." Other lost varieties described in the volume include the Marrowfats, which were very large, and the Scimitar varieties, which had curved pods and whose ancestry could be traced to the Sickle pea, known in 1688.

One of the few surviving smooth-seeded varieties is Alaska, though descriptions suggest that today's pea of that name bears little resemblance to the variety introduced in 1880. Wrinkle-seeded peas, which eclipsed their smooth cousins, have fared somewhat better. Wrinkle-seeded varieties introduced between 1880 and 1900 that are still available include Little Marvel, Thomas Laxton, Champion of England, Alderman, Telephone, and Lincoln.

Old pea varieties have disappeared largely because our tastes have changed. Most of the heirlooms being kept by seed savers are the sweet, wrinkle-seeded types, not their starchy, smooth-seeded predecessors. Yet some of the changes occurring today have little to do with flavor. For example, plant breeders now concentrate on determinate-vined peas, which can be harvested mechanically because they produce pods all at once at the end of a single main stem. Indeterminate-vined varieties, such as Laxton 8 and Alderman, develop and set pods over a much longer season, a habit that is preferable in home gardens. Despite that fact, fewer and fewer indeterminate-vined varieties are being offered in seed catalogues. Presumably, breeders are

Laxton's Alpha pea. *This pea is one of the best known and most extensively cultivated of the varieties raised by Mr. Laxton, whose name we have had frequent occasion to mention.* AV

keeping these varieties alive in working collections—Asgrow, for example, has more than 2,000 pea varieties in storage at its Idaho research station—but that will be little comfort to home gardeners if indeterminate-vined peas follow their smooth-seeded cousins into commercial exile.

Tomatoes (Lycopersicon esculentum)

Gardeners grow and collect old tomato varieties for one unambiguous reason—flavor. Supermarket tomatoes, with their thick skin, mealy consistency, and insipid flavor, have inspired more than a few gardeners to seek out tasty old varieties. Happily, tomatoes are self-pollinating; so it's easy to save seed from heirloom varieties of America's favorite vegetable.

Tomatoes were not always an American favorite, though the crop did originate in South America. By the time the Spanish arrived, the continent's inhabitants had been cultivating tomatoes for so long that they bore little resemblance to the wild plants that still grow in Peru and Ecuador. "From the earliest figure of the plant with fruit in European botanical literature, it is obvious that the fruits, for example, were already as large as they are now," writes Edward Hyams in *Plants in the Service of Man*. "We have, by selection, improved the shape of the fruit and nearly ruined its flavor, but we have not taken it any further from the wild species than the people of Central America had done."

The Spaniards didn't give the indigenous growers much credit for their accomplishment, but they did send the plant home, labeled with its original name, *tomatl*. Linnaeus later gave it the scientific name *Solanum lycopersicon*, which means "wolf peach," and emphasized its relationship to other members of the *Solanus*, or deadly nightshade, family. Years later, when the tomato's edibility had been established, it was renamed *Lycopersicon esculentum*. In the sixteenth century, how-

Early Conqueror tomato. *The product of one acre of this variety . . . was over one thousand bushels of tomatoes, all put into market before most other sorts had begun to ripen. After fully testing its good qualities, we unhesitatingly place it in the front rank of all the early varieties, and we do not think it has been surpassed, if indeed equaled, for a large producing, well-formed, smooth, handsome, early tomato for market or family use.* DM

ever, Spanish cooks weren't taking chances. The tomato's culinary possibilities were neglected until a visiting Moor took a
specimen to Morocco, where an Italian sailor spotted it and carried it home. The Italians lost no time incorporating the *pomo
dei mori* into their national cuisine, but the rest of Europe remained skeptical until the end of the sixteenth century.

Back in the New World, the tomato was being reintroduced
with mixed results, depending upon the prejudices in the home
country of the colonists. The Puritans shunned tomatoes, in
part because their sensuous shape and color made them suspect
as an aphrodisiac. French settlers in Louisiana didn't suffer
from such inhibitions and readily used tomatoes in their cooking. The shift in public attitude was illustrated by Thomas Jefferson, who grew tomatoes as an ornamental in 1781 but
brought them into the kitchen early in the nineteenth century.
By 1806, American nurseryman Bernard McMahon was writing that the "love apple is much cultivated for its fruit, in soups
and sauces, to which it imparts an agreeable acid flavor; and is
also stewed and dressed in various ways and very much ad-
mired." Despite such praise, McMahon did not include tomatoes on his seed lists.

The turning point for the tomato came in 1820, when Colo-
nel Robert Johnson, an eccentric but enthusiastic gardener, an-
nounced that he would eat a basketful on the steps of the court-
house in Salem, New Jersey. A large crowd gathered, expecting
to see Johnson "foam and froth at the mouth and double over
with appendicitis" as his own physician had predicted. Instead,
Johnson downed the entire basket, lived, and inspired an American passion for tomatoes whose intensity was suggested by this
recipe printed in the *Genesee Farmer* in 1839: "Daily Use of the
Tomato: Cut up with salt, vinegar and pepper (as you do cucumbers) and eat away as fast as you can."

The few tomato varieties available in Johnson's day usually
had generic names, such as Large Round Red or Yellow Pear

Shaped. During the next hundred years, a thousand new varieties were introduced, and breeders became more inventive
about names. Popular varieties in the mid-nineteenth century
included Cook's Favorite, Trophy, and Fiji Island, an egg-size
tomato with a yellow skin that was found on Fiji around 1840.
One of the most diligent of the early breeders was Alexander
Livingston, whose goal was to grow "tomatos smooth in con-
tour, uniform in size and better flavored." He was fortunate
enough to find a mutation with smooth skin and gradually up-
graded it until, in 1870, he introduced Paragon.

Breeders have since developed so many varieties that virtually no one misses the hundred varieties that are said to have
disappeared since 1950. In fact, some breeders are glad to see the
old varieties go. "Most of the old varieties don't have much merit
today," says Dr. Henry Munger, a highly respected breeder at
Cornell University. "They were susceptible to every disease.
They cracked. They had odd shapes. People who long for those
old varieties don't know what they're talking about."

One of the things they talk about is flavor, which was a primary goal of breeders during the early part of the twentieth century. With the advent of mechanized agriculture, breeding emphasis shifted to other characteristics, such as simultaneous
ripening, disease resistance, tough skins, and uniform shape.
Gardeners have benefited from the advances in disease resistance, but most of the other modifications have been to the advantage of commercial growers, who are now able to keep supermarkets stocked with tomatoes year-round. Impressive as
that accomplishment may be, it doesn't necessarily satisfy those
who have very individual ideas about how tomatoes should
taste.

Ben Quisenberry, for example, "fell in love with tomatoes"
when he was eight. For a while he sold tomato seeds, but now,
at the age of ninety-five, he raises them for his own pleasure. His
varieties include Golden Sunray, which makes beautiful tomato

Trophy tomato. *Un-*
doubtedly the best new
variety that has yet been
brought into notice. Is
medium early, of enor-
mous size, uniformly
smooth and well-formed;
solid to the center, and
very heavy. The seed we
offer is our own growth
from stock procured from
Mr. Waring, the
originator. DM

juice; Long Tom, which he calls a "dandy" salad tomato; and Mortgage Lifter, which is named for its size. His favorite variety is Brandywine, an heirloom that had been in a single family for a hundred years. "It has a kind of sharp taste to it," he explains, "and it's as fine a tasting tomato as ever was raised."

Lettuce (Lactuca sativa)

Like tomatoes, lettuce is a self-pollinating crop that is often included in home gardens because the home-grown varieties are so much superior to those available in most supermarkets. All the many types of lettuce are believed to be descended from the loose-leafed lettuce that grows wild in Asia Minor. The ancient origin of the upright *cos*, or *romaine*, *lettuce* is obvious from its names. *Romaine* is a corruption of "Roman," and *cos* comes from the name of a Greek Island, Kos, where the plant was first grown. Lettuce figured prominently in the Greeks' springtime festival, when pots of the plant were carried through the streets. The Romans also depended upon it to "relax the alimentary canal" before their notorious banquets.

In comparison, *head*, or *cabbage*, *lettuce* is a recent development, dating only to the Middle Ages. The Iceberg variety so ubiquitous in supermarkets today was not developed until the nineteenth century. By then, however, the preference for head lettuce was well established. Burpee's 1888 catalogue lists twenty-three head varieties, three cos varieties, and only one leaf lettuce.

One of the oldest named head varieties is Brown Dutch, which was mentioned as early as 1805 and recommended throughout the nineteenth century as a variety that did well in cold weather. Another very old variety is Tennis Ball, which was grown by Thomas Jefferson in 1809 and formed a tight, compact head. Burpee's 1888 catalogue praised it as a "fine, early sort," but Vilmorin dismissed it as being exceptional only for its

Early Tennis Ball lettuce. *A small, extremely hardy variety, extensively grown by marketmen in winter, in cold frames, for early spring marketing. Dark green, very solid, if grown in cool weather, but apt to be loose if grown during summer. It is slow in going to seed, and the head blanches white and tender.* DM

Simpson's Early Curled
lettuce. *One of the best
early sorts for market or
family use. Heads large,
loose, all the leaves tending to produce a head.
Leaves beautifully
crimped, dark green,
very tender and crisp.
Recommended for general
cultivation.* DM

deep green color. Hansen is another survivor; it grew very solid heads of "remarkable size," according to Burpee in 1888.

Though leaf lettuce is preferable in home gardens because it can be harvested in small amounts over several weeks, it receives little attention from breeders. The most popular leaf variety is a descendant of Early Curled Simpson, introduced by A. M. Simpson in 1864. If the number of synonyms for a variety is any indication of popular acceptance, this leaf lettuce was enthusiastically received—the American Seed Trade Association list of vegetable varieties notes forty-one other names for the black-seeded variety of Simpson. Few gardeners collect lettuce, but members of the Seed Savers Exchange are keeping alive several old leaf varieties, including Bronze Arrowhead, Dear Tongue, and Ruby Red Leaf.

Radishes (Raphanus sativa)

Is it necessary to save old varieties of a crop as seemingly insignificant as radishes? Perhaps if we paid more attention to the old varieties, the crop would not be so insignificant in this country. Cultures that depend upon radishes as a food rather than a relish have a much larger selection.

French Breakfast radish.
*A medium sized radish,
olive-shaped, small top,
of quick growth, very
crisp and tender, of a
beautiful scarlet color,
except near the root,
which is pure white. A
splendid variety, for the
table, not only on account
of its excellent qualities
but also for its beautiful
color.* DM

Botanists are not sure whether radishes originated in China or the Middle East. We do know that the Egyptians ate them while working on the pyramids and that they were important enough in ancient Greece for the physician Moschian to have written an entire book on them. Large-rooted radishes were a staple in Europe during the Middle Ages—one sixteenth-century author describes specimens that weighed forty pounds. Vilmorin also described many "keeping radishes," which grew long or fat and could be stored like turnips.

In this country, *keeping radishes* never caught on, but even *bunching radishes* were represented by more varieties in the past. Burpee's 1888 catalogue lists seventeen varieties and suggests that "for breakfast, dinner and supper, three times a day, they are a most appetizing and wholesome relish." Popular old varieties include the French Breakfast radish, introduced in 1879; the Long Scarlet, which has a taproot as long as six inches; Black Spanish, introduced before 1828, which has a strong flavor and startling black skin; and China Rose, which Vilmorin called "a very distinctive variety" because of its chunky root. Another interesting old radish, mentioned as early as 1863, is the Rat Tail radish, whose pods, according to Peter Sturtevant, make "excellent pickles."

Corn (Zea mays)

Lots of people raise their own corn so they can, as Mark Twain once put it, "boil a pot of water in the field and shuck the ears into it." The pick-and-cook approach is optimum for *sweet corn*, but sweet corn is a relatively recent development in the history of this ancient grain. For thousands of years, corn was valued not for its sweet flavor but for its nutritious kernels, which could so easily be dried, stored, and milled. Indeed, some scholars contend that the accomplishments of the Incan and Aztec civilizations would have been impossible without the discovery and domestication of this nutritious and productive crop.

Scientists are still arguing about how and when that discovery was made. There is no doubt about corn's antiquity—cobs have been found in caves inhabited thousands of years ago—yet scientists are baffled by its history because they cannot find a wild plant that is clearly corn's ancestor. Some scientists are convinced that corn developed from teosinte, a wild plant that has comparable kernels. Their case was strengthened not long ago when researchers in Mexico discovered a variety of perennial teosinte that crosses with domesticated corn and may eventually be used to convert corn into a perennial crop. Meanwhile, the debate continues about how corn could have evolved since do-

Black Spanish radish. *One of the latest as well as the hardiest of the radishes, and is considered an excellent sort for winter use. Roots oblong, black, of very large size, and firm texture. It is sown rather earlier than the fall turnips, and must be stored in sand in the cellar, for winter use. It will keep good till spring.* DM

mesticated corn is, in the words of George Beale, a "biological monstrosity" that cannot survive without human intervention.

Fortunately, the Native Americans were more than willing to intervene, and corn was firmly established from Canada to Chile before Columbus landed in the New World. For most tribes, *maize*, which means "our life," was regarded as a gift from the gods, and its cultivation was surrounded by elaborate rituals and legends. Most tribes had traditional varieties that, over the centuries, had adapted to the conditions of their regions. Scientists estimate that between two hundred and three hundred varieties of *dent*, *flint*, *flour*, and *popcorn* were being grown in the Americas during the fifteenth century. Descriptions of 104 of those varieties are included in *Corn Among the Indians of the Upper Missouri*, by G. F. Will and G. E. Hyde. First published in 1917, this valuable book was reissued by the University of Nebraska in 1964.

In the Northeast, the Indians grew slender ears of multicolored corn with twelve to fourteen rows, which they shared with the first English colonists. Through selection, the colonists lengthened the ears and fattened the cobs to hold fourteen to twenty-four rows. They also selected for the yellow color so thoroughly that soon a young man who found a red ear at a corn husking was entitled to kiss the girl of his choice. In the South, the dominant variety was a coarse, white dent corn that was called Gourd Seed because its kernels were shaped like miniature gourds.

During the late 1700s, gardeners, including the famous Cotton Mather, noticed that when different kinds of corn were grown in adjacent fields, the seed became mixed. By selecting only the best from the mixed seed, farmers could produce custom-made varieties. In the 1860s, James Reid applied this process to a corn variety created when his father took Gordon Hopkins corn to a new farm in Illinois and planted it in the same

Early Minnesota corn.
*Very early; a decidedly
excellent variety;
ears fair-sized and
uniform; plant rather
dwarf.* PH

field as a local variety called Little Yellow. Reid's Yellow Dent produced five times the yield of the other Illinois varieties and soon became the standard field corn.

In the nineteenth century, raising corn was complicated by the fact that open-pollinated varieties such as Reid's Yellow Dent were not at all uniform. Some ears would have a thick sheath of husks and others would barely be covered. The ears were borne on branches of varying lengths so that harvesting was difficult, and the roots were so variable that some stalks would be blown down long before harvest. Hybrids, developed early in the twentieth century, solved all of these problems and dramatically increased yields. Between 1930 and 1975, corn production more than tripled and hundreds of old varieties were lost. Today, virtually every cornfield is planted with hybrids, and 70 percent of all the corn in the United States is descended from six parent lines. The dangers of such a narrow genetic base in such a vital crop were dramatically demonstrated in 1970, when a new strain of fungus wiped out 15 percent of the U.S. corn crop. Scientists quickly stepped in with new, resistant varieties, but they acknowledge that today's corn crop is no less vulnerable.

Most backyard gardeners aren't acquainted with the old varieties of field corn. That's a shame, according to Carl Barnes, founder of CORNS, an organization that is preserving more than two hundred old corn varieties. The collection includes many famous old dent corns, such as Bloody Butcher, a red-kerneled corn that was sought after by Southern planters because "worms and birds do not bother it very much." Many of the organization's flint corns take their names from Native American tribes—Navaho, Papago, Pawnee, and Taos. Sweet corn is included in the collection, though Barnes thinks the flavor of a roasting corn like Old Hickory is better. Early in the nineteenth century, most Americans would have agreed with Barnes. Pop-

Tuscarora corn. *Plant five to six feet in height, moderately strong and vigorous; ears eight-rowed, and of remarkable size—exceeding in this respect almost every sort used for the table in the green state. The kernel, which is much larger than any other table variety, is pure white, rounded, flattened, and, when divided in the direction of its width, apparently filled with fine flour of snowy whiteness; the cob is red, and of medium size . . . considered a valuable sort by those to whom the sweetness of the sugar varieties is objectionable.* FB

ular old roasting corns included Adams, which had a reputation for flavor, and Tuscarora, which could be traced back to 1712, when the Tuscarora tribe planted it in New York.

Native Americans were also growing sweet corn, though scientists suspect that the gene for sweetness is a relatively recent mutation. The colonists seem to have discovered sweet corn in 1779, when Lieutenant Richard Bagnal brought a sample to Massachusetts after General Sullivan's campaign against the Six Nations. The variety, which was called Papoon, had a red cob and eight rows of white kernels. Small cobs and white kernels were typical of early sweet corn varieties. Stowell's Evergreen, introduced around 1850, was the first variety to have a larger cob, and Golden Bantam was the first to displace the public prejudice against yellow corn as "horse corn."

Sweet corn didn't catch on right away. It first appeared in seed catalogues in 1828 and was listed under generic names such as "sweet" or "sugar" corn. After 1850, the taste for the new corn had been established and many new varieties were introduced. Fearing Burr, Jr. praised Red Narragansett, a variety with red kernels, because "it is tender and of excellent quality"; today it is on Kent Whealy's Lost Vegetables List. Burr also had high regard for Old Colony, a hybrid that combined "the productiveness of the Southern with the sweetness of the Northern parent," and Rhode Island Asylum, which had "tender sugary" kernels. Peter Henderson, another influential nineteenth-century writer, recommended Dwarf Early Sugar for family use because its three-to-four-foot stalks allowed it to be grown in a small area; he appreciated Mammoth Sweet because its size dictated "one ear to the meal."

One of the most unusual old varieties is Black Mexican, whose kernels are white at the milk stage but turn jet black as they dry. This corn was so delicious that the authors of *The Corns of New York* wrote, "The epicure of vegetable morsels

Stowell's Evergreen corn. *This variety is intermediate in its season and if planted at the same time with earlier kinds, will keep the table supplied till October. It is hardy and productive, very tender and sugary, remaining a long time in fresh condition and suitable for boiling.* DM

may not rest in his search for the acme of all sweet corn until he has eaten Black Mexican fresh from the field."

Sweet corn is a challenging collectible because it cross-pollinates so readily. Even those who are raising only a single variety must have the cooperation of their neighbors or become adept at hand pollination. For that reason, it's all the more remarkable to discover heirloom varieties that have been kept alive by individuals or families. For example, Kent Whealy's Growers Network is preserving a purple-kerneled corn called Catawba corn that had been kept pure for forty years by Phil Hewitt. As it turns out, the variety is not represented in the National Seed Storage Laboratory even though it was prized for its flavor. Another heirloom is Aunt Mary's Sweet corn, which was discovered by Lee Bonnewitz on a visit to his Aunt Mary during the Depression. His aunt served the most delicious sweet corn he had ever tasted, and Bonnewitz asked if he could have the seed. After improving the variety, he made seed available for sale and attracted a following of loyal gardeners. Though seed companies dropped Aunt Mary's Sweet corn, gardeners didn't and today it has been reintroduced to a newly appreciative public.

Another rediscovered heirloom has the intriguing name of Howling Mob. The farmer who first developed the variety claimed to attract that kind of crowd every time he brought his corn to market. When the variety showed up on Kent Whealy's list of "lost" vegetables, several seed savers volunteered to share the seeds they had been keeping alive. Yet another heirloom is available from the Taos Pueblo Native Seed Company. Their Taos Pueblo blue corn has been handed down from generation to generation and is now grown on a mountain in New Mexico, where it can be watered with water from a lake that the Pueblos call sacred.

All of these varieties have been preserved by gardeners who

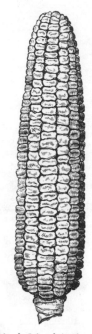

Rhode Island Asylum corn. *So named from its origin on the grounds of this institution. The plant is of medium size, producing one or two ears; foliage abundant; the ears are rather large, and eight or ten rowed; kernel yellowish-white at maturity, shriveled and indented. The variety is not early but is recommended for productiveness, and for the tender, sugary character of the kernel.* FB followed the advice of Peter Henderson. "Most persons who raise sweet corn have a favorite variety, or rather strain of their own," wrote Henderson. "By carefully selecting for seed each year those ears that have desirable peculiarities most strongly marked, a strain is soon established suited to the locality."

Because of its importance as a grain crop, corn has inspired many books. *The Corns of New York*, like other publications in the series, is an excellent source of information about varieties known in the 1930s. Two other classic references are *Corn: Its Origin, Evolution and Improvement*, by P. C. Mangelsdorf, and *Corn and Its Early Fathers*, by H. A. Wallace.

Carrots (Daucus carota)

Of the three biennial root crops, only carrots have attracted the attention of heirloom collectors. Gardeners often become intrigued when they learn that carrots can be purple, yellow, or white in addition to their familiar orange. Actually, the orange color is a recent development for the carrot, which descended from a roadside weed much like Queen Anne's lace.

Apparently, carrots were known by the Romans, who didn't think much of them. Around the seventh century, purple-rooted carrots started showing up in the Middle East, but they didn't become common in Europe until the fourteenth century. By that time a mutation had produced a variety with yellow roots. A mutation occurring in the seventeenth century resulted in carrots with orange roots. By 1620, Dutch breeders had produced two distinct types of orange carrots—Long Orange, which had large, long roots for winter storage, and Horn, which had finer flesh and sweeter flavor. Both varieties were raised by settlers in the New World and are often mentioned in nine-teenth-century gardening manuals.

Aside from Long Orange and Horn, few of the old varieties have survived. We can only speculate about the taste of Al-

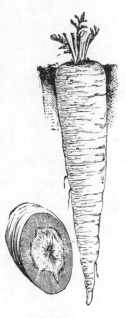

Long Orange carrot. *A well known standard sort; roots long, thickest near the crown, tapering regularly to a point; color deep orange; suitable for the table and main field crop. It requires a deep soil, and the plants should stand eight inches apart.* DM

tringham, a long, slender carrot with a bright red color and exceptional flavor, or the appearance of Lemon, a yellow variety that Vilmorin cites as being very old. On the other hand, variations on some nineteenth-century varieties are the stock in trade of today's seed companies. Danvers, for example, was developed in Massachusetts in 1870. Oxheart, or Guerand, a stumpy variety that grows well in dense soil, was introduced from France in 1884. And Nantes, a French variety developed near the town of that name, is still regarded almost as highly as it was when it was introduced, in about 1870.

Though there aren't many reference works devoted solely to carrots, varieties are described in USDA Publication 361, *Descriptions of Types of Principal American Varieties of Orange-Fleshed Carrots*, which was published in 1940.

Danvers carrot. *Originated in Danvers, Mass., where they raise from 20–30 tons per acre. It is of medium length, rich, dark orange in color, very smooth and handsome, and easily dug. It yields an immense bulk, with smallest length of root.* DM

Beets (Beta vulgaris)

Beets were raised for their greens long before anyone thought to taste the root. German gardeners were raising beets in the thirteenth century, but the rest of Europe was slow to catch on. In his seventeenth-century herbal, Gerard rhapsodized about "the great and beautiful beet . . . may be used in winter for a sallad herb, with vinegar, oyle and salt, and is not only pleasant to the taste, but also delightful to the eye."

Actually, to the modern eye, early beets look coarse, misshapen, and hairy. Most were turnip-shaped. The compact little balls growing in gardens today weren't developed until the nineteenth century. By that time, beets had firmly established their value for the typical homestead. The greens were valued as a fresh vegetable, and the roots had several purposes. Small, delicate varieties were eaten by people, who usually boiled them, though some cookbook writers recommended baking, which "retained and concentrated" the "sweet juices which inevitably

Bassano beet. *Bulb flat-
tened; six or seven inches
in diameter by three or
four inches in depth; not
very regular or symmetri-
cal, but often somewhat
ribbed and terminating
in a small slender tap-
root. The skin is of fine
texture; brown above
ground; below the sur-
face, clear rose-red.
Flesh white, circled or
zoned with bright pink;
not close-grained but
sugary and well-flavored
. . . Generally consid-
ered the earliest of the
garden beets.* FB

escape while boiling." Large, coarse varieties, known as mangel
wurzels, were grown as fodder for livestock.

Perhaps because beets served so many purposes in the nineteenth century, gardeners had a selection that makes today's varieties seem disturbingly uniform. They could choose round varieties, such as Early Blood Turnip, or long varieties, such as
Long Blood Red, whose root grew a foot long. Some, like Yellow Turnip, weren't even red. Other interesting nineteenth-
century varieties that are no longer commercially available include Bassano, which was regularly recommended by garden
writers as an unusually early variety, and Scarcity, a variety so
productive that it could be counted upon to avert famine. Fortunately, some varieties have fared much better. Egyptian, introduced around 1868, is still widely available, and Detroit can
be traced back to a variety introduced in 1892. Beet varieties
known in 1940 are catalogued in USDA Publication 374, *Descriptions of Types of Principal American Varieties of Red Garden
Beets.*

Turnips (Brassica rapa)

Turnips are another crop that has fallen out of favor. Native to
Europe, they were grown extensively during the Middle Ages
and were planted in the New World as early as 1540. During the
mid-nineteenth century, garden writer Robert Buist noted that
"During the great deficiency of the potato crop, they formed a
partial substitute for that valuable root." The varieties favored
by Buist included Early White Dutch, which produced "roots
fit for the table in six weeks," and Early Yellow Dutch, which
was a "beautifully formed variety."

Vilmorin describes the varieties of turnip as "exceedingly
numerous," but only a few have survived. Among these, the
most ubiquitous is the Purple-top Strap-leaved, introduced before 1865 and characterized by a purple blotch at the top of the

turnip. Other survivors include White Egg, which was prized for its thin skin and rapid growth, and Orange Jelly, which had, according to Burpee's 1888 catalogue, "rich, sweet, pulpy flesh."

Most of the other varieties are casualties of changing tastes. This problem was anticipated by *The Gardener's Manual*, published by the Shakers to accompany their seed packets. "Turneps are an excellent and very healthy vegetable, if properly cooked and dressed," the author noted. "But many people spoil them in the cooking." The author suggested that "good sweet turneps raised in a suitable soil" should be cut into small pieces and stewed and mashed. "When sufficiently done, take them up and dress them with a little salt and butter."

Potatoes (Solanaceae)

Collecting potato varieties requires unusual commitment since the entire collection must be replenished each year. Though potatoes do occasionally produce seeds, planting the seeds is a gamble because they will not reliably reproduce the parent plant. Potatoes have always been associated with the Irish, but they originated in Peru, where indigenous peoples began cultivating them as long as 4,000 years ago. When the Spanish came to Peru, they didn't know what to make of this lowly tuber, but Pizarro dutifully sent samples of the "earth nuts" to Europe.

There, the plant met with resistance because, like tomatoes, it was related to the deadly nightshade. In the seventeenth century, however, members of the Royal Society of London conducted scientific experiments with the tubers and concluded that they would make a nutritious food for the poor, who were always in danger of starvation from the failure of grain crops. Sir Walter Raleigh sent a shipment of potatoes to his estate in Ireland, where they became particularly popular. In fact, the allotment for Irish factory workers in the early nineteenth century was an astonishing twelve pounds of potatoes per day.

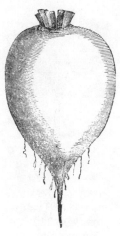

White Egg turnip. *A new, quick-growing variety, perfectly smooth, and nearly egg-shaped. In color, it is pure white; of extraordinary firmness and solidity. Grows about half out of the ground, has small top and rough leaves . . . The flesh is very sweet, firm and milky, never having the rank, strong taste of some varieties.* DM

Jackson White potato.
*This comparatively new
but very excellent variety
originated in Maine
. . . Tubers yellowish-
white, varying in size
from medium to large;
form somewhat irregu-
lar, but generally round-
ish, though sometimes ob-
long and a little
flattened; eyes rather numerous, and deeply sunk;
flesh perfectly white when
cooked, remarkably dry,
mealy, farinaceous, and
well-flavored. The vari-
ety unquestionably at-
tains its greatest perfection when grown in
Maine. . . . It is . . .
comparatively free from
disease; a good keeper;
and everything consid-
ered must be classed as
one of the best.* FB

The consequences of that dependence on a few varieties of a single crop comprise one of the most graphic lessons about the need for genetic diversity. When a fungus struck the potato in the 1840s, more than a million people died in Ireland alone. In the United States, where the potato didn't become popular until the early 1800s, officials of the Commonwealth of Massachusetts offered $10,000 to any person who could discover "a sure and practical remedy for the Potato Rot."

The remedy, when it came, was the introduction of new genes that were resistant to the blight. The Reverend Chauncy Enoch Goodrich of Utica, New York, obtained seed from a wild potato grown in Chile and began to cross it with domestic varieties. The result was Garnet Chili, a blight-resistant variety introduced in 1853. For the rest of the century, most of the popular potato introductions were descendants of Garnet Chili.

The nineteenth century had such a rich diversity of potato varieties that many garden writers refused to catalogue them, saying simply that each region had a favorite that was well suited to the growing conditions there. Mssrs. Vilmorin, who called the number of varieties "prodigious," estimated that as many as a thousand varieties had been grown in the nineteenth century. They described forty of the most popular, including Early Rose, which, Peter Henderson agreed, was a "universal favorite . . . unrivalled for earliness, quality and productiveness," and Snowflake, prized for its "neat symmetrical shape." Other nineteenth-century varieties that have survived are Burbank, a variety developed by the famous botanist, and Irish Cobbler, an unusually early variety.

Some potato collectors enjoy finding potatoes with unusual shapes and colors. Lady Finger, for example, is an heirloom introduced by German immigrants before 1850. Its small, slender tubers had such a fine flavor that it was considered a "fancy potato" by E. Emmons, author of *A Natural History of New York*, published in 1849. Others are attracted to brightly colored potatoes such as Hundred-fold, an old variety with violet skin.

Potatoes that deviate from the Idaho baking standard are dismissed as novelties by most Americans; yet these novelties may be in demand in the future. Researchers have recently discovered, for example, that potatoes with deeper eyes seem to be more nutritious. In other words, breeders who have been working to smooth out the potato may have inadvertently reduced its food value. Illustrations in Vilmorin's book show that old varieties such as Vitelotte and Chardon were deeply pitted, but because they were rejected by gardeners and growers, they have disappeared and are thus no longer available even for testing.

Squashes and pumpkins (Cucurbita)

Squashes and pumpkins are perhaps the most confusing heirlooms to collect because the common garden classification—winter squash, summer squash, pumpkin—does not correspond to the botanical classification—*C. maxima*, *C. pepo*, *C. mixta*, and *C. moschata*. All of these species were apparently known by the earliest Americans since the seeds have been found in pre-Columbian graves. When Europeans arrived in the New World, they were given both the seeds for this new vegetable and a name—*askuta squash*, which means "eaten raw."

Members of the *C. pepo* group, which includes ribbed pumpkins and summer squashes, were the first to be appreciated by the American colonists. A variety of *C. pepo* that is now called Connecticut Field pumpkin was being grown by North American tribes when the colonists arrived, and its prolific habit helped them through their first difficult winters. As one rhymester put it, "We had pumpkins at morning and pumpkins at noon. If it were not for pumpkins we should be undone." Years later there was a perhaps predictable backlash against the

Lady Finger potato. *The Lady Finger is a very old variety, of pretty appearance, and much esteemed as a Baking Potato; the tubers are long and slender, of nearly the same diameter throughout, and when cooked are as white as snow . . . Lost sight of as it has been for several years, there is no doubt that the coming season will revive all its popularity, as it fills a niche that no other potato can occupy.* PW

Boston Marrow squash. *Of oval form; skin thin; when ripe, bright orange; flesh rich salmon yellow, very dry, fine-grained, and for sweetness and excellence, unsurpassed; a very popular variety in the Boston market.* DM

Hubbard squash. *This is a superior variety, and the best winter squash known; flesh bright orange yellow, fine-grained, very dry, sweet and rich-flavored; keeps perfectly good throughout the winter; boils or bakes exceedingly dry, and is esteemed by many to be as good baked as the sweet potato.* DM

pumpkin. "The pumpkin is yet offered in large quantities for sale in our markets," wrote Peter Henderson in *Gardening for Profit* in 1893, "but it ought to be banished from them as it has for some time been from our garden. But the good lieges of our cities are suspicious in all innovations in what is offered them to eat, and it will be many years yet before the masses will understand the modest and sometimes uncouth looking squash is immeasureably superior for all culinary purposes to the mammoth, rotund pumpkin."

Among summer squashes, Henderson recommended White Bush Scallop, a variety Native Americans had grown, which he praised for "never presenting any variation"; Summer Crookneck, a very old squash that he called "the best flavored of the summer varieties"; and Boston Marrow, with flesh of "unsurpassed flavor." An apple-shaped pumpkin called Perfect Gem was the first specimen of *C. pepo* to be sent back to Europe, and the Europeans lost no time in importing other varieties and shaping them to their own national purposes. In England, the squash of choice was the bland *vegetable marrow*; in France, the slender *courgette*; and in Italy, the *zucha*. The *zucchini*, which now monopolizes most of the U.S. breeding effort, was first grown in California around 1920.

Varied as *C. pepo* may be, it seems bland beside the variety in shape, size, color, and flavor available in *C. maxima*. Many of the squashes in this group keep through the winter, so they were a mainstay in the early American diet. As canning and other forms of preservation became popular, *C. maxima* fell out of favor. Today, heirloom gardeners are rediscovering grand old squashes such as the Turban squash, which has a button on its blossom end that looks like the gathers on a turban; Delicious, a fat, round squash with a flavor so sweet that it is often used in commercial baby foods; and Sweet Meat, which has a reputation for delicious gold flesh inside a drab gray shell.

Though *C. maxima* originated in the Western Hemisphere, its culture was confined to the Andes, and several varieties were first introduced to the settlers by sailors. Hubbard is believed to have been brought to Massachusetts by a sea captain. The seed passed from gardener to gardener until Elizabeth Hubbard brought it to the attention of J. H. Gregory, the seedsman. "As the squash up to this time had no specific name to designate it from other varieties," wrote Gregory, "my father termed it the Hubbard Squash." In addition to variations on Hubbard—which included the Green, Blue, Golden, and Warted—Gregory, who wrote an 1893 reference work called *Squashes: How To Grow Them*, was also responsible for the introduction of Marblehead, which was brought to the town of that name by yet another sea captain. While Gregory was obtaining squash by sea, the Will Seed Company in North Dakota was obtaining seed from local Native American tribes. The company's squash introductions included Winnebago, which was like an elongated Hubbard, and Arikara, which grew well with minimal water.

Puritan squash. *Plant ten feet and upwards in length; fruit bottle-formed, fourteen or fifteen inches long, and ten inches in diameter at the broadest part; neck solid, four or five inches in diameter; average weight eight to ten pounds; skin thin, usually white, or cream-white, striped and marked with green . . . flesh pale yellow, dry, sweet, mild and well-flavored . . . It is hardy and productive, good for table use, excellent for pies and well deserving of cultivation.* FB

C. moschata was also being grown by North American tribes, who often labeled it "crane" or "crooked" neck. Very old varieties in this category include Large Cheese, which is a lovely buff color, and Puritan, which was grown early in the colony of Massachusetts. Today, the only representative of *C. moschata* that shows up regularly in seed catalogues is Butternut.

In the past, varieties belonging to the species *C. mixta* were often lumped together with *C. moschata* because there is a close family resemblance. Even the authors of *The Cucurbits of New York* didn't bother to distinguish between the two groups. For the heirloom gardener, the distinction is important because members of the two groups will not cross-pollinate and can be safely grown in the same garden. Old varieties of *C. mixta* include Tennessee Sweet Potato, which has creamy skin with green stripes, and members of the cushaw or cashaw group.

Though Robert Buist found the cushaw squashes superior to every other winter squash, they never achieved the popularity of other varieties.

Cucumbers (Cucumis sativus)

The standard supermarket cucumber with its straight cylindrical shape and its glossy green skin gives no hint of the diversity of which this vegetable is capable. In the Orient, cucumbers are long and thin. In France, cosmetics are made with fat, juicy cucumbers. In Russia, cucumbers have brown, netted skin.

The antecedents of all these varieties probably originated in North Africa. Cucumbers were appreciated by the ancient Romans, including Tiberius, who was proud of his system for growing them under glass out of season. Columbus introduced the first cucumbers to the New World in 1492. Native Americans adopted the crop so readily that when de Soto arrived in Florida in 1539, they were growing as if they were a native plant. The colonists enjoyed the "cold and moist nourishment" of cucumbers in the summer and pickled them for the winter.

For many years the most popular varieties were imported from Europe. In 1806, American nurseryman Bernard McMahon listed eight standard varieties—Early Short Prickly, Long Green Prickly, White Prickly, Long Green Turkey, Long White Turkey, Smyrna, Roman, and White Spined. Of those, Long Green Turkey was destined for greatness as the parent of Improved Long Green, a variety that was introduced around 1842. Breeders had little interest in cucumbers until Joseph Tailby crossed White Spine, an American cucumber, with Dickson's All the Year-round, an English forcing variety. Exhibited in 1872, Tailby's Hybrid stimulated interest in cucumbers because of its high yields and large fruits. Pickling cucumbers took a comparable leap forward in 1924, when the National Pickle Packers Association began a search for the perfect pick-

Early Russian cucumber. *Fruit three or four inches long, an inch and a half in diameter, generally produced in pairs; flesh tender, crisp, and well-flavored; comes into use about ten days earlier than any other variety and makes a fine, small pickle.* DM

Early Short Green cucumber. *Excellent variety for table use, being tender and well-flavored, and keeps green longer than any other variety; also makes splendid, hard green pickles.* DM

ling cucumber. The result was National pickle, a variety that is still available today.

Many old cucumber varieties disappeared because they were susceptible to disease such as mildew and scab. New introductions are, for the most part, resistant to these diseases, and so they have been adopted by home gardeners and commercial growers. Old varieties that are still available include Lemon, an 1894 variety with the shape and color of a lemon; West Indian Gherkin, which was introduced in 1793; and White Wonder, an 1893 variety with ivory skin.

Melons (Cucumis melo)

Heirloom melons are scarce because, like cucumbers, some were distressingly susceptible to disease. The species is believed to have originated in Persia and was known by the Romans. Melons were among the first plants introduced to the New World by Columbus and were soon being grown by Native Americans throughout the continent.

Gardeners in the nineteenth century grew green-fleshed melons that were said to have descended from a melon brought to France from Africa by a monk. A variety called Pineapple was listed by seedsman Grant Thorburn in 1824, but the standard varieties of the day were Citron and Nutmeg. Both were used in breeding other famous green-fleshed varieties, such as Skillman's Netted, introduced around 1834, and Hackensack, introduced in 1882.

Orange-fleshed melons did not become popular until the middle of the century. In 1851, the Massachusetts Horticultural Society hastened their acceptance by giving a premium award to Christiana, an orange-fleshed melon developed by Captain Josiah Lovett of Beverly, Massachusetts. Though Fearing Burr, Jr. recommended Christiana for its early maturity, he contended that Nutmeg and other green varieties surpassed it in

Skillman's Fine Netted melon. *This is a small rough netted variety, flattened at the ends, flesh green, very thick, firm, sugary, and of delicious flavor. Among the earliest of the green-fleshed melons.* DM

"firmness of flesh, sweetness and general excellence." Melon breeding hit its stride in about 1880, and nearly fifty new varieties were introduced during the next twenty years.

Nineteenth-century gardeners also experimented with other melons, such as Banana, a novelty that caused a sensation when it was introduced in 1883. "When ripe," wrote seedsman J. H. Gregory, "it reminds one of a large overgrown banana and, what is a singular coincidence, it smells like one." Seed for the Casaba melon was distributed by the U.S. Patent Office in 1850, but the melon didn't become popular until the 1920s. Honey Dew was discovered when a man named Gauger saved the seeds from an imported melon served in a New York City hotel. He planted the seeds of what was probably a White Antibes melon from France, selected for quality, and introduced the "new" melon in 1915.

In addition to disease resistance, breeders have developed melons to, in the words of one seed company, "meet requirements for packing in crates and shipping long distances to market." Perhaps that's why some gardeners are willing to pamper heirloom varieties that are delicate but flavorful. For example, the Cob melon, which gets its name from a fibrous "cob" that holds the seeds at the center of the melon, has never been sold commercially because it doesn't keep well. Gardeners, however, prize it for a flavor so special that it is sometimes called the Ice Cream melon. Though seed companies dropped it, this old variety was kept alive by heirloom gardeners and is now being offered again by a few discerning seedspeople.

Casaba melon. *One of the largest and best musk melons in cultivation. Its usual weight when well grown is from twelve to fifteen pounds. Flesh green, very sweet, melting and delicious.* DM

Cabbages (Brassica oleracea)

Because cabbage needs two years to produce seed, relatively few gardeners raise the heirloom varieties. Scientists hypothesize that cabbage probably evolved from a loose-leafed plant in Asia

Minor. The Greeks, who believed that cabbage prevented drunkenness, were also convinced that the first head had grown from Jupiter's perspiration. The crop was grown throughout Europe, with tight-headed varieties in the north and loose-leafed varieties in the south. In 1541, Jacques Cartier brought cabbage to Canada.

From the beginning, cabbage was valued by the colonists because it could be eaten fresh or pickled. They had a large selection of varieties. In 1806, Bernard McMahon listed six early and seven late varieties; in 1837, Thomas Bridgeman offered seventeen varieties. By 1866, Fearing Burr, Jr. described twenty-five varieties, including Early York, a popular variety with an elliptical head.

The shape of the head was the most common way of identifying cabbages. The drumhead cabbages, which are among the oldest, have compact, flat heads. Other varieties, such as Winnigstadt, Oxheart, and Early Jersey Wakefield, had pointed heads and matured early. One unusual variety from 1726 was called Sugar Loaf because it grew a long, loose-leafed head rather like cos lettuce. Vilmorin praised it because it "does not occupy much ground" and "is also slow in running to seed." Savoy cabbages were also available, and Peter Henderson recommended a variety called Drumhead Savoy in 1893. "Still," he noted, "such is the force of habit, that the public do not purchase one Savoy for every thousand of the coarse Drumhead class, although the difference in the quality of the two is as great as between the fox grape of the woods and the cultivated Delaware."

Many modern cabbage varieties are hybrids, descended from flat varieties, such as Large Flat Dutch, or round varieties, such as Early Dwarf Flat Dutch, which was round except for its flattened top. Commercial growers prefer the hybrids because the heads are uniform and they ripen simultaneously. These features are often an inconvenience to home gardeners, who

Early York cabbage. *A very valuable early variety. Heads small, rather heart-shaped, firm and tender, of very dwarf growth, and may be transplanted 15 or 18 inches apart.* DM

Early Winnigstadt cabbage. *This variety is the best in cultivation for general use. It comes both early and late, is remarkably solid and hard even in summer, and keeps well in hot or cold weather. The heads are regularly conical, exceedingly full and of excellent quality.* DM

may find more satisfaction with a variety such as Burpee's Surehead, introduced in 1877. Other heirloom cabbages are described in USDA Miscellaneous Publication 169, *Descriptions of Types of Principal American Varieties of Cabbage*, published in 1934.

Apples (Pyrus malus)

Whether or not apples originated in the Garden of Eden, they are very old. Apples sliced and dried for winter storage have been found carbonized in Switzerland and dated at 2000 to 3000 B.C. In the sixteenth century, the French became interested in the apple and developed varieties such as Lady and Fameuse, which still exist today. Apples reached their zenith in North America, where the first colonists planted them both as scions and as seedlings.

Apple seeds do not grow to be like their parents, and many of the colonists' seedlings were inferior trees whose crops were suited mostly for cider. Every now and then a seedling would distinguish itself by bearing fruit that was earlier, larger, or more delicious than its fellows. These chance improvements were often noticed by attentive nurserymen such as Robert Prince, who established his Long Island Nursery in 1730. Though he started with imported varieties, Prince was soon selling scions from his exceptional seedlings, and by 1845 his catalogue included 350 varieties.

Many apple enthusiasts believe that the world's finest apple varieties originated in this country between 1790 and 1900 and have since been neglected in favor of insipid varieties, such as Delicious, that keep and ship well. Fortunately, unlike vegetables, apples can survive human neglect for a while. During the last fifty years, dedicated collectors and nursery people have scoured the country looking for rare old varieties lurking in hedgerows or overgrown in orchards. A collection of apple va-

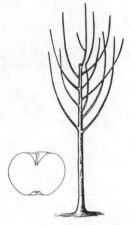

Northern Spy apple. *It is one of the most beautiful apples; having a rich, deep crimson skin, with purplish stripes, and covered with a soft bloom like the Red Astrachan. In its keeping-qualities, it is superior to the Baldwin; and although its flesh is remarkably tender and juicy, it keeps perfectly sound, and retains all its freshness, till June . . . {it} was raised in the town of East Bloomfield, N.Y., nearly fifty years ago {around 1800}, from seeds carried from Connecticut.* HOV

rieties at the New York State Agricultural Station in Geneva, New York, has recently been named the U.S. official repository for apple germplasm, and another fine collection has been established by the American Pomological Society at the University of Pennsylvania. Smaller collections that are accessible to the public are maintained at Old Sturbridge Village in Sturbridge, Massachusetts, and the Bybee-Howell House in Portland, Oregon.

The roster of old varieties is staggering—more than 8,000 have been described—and each has its partisans. One of the oldest varieties is the Roxbury Russet, which has mottled brown skin but makes sensational cider. Other important varieties introduced before the Revolutionary War include Rhode Island Greening, a variety that has survived commercially; Esopus Spitzenburg, which has been described as "the finest eating apple in the world"; and Newton Pippin, a fine keeping apple. In contrast, Red Astrachan doesn't keep a day but makes extraordinary jelly. Gravenstein, a variety that makes such fine pies that restaurants could double their pie sales by using it, is ideal for home orchards because the apples ripen gradually over several weeks. Other old varieties include Wolf River, noted for the enormous size of its fruit; Maiden's Blush, whose name comes from its delicate coloring; and Tolman Sweet, which is excellent for baking.

All of these and many other apples are described in exhaustive reference works written in the nineteenth and early twentieth centuries. Good places to start include *The Apples of New York*, written by A. S. Beach in 1905, and *Handbook of Hardy Fruits, Volume I*, written by E. A. Bunyard in 1920. More difficult to find but well worth the effort are the various editions of *The Fruits and Fruit Trees of America*, published by A. J. Downing between 1845 and 1900. Sources for old varieties are listed in the recently published *North American and European Fruit and Tree Nut Germplasm Resources Inventory*, compiled by the U.S. Department of Agriculture.

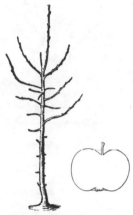

Red Astrachan apple. *If a fruit should be entitled to the attention of cultivators for its beauty alone, the Red Astrachan . . . would bear off the palm. It has not only a rich, deep crimson, skin, often heightened by the peculiar abruptness of the coloring from the sunny to the shaded side, but it is covered with a soft bloom, as beautiful as that of a plum . . . It is a hardy and exceedingly vigorous variety, admirably adapted for dwarf trees . . . It comes into bearing rather early, young and thrifty trees often producing fruit the fourth or fifth year.* HOV

Pears (Pyrus communis)

Sorting out old varieties of pears is almost as daunting a task as sorting out old apples. Pears have been in cultivation so long that it is difficult to trace their origins. The Romans were the first to cultivate them, and Pliny described forty-one varieties. The number of varieties grew gradually until the eighteenth century, when enthusiasm for the fruit created a great increase in the number of available varieties. In Great Britain, for example, sixty-four varieties were cultivated in 1640, but more than seven hundred varieties were being grown in 1842. The French were even more enthusiastic, which explains why so many desirable old varieties have French names.

In the New World, pears were a favorite crop among the early settlers, who promptly planted trees throughout the colonies. Most of the varieties were imported from Europe. Even in 1858, when Thomas W. Field published his comprehensive book on *Pear Culture*, 683 of the 800 varieties he mentioned came from Europe. Another excellent source of information on old varieties is *The Pears of New York*, edited by U. P. Hedrick and published in 1921.

Unfortunately, many old varieties have disappeared. The Department of Agriculture reports that large collections were accumulated in the search for a gene to resist fire blight and then discarded when none of the varieties proved resistant. Fire blight continues to be a problem for those who want to raise old varieties in the East and South. Pacific Coast fruit growers have an advantage because the disease does not do as much damage during their dry summers.

Despite the problem of blight, the descriptions of old pear varieties are lush and tempting. U. P. Hedrick was particularly extravagant with his praise. He said of Sheldon that it "deserves more than any other pear the adjective luscious." Flemish Beauty, another nineteenth-century pear, won his praise for

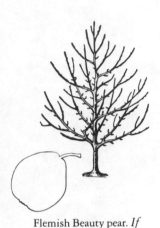

Flemish Beauty pear. *If large size, beautiful appearance, and delicious flavor, constitute a fine fruit, the {Flemish Beauty} possesses them all in a remarkable degree . . . Under the name of the Barnard pear, {it} has been known in Dorchester, Mass., for nearly twenty years {since 1830} . . .*

One peculiarity . . . should always be borne in mind by cultivators. If the fruit remains upon the tree until fully ripe, it loses most of its flavor.

It should always be gathered while it adheres firmly to the tree; it then becomes extremely melting and luscious. HOV

being "almost unapproachable in quality," while Vermont Beauty pears "best satisfy the eye for color." These three varieties are still available from Grootendorst Nurseries (see Appendix II), and source information for other old varieties is included in the *North American and European Fruit and Tree Nut Germplasm Resources Inventory* published by the U.S. Department of Agriculture.

Though experienced heirloom gardeners may find these historical sketches distressingly brief, beginners are more likely to feel overwhelmed. There's no question that it's simpler to remember the names for only a few varieties. In fact, supermarkets and seed companies assume that once people associate Delicious apples with flavor or Iceberg lettuce with quality, they won't want anything else.

At the very least, the descriptions of old varieties should make most gardeners wonder if those judgments are valid. The only way to find out is to raise a few heirlooms to see how they compare with modern varieties. If, like hundreds of other gardeners, you find the old varieties more satisfying or simply more interesting, you'll need—and want—to learn the seed-saving techniques that will enable you to keep those heirlooms growing year after year.

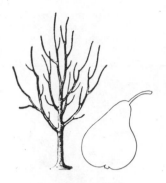

Beurre Bosc pear. *It is a moderately vigorous and healthy growing tree, with large, glossy, and ample foliage . . . and when loaded with its large, bell-shaped, rich-looking russety fruit, distributed evenly, but not thickly, over the branches, no pear has a more noble and attractive aspect. The Beurre Bosc was raised as long ago as 1807.* HOV

9
Bringing in the Seeds

THERE'S NO WAY AROUND IT. GARDENERS WHO WANT to grow heirloom varieties must master the techniques for raising and saving good seeds. To many people, the idea of raising their own seed is intimidating. For nearly a century, Americans have been buying seeds in packets, and, by now, many people are convinced that home-grown seed is inferior. Few things could be further from the truth. Home-grown seed was the rule in this country before 1850 and still is for much of the world. The techniques aren't that difficult—as one wise seedsman put it, "You just follow what the plant does naturally"—and the satisfactions can be tremendous.

Few gardeners will want to raise *all* their own seed. Buying seed is convenient for many varieties and necessary for hybrids. Nevertheless, raising even a small amount of seed adds a new dimension to gardening. Gardeners who grow their own seed enjoy a very special kind of self-sufficiency. For one thing, the seed is free, a consideration now that the price of heavily advertised hybrids often exceeds a dollar per packet. For another, seed that is carefully selected eventually produces varieties that are subtly adapted to a particular gardener's taste, soil, and climate. Finally, saving seed provides a sense of continuity because each year's garden grows quite literally from the one the year before.

These reasons for raising seed apply to any open-pollinated vegetable; yet they pale beside the fact that heirloom varieties will simply disappear if no one saves their seed. As a result, saving seed from an heirloom becomes a special opportunity—and responsibility. Seed that is carelessly propagated may become disease-ridden or, worse yet, "run out," losing the special characteristics that made the variety worth keeping. Some seed-saving guides simply advise a gardener to reorder when a variety loses vigor. That, of course, is impossible for heirloom varieties; so the gardener who decides to grow a vegetable that is old or rare has an obligation to keep it true and vigorous.

Fortunately, the techniques for raising high-quality seed are no more difficult than those for raising first-rate fruits and vegetables. The cookbook instructions for propagating various vegetables and fruits appear later in this chapter. They can be followed by rote but are more likely to produce good results for those who understand the botany behind them.

How Plants Make Seeds

All seeds start with some sort of flower, though in some cases, such as corn, the flowers don't look like anything you'd arrange in a vase. The male parts of a flower are called *stamens*; they consist of long stalks, called *filaments*, with pollen sacs, or *anthers*, on their tips. Female parts of the flower, called *pistils*, include the *stigma*, which receives the pollen; the *ovary*, which contains the *ovule*; and the *style*, a tube connecting the two. Flowers that contain both male and female parts are called *complete*. *Incomplete* flowers contain male or female parts but not both.

For all flowers, the goal is to get pollen from the male parts to the female parts. Complete flowers often have the easiest time

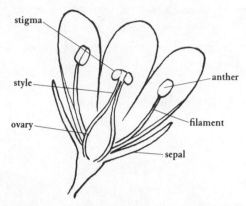

A complete flower with female and male parts labeled.

of it since, in many cases, they are designed so that pollen from the anthers brushes against the stigma before the flower even opens. A few complete flowers won't accept pollen from themselves and must, like incomplete flowers, depend upon enterprising insects, particularly bees, who in poking around the flowers, pick up pollen from one and deposit it on the stigma of another. In other plants, the pollen is so fine that it is distributed by the wind.

The problem, from the point of view of the heirloom gardener, is that wind- and insect-pollinated plants are not very discriminating about the pollen they accept. True, a carrot flower won't accept pollen from a cabbage, but it will accept it from other varieties of carrot and even related weeds. The resulting seed will have genes from both parent plants. In other words, random pollination produces characteristics that are, at best, irrelevant and, at worst, undesirable. For example, an heirloom carrot may be valued because it has an unusually sweet flavor. If the carrot is pollinated by a less flavorful neighbor, some of the seeds will no longer carry the genes for exceptional flavor. If the cross-pollination goes on for several years, the exceptional quality may occur so rarely that it will seem to have disappeared.

This process, often called *running out*, occurs in part because nature and people are working at cross-purposes when it comes to plants. Nature's ideal plant is a tough, resourceful survivor—a weed. To produce that kind of plant, nature is willing to experiment constantly with new combinations of genes because at least some of the offspring will be even better survivors than the parents. People, on the other hand, prefer plants with large fruits, nutritious seeds, edible roots, or sweet leaves, characteristics that do not necessarily contribute to the plant's ability to survive. In fact, survival is a relatively low priority for people who are willing to pamper plants with weeding, watering, and other attentions. In order to preserve genetic combinations they find desirable, gardeners must thwart nature's tendency to recombine genes at the slightest opportunity.

As an analogy, consider a painter mixing colors. Mixing selected shades of the same color can intensify and brighten the hue. But mixing colors at random will eventually produce a muddy black pigment that is, for the painter's purposes, worthless. Similarly, the goal of seed saving is to mix up the genes that make a particular variety unique but to exclude other genes that will overwhelm or dilute a variety's best characteristics. In some cases, the genes become hopelessly muddled whenever seed is produced by cross-pollination. Potatoes, apples, and many other fruits rarely produce true seed no matter what precautions are taken, so heirloom varieties must be cloned, using techniques described later in this chapter.

Controlling Pollination

For most vegetables, gardeners can preserve the purity of an old variety by arranging marriages for seed-producing plants. The easiest approach is isolation—either by time or space. Separating plants by time means scheduling them so that they will flower in different weeks. Because plants don't grow on precise timetables, this can be tricky. Still, it is possible to save pure seed from a very early sweet corn and a very late variety even when they're grown in the same garden.

Cross-pollination can also be prevented by putting space between different varieties of the same species. The amount of space depends upon the style of pollination. Self-pollinating plants such as beans, peas, lettuce, and tomatoes can be separated by a relatively small distance since, in most cases, their flowers will be pollinated before they open. Plants that are pollinated by wind or insects are more difficult to isolate. Some experts recommend a space of two hundred feet between varieties, though others insist the varieties will be in danger of contamination if another variety is growing within a quarter of a mile. The safe distance can be reduced if the plants are separated by a barrier such as a hedgerow or even a taller crop.

Because isolation requires lots of space, gardeners who don't have it may have to raise seed from only one heirloom per species each year. Collectors fortunate enough to have lots of space often plant separate gardens, as much as an acre apart. Those with near neighbors distribute free seed in the hope that their neighbors will raise the same variety. Still, despite these precautions, plants protected by isolation are always vulnerable to a particularly industrious bee or an unusually powerful gust of wind.

As a result, most heirloom gardeners eventually master other techniques for guaranteeing appropriate pollination. One alternative is to segregate seed-producing plants in cages that exclude insects and/or pollen. Caging is best suited to plants that have small flowers, fine pollen, or flowers that produce only a few seeds. Examples include spinach, root crops such as beets, carrots, and onions, and cole crops such as cabbage and broccoli. Cages must be custom-built for each crop—obviously, broccoli needs a taller cage than lettuce. The best approach is to devise a structure of the right height with scrap wood or metal. Cover it

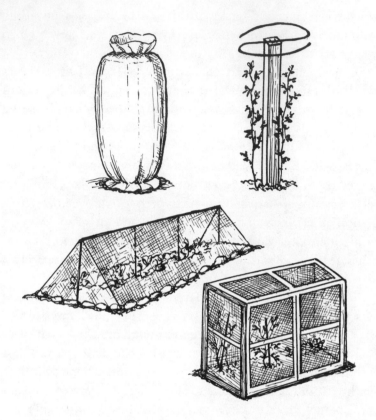

Cages to prevent cross-pollination must be tailored to the height of the seed stalk and the method of pollination. Low-growing plants such as lettuce can be protected with a tentlike enclosure; taller plants can be "bagged" or "boxed" as shown. Cages for wind-pollinated plants must be covered with muslin; insect-pollinated plants are adequately protected by cheesecloth or screening.

with hardware cloth or cheesecloth to exclude insects, or muslin to keep out wind-borne pollen. Place the cage over the plants before the flowers open and leave it in place until after the seed pods have formed.

In some cases, insect-pollinated plants need to be tied so that their flowers don't brush against the cage. It may also be necessary to introduce some insects into the cage. Flies are a perfectly adequate substitute for bees. To catch living flies, place a piece of raw meat on a piece of paper outdoors in the sun. Set two small sticks of wood on either side of the meat and place a large-mouthed jar upside-down on top of the sticks. When the flies congregate on the meat, simply tap the sides of the jar. The flies will instinctively fly upward. Slip another piece of paper over the mouth of the inverted jar to keep the flies inside while you transport them to the garden.

Hand pollination is a better alternative for vegetables with large flowers and fruits that contain many seeds, particularly cucurbits. This procedure is regularly used by plant breeders. Though it seems complex at first, gardeners can quickly become adept at it. Its advantage is absolute certainty about a seed's pedigree. To hand-pollinate, first identify a female flower—usually it has what looks like a miniature vegetable at the base of the flower. Before the flower opens, clip it shut with a rubber band, paper clip, or piece of tape. Richard Grazzini, who writes about hand pollination for the *Seed Savers Yearbook*, recommends looking for flower buds that are firm and yellow and clipping them shut late in the afternoon. The next day, identify a freshly opened male flower, pluck the flower, and remove the petals. Remove the clip on the female flower and gently spread the petals. Some gardeners then brush the anthers of the male flower over the stigma of the female. Others use a fine artist's brush to daub pollen on the stigma. When the pollen has been transferred, clip the female flower shut again, tag it so that it won't be disturbed, and leave it alone so the fruit will develop. It's best to hand-pollinate several flowers in case the fruit from one doesn't develop, rots for some reason, or gets picked accidentally.

SPECIAL CARE FOR SEED PARENTS

When selecting the parents for heirloom seeds, it is important to consider the entire plant. It may be tempting to use "leftovers"

A squash plant with flowers clipped shut in preparation for hand pol-
lination. The central flower can be identified as a female by the bulge
at its base. The male flower at right may also be clipped shut to pre-
serve its pollen.

Daubing pollen directly from the anther onto the stigma of the female flower. Some breeders remove the petals for easier access to the stigma, as shown here; in that case the pollinated female flower must be covered with a bag or envelope. Petals may also be left on and clipped shut after pollination.

as seed parents—the cucumber that didn't get picked in time or the last few beans in the row. Remember, however, that the quality of successive crops will depend upon the quality of the seed; so select parent plants that epitomize the variety's good points. In addition to flavor, consider the size of fruit, date of maturation, productivity, resistance to insects and diseases, storage qualities, general vigor, and tolerance for stressful conditions such as cold or drought.

Obviously, plants that are defective in some way should be disqualified as seed parents. Commercial seed producers call deviant plants *rogues* and destroy them so that they won't accidentally pollinate other plants. Home gardeners can harvest food, but should not harvest seed, from rogues. Of course, some vegetable problems are caused by environmental factors and cannot be inherited. For example, tomatoes split because of uneven rainfall, not bad genes; so seed gathered from a split tomato will not produce tomatoes more likely to split. Disease is an exception to this rule. In general, disease saps the strength of the parent plant so that its seed will be less vigorous. Also, some diseases are carried by seeds; so seeds harvested from infected plants may themselves be infected.

In general, the best approach is to choose the most nearly perfect plants as seed parents. One result of this attention to seed parents is that the qualities that made a variety an heirloom are kept alive. Another is that, over the years, the plant will become more and more attuned to a gardener's personal preferences and local growing conditions. By selecting what he or she regards as the best plants, the gardener makes subtle modifications in the genetics of the variety, eliminating plants that don't thrive in the local soil and encouraging those that match a personal vision of perfection. Over time, careful seed saving produces an heirloom fine-tuned to do its best in a particular garden.

Be sure to label the seed parents so they won't be harvested prematurely. Some gardeners tie a ribbon or string around the

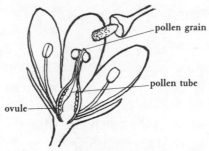

During fertilization two male nuclei from the pollen grain travel down the pollen tube to fertilize an ovule.

chosen few. Tagging the plant with a plastic marker is also a good idea. Markers can easily be cut from empty plastic containers. Write the name of the variety on the marker with indelible ink and poke a hole in it so that it can be tied to the plant. Take special care of the parent plants. See to it that they get necessary water and extra fertilizer. Stake the seed stalk if necessary and mulch to keep the fruits from rotting. Though it may be tempting to save the seed from a single specimen—one cucumber, for example, yields about three hundred seeds—keep seed from several. Mixing a hundred seeds from three plants of the same variety will preserve genetic variations within the variety.

RIPENESS IS ALL FOR SEEDS

Times and techniques for harvesting seed vary from plant to plant and are described in detail at the end of this chapter. There are, however, general guidelines that should be kept in mind. First, don't harvest until the seed is fully mature. The importance of this rule becomes more obvious if you understand how a seed develops. When a grain of pollen touches the stigma of a flower, it promptly germinates and grows a long tube that extends down the style and penetrates the ovule. Two male nuclei travel down the pollen tube. One unites with the ovule to form the embryonic plant, or *embryo*; the other fuses with special polar nuclei within the ovule and develops into a food supply called the *endosperm*.

Living off the nourishment in the endosperm, the embryo grows rapidly until it has three distinct parts—the *epicotyl*, which will become the plant's stem; the *hypocotyl*, which will become its root; and the *cotyledons*, which will become leaves. Once the embryonic plant is fully developed, the seed begins to accumulate reserves of food—protein, starch, sugar, and oil. In the mature seed, as much as 95 percent of the bulk consists of stored food. Sometimes the food is stored in the cotyledons, which become thicker, and sometimes in the endosperm. Either way, food is crucial to the survival of the seed. If the seed is harvested before it has stored adequate food, it may die in storage or be unable to germinate properly. In many plants, the seed itself signals the end of the food-storage stage. Inside, the embryo goes dormant, and outside the seed coat hardens and dries.

The goal of harvesting seeds is to continue the seed's natural processes of dormancy and drying with as little disruption as possible. Throughout the harvesting, cleaning, and storing procedures, it is important to remember that the seed is, as a student once put it, "a young plant in a box with its lunch." Though there may not be visible signs of it, the plant continues to live. Its metabolic activities depend upon moisture combining with the food in the endosperm to nourish the plant. Minimizing the amount of available moisture slows down the metabolic rate and conserves the plant's food supply. The goal of seed storage is to reduce the seed's moisture content as much as possible so that the plant inside will live as long as possible.

When it comes to saving seeds, dryness is all. Dr. Louis Bass, director of the National Seed Storage Laboratory in Fort Collins, Colorado, says simply, "The moisture content of seeds is no doubt the most influential factor affecting their longevity." Judge every piece of seed-saving advice in light of that fact. For example, bean seeds are usually allowed to dry on the plant. In a particularly rainy year, however, break that rule and pick the pods early so they can dry in a a well-ventilated building. Standard procedures must also be varied according to the local climate. For example, most commercial seed growers choose to locate in the West because the arid climate is ideal for seed growing. Gardeners in more humid regions, such as the East and South, may have to take extra steps in drying their seed.

In general, the seed-bearing habits of vegetables fall into one of three categories, depending on which part of the plant is edible. Seeds enclosed in fleshy fruits such as melons or tomatoes are usually ripe when the fruit is ready to be eaten. Edible seeds such as corn, peas, and beans usually need to ripen several weeks beyond the tender eating stage. Plants that produce edible roots, leaves, or flowers often have small seed pods that scatter their tiny seeds by shattering when the pods are dry. Obviously, these pods must be harvested before they are thoroughly dry or the seed will be lost.

Cleaning, Flailing, and Winnowing Seeds

After seeds have been harvested, they should be cleaned. There are two reasons for this: Clean seed is easier to store, and cleaning minimizes potential problems by helping to get rid of disease organisms and insect eggs. Seeds from fleshy fruits should be promptly separated from the fruit, rinsed with water, and allowed to dry on blotters or paper towels. Seeds in pods can be allowed to dry in the pod. Place smaller pods in paper bags so that the seeds won't be lost if the pods crack. Tie plants with large pods still on them in bunches and hang them over a piece of canvas or burlap. These seeds can be cleaned during the winter, when most gardeners have extra time.

The first step in cleaning large-podded seeds such as beans and peas is crushing the dried pods. Many techniques are pos-

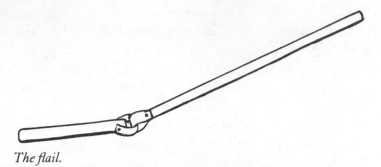

The flail.

sible, but those who recommend filling a burlap sack with bean plants and running a car over it have forgotten the vital fact that the seed is alive. Careful handling is necessary to avoid external or internal injuries to the seed. For the small quantities of seed that heirloom gardeners often raise, cleaning by hand is adequate. Simply crack the pods and pick out the seeds.

For larger batches of seed, try *flailing*, a time-honored technique. The basic tool, a flail, is made by fastening a short, hardwood dowel to a longer handle with a swivel. The simplest swivel is two interlocking loops of leather, though some people use a large fish-line swivel on the end of the longer pole. Spread the pods or plants on a piece of canvas or other fabric—an old sheet or shower curtain will do—then beat the pods with the flail. When the pods are broken, the seeds, which are heavier than the other plant material, will drop out on the fabric, so the debris can be skimmed off. Gardeners in dry climates should flail their seeds before they are totally dry since very dry seeds are more likely to break.

After cleaning by hand or flailing, seeds are likely to be mixed with bits of plant dust and other debris. To separate out extraneous plant matter, use kitchen strainers or screens made by tacking hardware cloth on a wood frame. Of course, someone who is saving tiny carrot seeds needs a different size screen from someone who collects peas or beans. "Obtain as many dif-

Winnowing: the lighter chaff is blown away.

ferent-sized sieve materials as possible," recommends Albert Vasquez, a Virginia seed saver. He notes that hardware stores often don't stock anything finer than fly screen, but he has found alternatives in dime stores. "If one is observant and obsessive about sieves," he adds, "it is surprising what can be turned up." The goal is to have two different screens for each seed you save—one with holes a little larger than the seed so that the seed drops through, leaving the debris behind, and one with holes a little smaller than the seed so that chaff and dust fall away, leaving the seed behind.

To get rid of dust and other plant materials smaller and lighter than seeds, try *winnowing*, another ancient technique. Find a large, shallow container with a rounded bottom—a basket is traditional. For small seeds, which get caught in basket fibers, a shallow metal basin may work better. Take the container outdoors on a day when there is a gentle breeze, place the uncleaned seeds into it, and toss them in the air. The seeds will fall back into the basket, and the chaff and debris will be blown away. Since wind can be unpredictable, some gardeners create their own breeze by turning on an electric fan or, in the case of tiny seeds, by simply blowing on them. As an alternative to tossing the seeds in the air, try this: Standing over a newspaper, pick up a small quantity of uncleaned seed and rub it back and forth between your hands, allowing it to fall in a fine stream. The seed will end up on the newspaper, and the chaff will be blown away.

AVOIDING SEED-BORNE DISEASES

One problem with home-grown seed is that some diseases, particularly those caused by bacteria, can live on the seed and infect the crop the following year. One way to guard against this is to become familiar with problem diseases in your region by talking to the local cooperative extension agent. Learn to recognize the symptoms of these diseases, particularly those transferred by seeds, and rogue out any plants that are suspicious.

Crop rotation is also important for heirloom gardeners. After using a patch of the garden for one crop, plant something different in that space for the next two years. Rob Johnston of Johnny's Selected Seeds also recommends having a separate plot away from the main garden where you test new varieties acquired from other gardeners. "Grow new seeds in isolation first," he cautions. "Then if there is a disease present, you won't have it spreading around to your other crops."

Some seed-borne disease organisms can be killed with hot water, but the treatment must be done carefully or the seeds themselves will be damaged. Kent Whealy of the Seed Savers Exchange recommends creating a sort of double-boiler by putting a saucepan in an electric frying pan filled with water. Turn on the frying pan and experiment with settings until you can maintain the temperature in both containers at a very steady 122°F. If the water gets too hot, the seeds may be irreparably harmed; so be sure you can keep the temperature constant. Then pour in the seeds. Stir them gently and continuously throughout the treatment, which lasts from twenty to thirty minutes depending on the species. Finally, strain the seeds and dry them thoroughly. This hot-water treatment is helpful in preventing bacterial diseases in tomatoes, cabbage, broccoli, cauliflower, eggplant, spinach, and turnips.

Some diseases live on the surface of seeds, including the fungi that cause "damping off." These fungi won't hurt the seed in storage, but they will cause the seedlings to die soon after sprouting in the spring. Commercial growers take care of this problem with Captan, a fungicide that is available in garden-supply stores. A less dangerous approach is to disinfect the seeds with household bleach. Use one part bleach to nineteen parts water, or two-and-a-half teaspoons per cup. When ready to plant the seeds, soak them in the solution for ninety seconds; then rinse them in clear water and plant as usual.

DRYING SEEDS FOR STORAGE

Proper storage is equally important in assuring a seed's survival. Those who plan to grow the seeds the following year can simply put them away in envelopes in a cool, dry place. Many heirloom gardeners find that they have seed from more varieties than they can grow each year. Unlike collectors of inanimate treasures such as Depression glass or books, heirloom seed collectors must face the fact that their "collectibles" lose vigor in storage. Although viable seeds have been found in ancient tombs, collectors cannot count on that sort of longevity. In fact, standard viability charts list two to five years as the life span for most vegetable seeds. Fortunately, that period can be extended through careful storage. Though the newly discovered techniques that keep seeds alive for a hundred years aren't available to home gardeners, heirloom gardeners owe it to future generations to devise storage systems more sophisticated than a shoebox full of envelopes.

In storage, the goal is to keep the moisture content of the seeds as low as possible. Dryness keeps potentially damaging fungi dormant and prolongs the life of the seed. "Seed is alive,"

White Globe onion. *Form nearly ovoid, very regular and symmetrical; skin greenish-yellow, marked with rose-colored lines—the pellicle changing to white on drying. The bulb measures four inches in depth and two inches and three fourths in its largest diameter. It keeps well and is an excellent variety.* FB

explains Albert Vasquez. "It breathes. Respiration produces carbon dioxide and water. The more moisture in the seed, the faster it breathes. The warmer it is, the faster it breathes . . . The water produced from respiration just hangs around and makes the seed damper, thereby increasing respiration. Next thing you know, you have moldy, heating seed." The best way to prevent that catastrophe is to dry the seed. According to studies by Dr. James Harrington of the University of California, seeds will survive with a moisture content of as low as 5 percent. Unfortunately, measuring the moisture content of seeds requires special equipment unavailable to home gardeners. However, because this factor is so critical to the survival of seeds, heirloom gardeners must do all they can to control it.

Start by drying the seeds in the open air. After cleaning, spread the seeds on blotting paper or screens for a few days in a well-ventilated room. If necessary, put a fan near the seeds so the air will move, carrying away moisture as it evaporates. Stir the seeds once a day so they will dry evenly. Within two weeks, the seeds will reach equilibrium with the surrounding atmosphere. Purchase an inexpensive hydrometer at a hardware store to measure the relative humidity. Then use Table 1 to determine the moisture content of the seeds.

Open-air drying may be adequate for gardeners who live in arid climates, but anyone who lives in an area with a relative humidity of more than 40 percent will have to reduce the seeds' moisture content further. For example, some gardeners with wood-burning stoves wait until the wood-burning season begins and then leave the seeds in the room with the stove, where the air quickly becomes very dry. Others put a light bulb above the seed—its low-level heat further dries them. Don't try drying seeds in an oven. Temperatures as low as 100°F can damage many seeds, and few ovens have controls sensitive enough to prevent such accidents. To calculate the moisture content of seeds dried by these methods, weigh the seeds when they are at

TABLE I. *Guidelines on the Moisture Content of Seeds*

Vegetable	Recommended Moisture Content for Storage (Percent)	Normal Viability (Years)	Moisture Content (Percent) of Seed at Relative Humidity of					
			10%	20%	30%	45%	60%	75%
Bean	7.0	3	3.0	4.8	6.8	9.4	11.2	13.8
Beet	7.5	4	2.1	4.0	5.8	7.6	9.4	11.2
Cabbage	5.0	5	3.2	4.6	5.4	6.4	7.6	9.6
Carrot	7.0	3	4.5	5.9	6.8	7.9	9.2	11.6
Corn	8.0	2	3.8	5.8	7.0	9.0	10.6	12.8
Cucumber	6.0	5	2.6	4.3	5.6	7.1	8.4	10.1
Lettuce	5.5	5	2.8	4.2	5.1	5.9	7.1	9.6
Onion	6.5	1	4.6	6.8	8.0	9.5	11.2	13.4
Parsnip	6.0	1	5.0	6.1	7.0	8.2	9.5	11.2
Pea	7.0	3	5.4	7.3	8.6	10.1	11.9	15.0
Pepper	4.5	3	2.8	4.5	6.0	7.8	9.2	11.0
Radish	5.0	4	2.6	3.8	5.1	6.8	8.3	10.2
Spinach	8.0	4	4.6	6.5	7.8	9.5	11.1	13.2
Squash	6.0	5	3.0	4.3	5.6	7.4	9.0	10.8
Tomato	5.5	4	3.2	5.0	6.3	7.8	9.2	11.1
Watermelon	6.5	5	3.0	4.8	6.1	7.6	8.8	10.4

Compiled from information in *Principles and Practices of Seed Storage*, by Louis Bass and Oren Justice (USDA, 1978).

equilibrium with room conditions; then weigh the seeds again after drying. Subtract the second weight from the first to figure out how much moisture was lost.

Recognizing the problems gardeners have with these make-shift drying techniques, Dr. John Rahart, a member of the Seed Savers Exchange, and Dr. Bruce Bugbee of Utah State University have been looking for a simple, reliable way of drying seeds. Though their experiments are not complete, they believe that gardeners can safely and consistently dry their seeds by using silica gel, a chemical that is available in some pharamacies and most large camera-supply stores.

Weigh the seeds to be dried and weigh out an equal amount of silica gel. Package the gel in a small bag of loosely woven fabric such as cheesecloth. Place both the seeds and the gel in a large jar—Dr. Rahart recommends institutional-size mayonnaise jars. The silica gel is a desiccant and essentially sucks up the moisture remaining in the seed. The seeds reach a moisture content of 6 to 8 percent after eight to twelve days for small seeds, such as tomatoes, and twelve to sixteen days for larger seeds, such as beans. "At this point," writes Dr. Rahart in the *Seed Savers Yearbook*, "the seeds are dry enough to substantially increase their storage life without getting into the potential dormancy problems experienced when large seeded legumes are dried to under 5% seed moisture."

The dried seeds should be transferred quickly to their permanent, airtight storage containers since exposure to normal air will increase their moisture content. Although a few heirloom gardeners have invested in canning machines, which allow them to pressure-seal their seeds, most make do with found containers. Metal is good because it protects seeds from rodents and insects, but it is difficult to find a metal can with an airtight seal. To make a coffee can with a plastic lid airtight, wrap several layers of electrical tape around the seam. Small seeds can be safely stored in the metal canisters that film used to come in.

Citron watermelon. *Fruit nearly spherical, six or seven inches in diameter; color pale green, marbled with darker shades of green; flesh white, solid, tough, seedy, and very unpalatable in its crude state. It ripens late in the season and will keep until December. "It is employed in the making of sweetmeats and preserves by removing the rind, or skin, and seeds, cutting the flesh into convenient bits and boiling in syrup which has been flavored with ginger, lemon, or some agreeable article."* FB

Plastic containers, including plastic bags, are not suited for seeds because they can be permeated by air. Kent Whealy of the Seed Savers Exchange does, however, recommend laminated bags like those used by the National Seed Storage Laboratory. These bags, which are made of layers of paper, foil, and plastic, can be heat-sealed with the Seal-a-Meal appliance some gardeners use when freezing foods or with a household iron placed on a very low setting. "You can cut the edge off them with a pair of scissors and use them again and again," writes Whealy in the *Seed Savers Yearbook*, "and they take up relatively little space compared to jars."

On the other hand, jars are free for the asking and permit a clear view of what's going on inside. For saving seeds, use a jar whose lid has a rubber gasket or make your own gasket out of inner-tube rubber. Screw the cap on tightly. Gardeners who haven't followed the silica gel procedure described above may want to include a desiccant in the jar. Some seed savers use powdered milk as a desiccant, but silica gel is a better alternative because it absorbs more than ten times as much moisture per unit of weight as powdered milk. Silica gel is usually treated to turn pink as it absorbs moisture. As long as the gel is deep blue, the moisture level in the container is acceptable. Dr. Bugbee notes that silica gel can be reused year after year if it is dried in a 200°F oven for about eight hours.

THE LONGEVITY OF SEEDS

All the drying and storing procedures may sound like a lot of trouble, but they make a big difference in how long seeds survive. Dr. Harrington of the University of California states that when the moisture content of a seed is between 5 and 14 percent, a 1-percent reduction in moisture content doubles the life of the seed. The temperature at which seeds are stored also affects their longevity because lower temperatures slow down the life

Cowhorn turnip. *This variety is carrot-like in form, growing nearly half out of the ground and generally slightly crooked. It is pure white, except for a little shade of green near the top. Is delicate and well-flavored, of very rapid growth, and has obtained considerable favor as a market sort for fall and early winter use. It is in increasing demand every year.* DM

processes of the seeds. Freezing is an ideal storage situation for dry seeds, though if a seed contains too much moisture, the water will crystallize and damage the embryo. Seeds dried with silica gel are not susceptible to such damage and can be safely frozen. Seeds dried in the open air and stored without a desiccant will do better at temperatures between 38°F and 40°F, which happens to be the temperature of the average home refrigerator. If refrigerator space cannot be reserved for seeds, store them in a cool, dry place. Most basements won't do because they are damp. The attic is probably okay in the winter but may be too hot in the summer. Another of Dr. Harrington's guidelines is that the sum of the relative humidity and the temperature in degrees Fahrenheit should not exceed 100. In other words, if the relative humidity is 50 percent, the seeds will be safe at a temperature less than 50°F.

Table 1 lists the number of years seed will remain viable when stored in a cool, dry place. Dr. Bugbee is convinced that gardeners can multiply those figures by five if they use the silica gel treatment and freeze their seeds. Despite such assurances, those who hope to store their seed for more than five years should store extra for germination tests. Some seeds die under the best storage conditions, but if too many seeds lose vigor, it may be difficult to replenish the variety. Germination testing is the best way to know how the seed is doing in storage.

To perform a germination test, remove only the seeds to be tested from storage, as frequent fluctuations in temperature can damage seeds. Remember that whenever a storage container is opened, the seeds can absorb moisture from the air; so work as quickly as possible and then reseal the container. If the seeds have been dried with a desiccant, give them a few days to adjust to the relative humidity outside storage.

Though there are many ways to do germination testing, professionals generally use a hundred seeds and a ten-by-ten-inch piece of felt or blotting paper. If these materials aren't available, a double paper towel will do. Use a waterproof marker to divide the paper into a hundred one-inch squares. Place the paper on a cookie sheet and moisten it by misting with water from a clean spray bottle like the ones that come with window-washing solution. Put a seed in each square and cover with several wet paper towels; then place the cookie sheet in a warm, dark place where the temperature is between 70°F and 80°F. Throughout the test, the towel should be damp but not soggy.

Find out the normal germination time for the seeds—it varies from plant to plant—and allow the seeds to sit for an extra five days. Then count the number of seeds that germinated. If a hundred seeds were tested, the math is simple: the number of seeds that sprout is the percent of germination. If fewer seeds were used because of limited supplies, divide the number of sprouts by the original number of seeds to get the percent of germination. Most experts agree that when germination dips below 50 percent, it is time to replenish the seed.

If the germination rate is very low, drastic action may be necessary. Sometimes bean and pea seeds become dormant if they are too dry but may be coaxed into germinating if they are placed in a humid atmosphere for two weeks. Other seeds become damaged because their inner membranes deteriorate, allowing the seeds to absorb too much water when they are planted. Scientists at the Seed Research Laboratory in Beltsville, Maryland, have found that coating seeds with polyethylene glycol antifreeze shortly before planting may, in some instances, slow absorption of water enough for the seeds to germinate. This technique, which is still experimental, may be worth trying when all other attempts to grow out an heirloom variety have failed.

GETTING STARTED

At first, the techniques for saving heirloom seeds may seem demanding; yet they are no more difficult than the procedures that must be followed in preserving rare books or antique furniture. Heirloom gardeners are custodians of an extraordinary legacy and must do their utmost to preserve it. For that reason, two cardinal rules must be observed.

First, never plant all the seed of a rare variety. Even the best gardener is helpless in the face of drought, hailstorms, heat waves, and insect infestations. At least those who hold back some of their seed have the consolation of knowing they can try again. Reserving a seed sample also enables a gardener to compare newly harvested seed with the original. Though that may not matter much with radish seeds, it can be an indicator of purity in vegetables such as beans and corn. Discard all seeds that don't duplicate the color and size of the original. If you choose to grow variant seeds out of curiosity, don't label them with the heirloom name.

Second, keep accurate records. Label everything from the rows in the garden to the plants hanging upside-down in the tool shed to the seed envelopes in the refrigerator. Though the genes inside may be dramatically different, from the outside, one tomato seed looks a lot like another. Mislabeling seed in your own collection breeds confusion. Mislabeling seed that is being shared with other gardeners results in disappointment and, perhaps, loss of a variety that someone thought you were saving.

The best way to master seed saving is to try it, according to Rob Johnston of Johnny's Selected Seeds. "People think there's a lot of stuff they have to study and learn," he says, "but it's not difficult." True as that may be, a gardener who is saving seed for the first time should try an open-pollinated variety that is readily available. Then, if the variety crosses with what a neighbor is growing, or a flood destroys the crop just as it sets seed, the novice will have lost time but not an endangered old variety. The following advice on specific groups of plants is gleaned from garden publications, heirloom collectors, and professional seedspeople.

Beans and Peas

Beans and peas are among the easiest seeds to grow because they are self-pollinating, and most pollination occurs before the flowers ever open. Occasionally, bees interfere, but gardeners who plant only a few varieties can guarantee true seed by separating beans with a tall crop, such as corn, or by placing them about twenty-five feet apart. Peas, which cross a little more easily, should be separated by more distance. Bean collector John Withee, who plants as many as five hundred varieties a year, doesn't have enough space for that, so he plants beans with decidedly different seeds side by side. Then, if bees do cross-pollinate adjacent plants, the seeds of the crosses will look different.

In general, bean seeds are ready to harvest six weeks after the eating stage; peas take four weeks. Peas should be harvested promptly because they will germinate if the pods become moist after the seeds have matured. Pole beans ripen from the bottom to the top of the vine; so you need to pick pods as they dry. Bush beans can be picked when the leaves are yellow and the pods become dry and brittle. One way to tell when seeds are mature is to bite one—if the seed is so dry that your teeth can't dent it, it's ready for harvest.

Some people pull up the entire bean or pea plant, but that disturbs the nitrogen-producing nodules in the roots. An alternative is to cut off the bushes, tie them together, and hang them upside-down to dry. Put a drop cloth or bushel basket underneath to catch seeds from pods that pop. If that's inconvenient, pick the pods and spread them on screens to dry. When the pods are utterly dry, remove the seeds. For small amounts, this job can be done by hand. For larger batches, John Withee recommends

Long Yellow Six Weeks bean. *Extra early, vines large, vigorous, branching and very productive. Pods straight and flat and of fair quality; beans long, kidney-shaped, yellow, with darker marks around the eye. Excellent variety for general crop.* NBG

a funnel-shaped "bean bag" made of burlap. Withee ties off the narrow end of the bag and stuffs the bean plants in the other end. Then he hangs the bag and beats it with a stick. When the plants have been crushed, he raises the bag and opens the narrow end. The beans pour out and the chaff blows away.

Although beans are easily grown, they are subject to several seed-borne diseases. The most serious are anthracnose and bacterial blight, which, during the damp years that encourage their growth, have claimed up to 30 percent of the crop in states where the diseases are prevalent. Today, commercial seed growers avoid both diseases by raising all their seed in the arid areas west of the Rockies. Heirloom gardeners should make every effort to select seeds from healthy plants. Signs of anthracnose include small, brown specks on the pods that gradually enlarge to black sunken spots. For bacterial blight, symptoms include dark green spots on the pods, which gradually become dry and brick red. Avoid handling plants when they are wet since that may spread both diseases. Weevils are another seed-related problem since the pests lay their eggs under the seed coat. As a preventive measure, place the thoroughly dried beans in a sealed jar and freeze for at least twenty-four hours.

For peas, seed-borne diseases include bacterial blight and ascochyta blight. The first is recognized by dark green, water-soaked spots on leaves; the second by purplish specks on leaves and pods. Again, avoid harvesting seed from infected plants and stay away from the plants when they are wet from rain or dew. Since the disease can overwinter in leftover plant material, plant peas in a different place each year and destroy dead plants.

Unlike other seeds, beans and peas should not be stored in airtight containers since they may be troubled by fungus. Some collectors keep their seeds in small burlap sacks or envelopes. Under ordinary conditions, legume seeds remain viable for three to five years.

Tomatoes

Tomatoes are also self-pollinating, though occasionally insects try to help spread the pollen around. The best way to get true seed is to separate varieties by about twenty-five feet. Select representative tomatoes from three plants to get a good cross-section of genes. Some collectors feel that the most desirable seed tomatoes are the first set in the second set of branches. After selecting the seed tomatoes, tie a ribbon around each one so that it won't be harvested and eaten by accident. The tomato seed will be ready for harvest when the fruit is ripe but not rotten.

After picking the seed tomatoes, cut them in half and scoop out the jellylike material that holds the seeds. If you like, use the meat of the tomato in sauce or stuff the empty tomato shell. Put the tomato seeds and jelly into a jar, add a small amount of water, and allow the concoction to ferment for about four days. Stir it once or twice a day. At the end of the fermentation period, the good seed will be at the bottom of the jar and the bad seed and pulp will be floating on top. Scoop off the pulp and discard it; then strain the water off the seeds and dry them. This fermentation process is easier than cleaning slippery tomato seeds, and it destroys the bacteria that cause tomato canker.

Allow the seeds to dry on paper towels or a fine screen; then store in an airtight container. Tomato seeds are viable for about four years. The average tomato produces 250 to 300 seeds; so if seed is saved from three tomatoes, there's plenty to share with neighbors.

Cucurbits: Cucumbers, Melons, Squashes, and Pumpkins

Members of the Cucurbitaceae family require special attention from seed savers. All have separate male and female flowers and thus depend on insects for cross-pollination. Unfortunately, insects don't necessarily discriminate among various members of the family; so crosses are common. Though half-breed vegetables are fine for eating, they are a disaster for those who are trying to save true seed. Not all cucurbits cross; therefore one way to keep things straightened out is to plant only one from each of the following categories:

Autumnal Marrow squash. *Plant twelve feet or more in length, moderately vigorous; fruit ovoid, pointed at the extremities . . . stem very large, fleshy and contracted a little at its junction with the fruit . . . skin remarkably thin, easily bruised and broken, cream-yellow at the time of ripening, but changing to red after harvesting . . . flesh rich, salmon yellow, remarkably dry, fine-grained, and in sweetness and excellence surpassed by few varieties . . . Introduced by Mr. John M. Ives of Salem, Mass., in 1831; now universally esteemed and cultivated.* FB

Cucumbers (picklers and long varieties cross)
Cantaloupes (also called muskmelons)
Watermelons
C. maxima (squashes with long vines, huge leaves, and hairy stems, such as Hubbard)
C. moschata (squashes with large leaves, spreading vines, and five-sided stems, such as Butternut)
C. mixta (similar to *C. moschata* but won't cross with it; members include Cushaw and Tennessee Sweet Potato)
C. pepo (all summer squashes; a few winter squashes, such as acorn; and most traditional pumpkins)

Even experts have trouble with the distinctions among squashes; so ask a cooperative extension agent if in doubt. The *Seed Savers Yearbook* also includes lengthy lists of squashes in each of the categories. Planting only one variety from each category minimizes the likelihood of unintentional crosses—as long as there's no other squash-growing garden for a quarter of a mile.

Many gardeners can't ensure that kind of isolation, however, and others want to keep more than one or two squash varieties. The solution is hand pollination, a technique that may seem complicated at first but is really quite easily mastered. Though the process is a bit time-consuming, the reward is peace of mind. With hand pollination there is no risk of having the genes for a precious heirloom hopelessly mixed with the genes from a neighboring plant.

To hand-pollinate cucubits, start by closely observing their flowers. A female flower has a bulge at the base that will eventually grow into a cucumber, squash, or melon. A male flower has a thin stem that leads directly to the bud. To keep the female flower from being pollinated at random, clip the flower closed the day before it opens. Mature flower buds will be firm but not wilted, with fully developed yellow petals. Depending upon the size of the flower, you can use a clothespin, paper clip, or even tape. Some gardeners prefer to cover the entire flower with a paper bag. The goal is to keep the petals closed so that no insect can get inside the flower.

The next day, select a male flower from a different plant of the same variety. Remove the petals to expose the anthers, which should be golden with pollen. Carefully open the female flower and transfer the pollen to the stigma—either brush the anthers against the stigma or use an artist's brush to daub the pollen onto the female flower. When the task is accomplished, close the female flower again. Pollinate at least half a dozen flowers since it is advisable to mix seed from several different fruits.

Allow the fruit to ripen naturally. Cucumbers and summer squashes should become overripe and yellowed before harvest. Melons, winter squashes, and pumpkins should be eating-ripe so that the flesh can be enjoyed after the seeds have been harvested. For each cucurbit, cut the fruit in half and scoop out the pulp and seeds. Rinse out the pulp and allow the seeds to dry thoroughly on a screen or blotter. Stored in an airtight container, cucurbit seeds can be kept for up to five years.

Seed-borne diseases in cucumbers, squashes, and melons include cucumber mosaic, which causes dwarfed plants and misshapen fruit. Avoid harvesting seeds from any plants infected by disease. Also, cucumber and melon seeds benefit from

Turban squash. *Plant running; fruit rounded, flattened, expanding about the stem to a broad, plain, brick red or reddish cream surface, often of twelve inches in diameter. At the blossom-end, the fruit suddenly contracts to an irregular, cone-like point or termination, usually of greenish color, striped with white, but sometimes yellowish-white, without the stripes or variegations, and thus in form and color somewhat resembles a turban, whence its name. Flesh orange-yellow, remarkably thick, fine-grained, sugary and well-flavored.* FB fermentation. Scrape the pulp and seeds into a glass, add a little water, and ferment for four to seven days. At the end of that time, the pulp will be at the top of the glass and the good, disease-free seeds will be at the bottom.

Corn

Raising seed corn requires skill and patience because corn has an unusual system for pollination. The pollen for corn is produced by the tassel at the top of the plant. The silks in each ear are conduits for carrying pollen to the seeds, and each kernel must be pollinated if it is to develop. Most pollen reaches the ear by being dropped from the tassel of the same plant. But the kernel will accept any stray corn pollen that happens to blow by, which is why gardeners who plant yellow and white varieties side by side end up with checkerboard ears of corn.

The situation is further complicated because seed from corn that is self-pollinated shows inbreeding depression. Richard Grazzini believes it is important to mix the genes from plants within the variety while excluding pollen from other varieties; so he recommends the following procedure. As soon as a tassel pushes out from the top leaves, cover it with a paper bag and tie the bag opening shut. As soon as an ear begins to push away from the stalk and before the silk emerges, cover it too. When the tassel is mature, but before it begins to drop its pollen, bend it over so that the pollen will fall into the bag. After the pollen begins to fall, cut off the tassel and shake it inside the bag. Combine the pollen from fifteen to twenty-five plants of the same variety and store in a cool place until the silks emerge on the ears—usually about three days later. Uncover the corn ears, shake some pollen over the silks, and replace the bags. Do this once a day until the silks are dry and brown.

The pollinated ears should be allowed to ripen on the stalks

Corn plant showing tassel and ear covered with paper bags to prevent cross-pollination. Lower right: After silks emerge, pollen gathered from different tassels is shaken onto them.

until the kernels are hard and dry, usually about four weeks after the eating stage. Frost won't hurt the seeds; so the ears can continue to dry in the field. When the ears are dry, pick them, pull back the husks, and tie them together with twine. Hang in a dry, airy place. During the winter, remove the kernels by pressing them with the thumb on one hand while twisting the cob with the other hand. Be gentle because even a small crack in the kernel may kill the seed. In airtight containers, corn seed should keep for two or three years.

Root Crops

Radishes, turnips, beets, carrots, parsnips, and onions don't belong to the same biological family, but they all produce small seeds in narrow pods on tall stalks. Radishes are the easiest to grow because they set their seed in a single season. The others require a cool spell before setting seed; thus the techniques for growing them vary according to climate.

All, except beets and onions, are pollinated by insects; so they need to be caged to assure true seed. This is particularly true for carrots, which can cross easily with Queen Anne's lace, and for turnips and radishes, which cross with wild mustard, horseradish, and wintercress. Many gardeners find it most convenient to arrange their seed-producing plants in a circle around a stake that is slightly taller than the plants will be when full grown. A cross piece is fastened to the top of the stake, and the framework is draped with a roomy cheesecloth bag that falls all the way to the ground. Beets and onions also need to be caged but, because they are pollinated by wind, their covering must be made of muslin, which is more tightly woven.

To grow radish seeds, plant in the early spring and select the best plants for seed production. Since the root is the most important part of the plant, some gardeners pull the radishes to de-

Long White radish. *Root long and slender, nearly of the size and form of the Long Scarlet; skin white—when exposed to the light, tinged with green; flesh white, crisp and mild. It is deserving of cultivation, not only on account of its excellent qualities but as forming an agreeable contrast at table when served with the red varieties.* FB

cide which will be seed parents. Cut off the upper leaves of the radishes and replant the roots about eight inches apart. The two- to three-foot seed stalks will produce unspectacular white flowers. The little, pointed seed pods don't shatter—they may actually be difficult to break—so they can be left to dry on the plant. Radishes may be reluctant to set seed when the temperature is more than 90°F or rainfall is scarce; so give the plants an early start and water well. The seeds, which can be cleaned with an ⅛-inch screen, keep for about four years.

In warm climates, the procedure for growing seeds of carrot, beet, turnip, and parsnip is similar to what has been described for the radish. The seeds should be planted late in the season, however, since these plants need cool weather before they can produce seeds. By planting in August or September, the plants can become established before winter and will produce seed the following summer.

In cooler climates, the roots of these plants will die if left out all winter; so seed savers face the additional work of digging the roots and storing them until spring. Select the best plants as seed parents, saving about twice the number you expect to grow. Trim the tops of the roots one inch above the crown and pack in moist sand. Store over the winter at a temperature between 45°F and 50°F. In the spring, replant the roots with the crowns just beneath the surface of the soil. Allow eighteen inches between roots because they will send up new leaves and seed stalks.

Beets grow long, graceful branches that flower and then produce seed balls. The balls, which actually contain several seeds, first ripen near the main stem. When the inner seed balls become dry and corky, pull out the plants and put each one in a paper bag to dry. As the seed balls ripen, they can be stripped off by hand into the bag. Separate the beet seed from debris by rubbing it over ¼-inch hardware screen. Beet seed remains viable for about four years.

Carrots send up root stalks that are two to six feet tall. The

Barkskinned beet. *Root broadest near the crown and tapering regularly to a point . . . Skin dark-brown, thick, hard, and wrinkled, much resembling the bark of some descriptions of trees. Flesh deep purplish-red, fine-grained, sugary, and tender. It is an early French variety of fine flavor, excellent for summer use.* FB

flowers form in lacy umbels that ripen into brown seed heads. The king umbel is the largest and ripens first; so some gardeners cut off the side flowers and cage only the king umbel. The seeds are ready for harvest when they turn brown, usually six to nine weeks after flowering. Snip off the individual umbels and put them in a paper bag. Later, crush the seed heads by rubbing them through your hand. Rubbing also removes the tiny spines on the seeds. Clean the carrot seed through ⅛-inch screen to get rid of most debris. The seeds keep for three years.

Parsnip seed lives for just one year; so only those who are true fans of this vegetable are likely to save the seed. The techniques are similar to those for other root vegetables. Parsnip seed heads, however, shatter easily; they should be picked early and put in paper bags so that the seed will not be lost.

Turnips cross with everything from cabbages and rutabagas to radishes and wild mustard. To obtain true seed, cage the plants when they flower and cut the seed pods when they turn yellow. Crush the pods and clean the seed by rubbing through a ⅛-inch screen. As a member of the Cruciferea family, turnips are subject to black rot and black leg. Prevent the diseases by subjecting the seeds for twenty-five minutes to the hot-water treatment described earlier. Seeds remain viable for five years.

Unlike the other root crops, onions should not be stored in sand. In cold climates, the bulbs should be pulled and left in the sun to cure as they would be for winter storage. In the spring, replant the largest bulbs. Some gardeners make a small gash in the top of each bulb to help the seed stalk emerge. Onion flower stalks are hollow and topped with a round flower. Cage the plants during the flowering period, which lasts a couple of weeks. When the black seeds are exposed, harvest the seed heads. If the heads are left on the stalks too long, they will shatter and spill the seed. The onion is notorious for the short life of its seeds—they rarely live more than one or two years under ordinary storage conditions.

Danvers Yellow onion. *This somewhat recent variety was obtained by selection from the Common yellow. It is above medium size, and inclined to globular in its form. Average bulbs measure three inches in diameter and two inches and three fourths in depth. The skin is yellowish-brown, but becomes darker by age, and greenish-brown if long exposed to the sun. The flesh is similar to that of the Yellow— white, sugary, comparatively mild, and well-flavored. Its superiority over that variety consists principally in its greater productiveness . . . It is, however, not so good a keeper.* FB

Leafy Crops

Lettuce seed is easy to keep pure because it is self-pollinating, but it is hard to collect because the seeds are very tiny. Most gardeners are acquainted with the appearance of leaf lettuce that has gone to seed. The plant sends up a coarse stem with yellow flowers that fluff up into feathery seed heads. Head lettuce sends up a similar stalk, but some of the top leaves may need to be pulled aside to give the stalk an opportunity to emerge. Remember not to take seed from the plant that goes to seed first, since lettuce that doesn't bolt is more desirable as a food plant.

Lettuce seeds mature over a period of several weeks; so cut the stalk when about half the seeds are ripe. Put the stalk into a paper bag and crush the seed pods. Strain the seed through ⅛-inch screen. Some chaff will still be mixed with the seed, but that can be a help in sowing the seed more thinly the following season. Lettuce seed remains vigorous for about five years.

Early White Head lettuce. *An excellent variety for hotbed culture, as well as open air; early and hardy. Heads small, white, crisp, very compact and closely cabbaged.* DM

Cole Crops

All the cole crops are biennials, except broccoli, which goes to seed in its first year. Most gardeners know that a head of broccoli left on the plant too long will turn into small, yellow flowers. If the flowers are left to mature, they will produce long, thin seed pods. To be sure the pods have plenty of time to ripen, start the broccoli extra early. In the North, start the plants indoors or in a cold frame eight weeks before the last frost; in the South, plants started in October will produce seeds the following May or June.

Bees cross-pollinate broccoli; so separate it from flowering cabbage, brussels sprouts, kale, cauliflower, and kohlrabi with 100 feet of space or a tall crop such as corn. Broccoli flowers are not self-pollinating; so place at least two plants side by side. When the seed pods begin to dry, cut the plants and pile them on a sheet so that if pods burst the seeds will be caught. Clip off

Early Jersey Wakefield cabbage. *Heads of medium size, generally somewhat conical, but sometimes nearly round and very compact. A fine early variety, heading readily, and a great favorite with eastern market gardeners.* DM

the seed pods, put them in a bag, and crush them. The seed can be cleaned with ⅛-inch screen.

The procedure for growing cabbage seed is similar, though gardeners in the North must store the cabbage over the winter. Select large, solid cabbages, cut off the outer leaves, and store the cabbages in a root cellar with the root in cool earth. Water periodically so the cabbages won't dry out. In the spring, plant the cabbages, setting the roots deep enough so the heads rest on the ground and cut a two-inch X in the top of each head so the seed stalk can emerge. Cabbage produces very tall seed stalks; so some gardeners stake them. Cabbage must be separated from other cole crops by at least 100 feet.

Both cabbage and broccoli seed can carry bacterial diseases and therefore should be given a hot-water treatment. Cabbage should be heated for thirty minutes, broccoli for twenty minutes. If dried thoroughly after the treatment, seeds should last for five years.

Potatoes

Some potatoes produce seeds in little, round fruits, but for the most part they are not true to the parent plants. As a result, potato collectors have to store the tubers themselves and plant every variety every year. Gardeners have different opinions about whether it is best to plant potatoes that are cut or whole, large or small, sprouted or unsprouted. Potato collector Robert Lobitz eats the big potatoes and plants the small ones.

Potatoes can be harvested when the vines dry. Leave them exposed to the air for a week to toughen the skin; then store them in shallow bins that allow air to circulate around them. Potatoes keep best in dry storage where the temperature is 34°F to 35°F. Don't allow them to freeze.

The most serious problem for potato collectors is potato scab, which produces rot-filled pimples on the potatoes. The

State of Maine potato. *Quite early, but more liable to disease than the Davis Seedling and some other varieties. In Maine, it is grown in great perfection . . . On light soil, it is only moderately productive; but on strong land, in high cultivation, yields abundantly.* FB

best prevention is crop rotation. Once potatoes have been planted in a particular spot, use that patch for something else for at least two years—longer, if possible. Do not plant in low, soggy areas.

Fruit Trees

Like potatoes, fruit trees cannot reliably be propagated from seed. With a few exceptions, fruit trees are not self-pollinating—at least two trees are needed to produce a good crop—so the seeds inside an apple will not duplicate the parent tree. Trees grown from seed may be good for cider or sauce, and every now and then the genes will combine in a seedling to produce a superior variety like the Jonathan apple, which was a seedling from Spitzenberg. Still, raising seedlings for anything but rootstock is like playing roulette with the odds heavily against the bettor.

Fortunately, several nurseries now specialize in heirloom fruits, particularly apples, and many fine old varieties are available. These can be ordered and planted like any other fruit tree. Remember that heirloom fruits are often extremely sensitive to local climatic conditions; the variety that does well outside Boston may be a disaster in Virginia. Before selecting an old variety, try to obtain as much information as possible about where it was developed.

Those who want a rare old variety not sold by any nursery will have to locate a collector who is willing to share scions. In addition to seeking collectors locally, it may be possible to obtain scionwood from members of the North American Fruit Exchange, the Home Orchard Society, or other organizations of fruit enthusiasts (see Appendix I for addresses). In order to use material obtained in this way, it is necessary to master grafting techniques.

Although grafting, like seed-saving, seems mysterious to

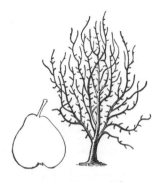

Winter Nelis pear. *The Winter Nelis deservedly ranks among the very best winter pears which have yet been produced. Though of only medium size and rather unprepossessing appearance, its peculiarly rich, sugary, and high-flavored qualities have gained for it a popularity surpassed by no other pear. As a hardy, vigorous, and productive tree, ripening its fruit freely and keeping well, it must be classed with the very few first-rate pears we yet possess . . . This fine pear was raised by the Chevalier Nelis, of Mechlin {France} . . . For its first introduction to our gardens, we are indebted to the late Mr. Knight, who sent it to Mr. Lowell, in 1823.* HOV

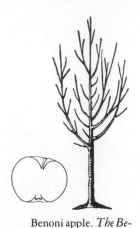

Benoni apple. *The Be-noni is a summer apple, of superior quality. It is not quite so large as the Williams, which ripens about the same time— nor has it the prepossess-ing appearance of that showy and excellent va-riety—but it is fully equal to it in quality. It has a firm and crisp flesh, and a rich, pleasant subacid and sprightly flavor, which combined with the pro-ductiveness of the tree, claim for it a prominent place in every fruit gar-den or orchard . . . it originated in Dedham, Mass., upwards of twenty-five years ago {around 1825}, where the original tree, we believe, is still growing.* HOV

many amateurs, it can be mastered with practice and patience. Grafting means uniting a young branch, or scion, with a rooted tree, usually called rootstock. To be successful, a graft must connect the cambium of the rootstock—the cambium is the ring of growing tissue immediately under the bark—to the cambium of the scion. Grafts are usually made in the spring, when the sap is flowing, so that sap will travel from the rootstock into the scion, eventually fusing them into a single plant.

The rootstock for a graft can be a full-grown tree or a seedling. Whichever is used, the fruit will always take on the characteristics of the scion, and the size of the grafted tree will be determined by the rootstock. Today, many heirloom gardeners graft old varieties onto specially bred dwarf rootstock, because the smaller trees are easier to tend and harvest and also because they allow a larger selection of varieties in a small space.

Once the rootstock tree has been established, it must be cut to within a few inches of the ground so that a scion can be grafted to it. In general, scions should be cut when the donor tree is still dormant (before the sap runs in the spring). They can be kept moist in peat moss, and refrigerated in a plastic bag until the time is right for grafting. Scions should be taken from year-old growth at the end of the branch. Cut a section that contains about eighteen buds. Then trim off the six buds at the top and the six at the bottom. The middle section will be the scion.

Heirloom fruit growers use several grafting techniques. A *whip graft* is most effective when rootstock and scion are approximately the same size. Cut both pieces at complementary angles and fasten them together so the layers of cambium are perfectly aligned on at least one side of the graft. Wrap the two sections with rubber tape, grafting wax, or some other material that will hold them firmly in place but will allow the branch to grow as it needs to.

Cleft grafting is another technique, used when the rootstock is considerably larger than the scion. Depending upon the size

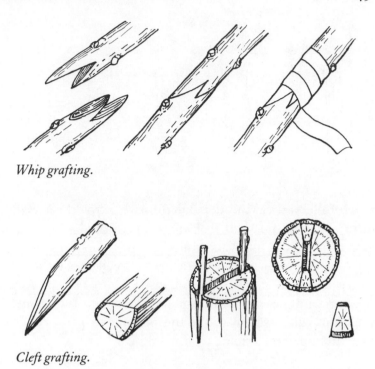

Whip grafting.

Cleft grafting.

of the scions, one or two may be used. A two-inch cleft is cut in the rootstock—with a knife, if the tree is small enough, or with a hammer and chisel. Cut the bottom of each scion into a wedge shape and insert into the cleft. Again, be sure to line up the cambium layers on at least one side of each scion so the sap can flow from rootstock to scion, and cover all cut parts with grafting wax or rubber tape so the interior won't dry out.

Since cleft and whip grafts require careful matching of the cambium layers, some gardeners prefer to do *bark grafts*. These grafts require pencil-sized scions and somewhat larger rootstock. Though they "take" readily, they do not produce as strong a graft as the other methods, and the resulting tree is more susceptible to wind or other damage. To make a bark graft, cut the rootstock horizontally across the top. Now make

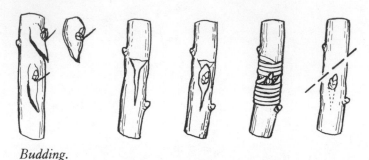

Budding.

two parallel vertical cuts through the bark, about three-eighths of an inch deep and a half-inch apart. You can make several pairs of cuts at regular intervals around the trunk to accommodate multiple scions. Carefully peel back the bark at each cut. Sharpen the end of each scion and insert it into the gap between the bark and the cambium. Again, tape the grafts carefully so the scions will stay in place and the incisions are protected from dehydration or infection.

Like bark grafting, *budding* involves inserting new plant material into the space between bark and cambium on the rootstock. As its name implies, budding uses, instead of a scion, a young bud that appears just below the union of leaf and branch. This type of grafting must be done after the buds are fat and fully developed but before the sap stops flowing in the fall. Using a knife, cut the bud off the branch, slicing carefully under the bark. Leave about one-quarter inch of bark (including the attached leaf) above the bud and three-quarters below. On the rootstock, use a very sharp knife to make a "T" cut in the bark. The two flaps created by this cut should slip away from the underlying wood so the bud can be inserted into the space. Maneuver the bud by using the lower part of the leaf stem as a handle. When the bud is in place, tie it securely with rubber bands.

No matter what kind of graft you make, rub off all sprouts on the rootstock below the graft so that all the plant's growth will go into the scion. Keep the graft wrapped for several months and don't expect to see new growth right away. Grafting is a delicate art, and results are never guaranteed. Fortunately, scionwood is easily obtained from a healthy tree, so the gardener can experiment until a graft succeeds.

These instructions are necessarily sketchy and gardeners who want further information should consult the book *Fruits and Berries for the Home Garden* by Lewis Hill (Knopf, 1977) as well as publications from the North American Fruit Explorers. For more information about seed-saving, consult any of the following books, which are devoted entirely to the subject of growing and saving good seed:

Sheldon pear. *First quality, large, round, russet and red, melting, rich and delicious. Tree vigorous, erect and handsome, and bears well when grown. As a standard, should be more largely planted. The best of all pears for high quality, and very vigorous and productive. It is better than Bosc.* GR

Bubel, Nancy. *Seed Starter's Handbook*. Emmaus, Pa.: Rodale Press, 1980. Explains how to grow seedlings as well as save seeds.

Fitz, Franklin. *A Gardener's Guide to Propagating Food Plants.* New York: Charles Scribner's Sons, 1983. Describes propagation techniques and includes information about pollination procedures and seed viability for 130 cultivated food plants.

Johnston, Rob. *Growing Garden Seeds*. 1976. $2.30. Write to: Johnny's Selected Seeds, Albion, ME 04910. A pamphlet written by a seedsman to satisfy customer curiosity about seed saving.

Miller, Douglas. *Vegetable and Herb Seed Growing for the Gardener and Small Farmer*. 1977. $3.25. Write to: Bullkill Creek Publishing, Hersey, MI 49639. A pamphlet with very good information about caging as well as detailed advice about specific varieties.

Rogers, Marc. *Garden Way's Growing and Saving Vegetable Seeds*. Charlotte, Vt.: Garden Way, 1978. Good information about hand pollination.

PART FOUR

Plants for the Future

10
Heirlooms in Perspective

THE HEIRLOOM GARDENER WHO INCLUDES A RARE BEAN variety in his or her vegetable patch or cares for an ancient apple tree is participating in a worldwide effort to preserve plant resources. In every country, plants—both domestic and wild—are being allowed to become extinct. Sometimes these plants are lost to human greed; sometimes they are sacrificed to human necessity. Often, they are destroyed simply because human beings are ignorant of their value. Whatever the reasons, the loss of these plant resources has dire consequences for the human race, and gardeners who care enough to pursue and plant an heirloom variety in the backyard cannot help but be concerned.

Those who are distressed about the extinction of plants have tended to divide themselves rather arbitrarily into two groups. Conservationists are traditionally concerned about wild species, such as the celebrated Furbish's lousewort; most plant breeders are disturbed by the loss of domesticated varieties and their wild relatives. The distinction hinges on whether humans have discovered an economic use for a particular plant. Yet the line between wild and domesticated plants is not as sharp as it might seem. Nearly all domesticated plants can be traced back through increasingly primitive variations to the wild species from which they are descended. Earlier incarnations usually do not live up to contemporary standards for flavor and productivity; yet they often contain specialized genes that may be invaluable to plant breeders.

A few examples illustrate the point. In the early 1970s, researchers at Purdue University wanted to increase the protein content of sorghum. After screening 9,000 samples, they found a "primitive" strain grown by Ethiopian peasants that contained three times the customary protein. In another instance, a plant explorer in Iran spotted an unusual onion with a tight neck in the market of Kashan. He sent samples to American plant breeders, who soon discovered that the tight neck frustrated the onion thrip, a major problem for onion growers. By transferring the tight-neck trait to contemporary onion varieties, breeders were able to save onion growers millions of dollars normally spent to control the pest.

THE ORIGINS OF GENETIC DIVERSITY

Specialized characteristics often evolve in centers of genetic diversity. First identified in the 1920s by the Russian scientist N. I. Vavilov, these centers are usually the places where specific edible plants were first domesticated and grown deliberately as crops. Over the centuries, through natural and human selection, these crops evolved into varied forms that helped them thrive under local conditions. In a valley, a crop might develop tolerance for cooler temperatures; on a hillside, it might grow with a stronger stem less likely to be broken by the wind. Even in the same field, these primitive crops often display genetic variation.

These richly varied crops, which are usually passed from one generation of farmers to the next, are called *land races*. Un-

Wethersfield Large Red onion. *Bulb sometimes roundish, but, when pure, more or less flattened. It is of very large size, and when grown in favorable soil, often measures five inches or more in diameter, and three inches in depth. Skin deep purplish red; neck of medium size; flesh purplish-white, moderately fine grained and stronger flavored than the yellow and earlier red varieties. It is quite productive; one of the best to keep.* FB

like contemporary crops, which are bred to be as uniform as possible, land races contain subtle genetic variations that enable the crop to produce fruit regardless of the environmental conditions. "When we travel in primitive parts of the world where modern varieties don't occur at all, or didn't until quite recently, we notice that there is no crop ever completely free of disease," notes Dr. Erna Bennett, a genetic resources expert for the United Nations. "And there is no crop ever completely devastated by the disease. Disease and variety live in a kind of genetic balance with each other." This equilibrium with nature assures that at least part of a crop will survive through every growing season. Though land races rarely are phenomenally productive, they produce subsistence crops year after year.

Land races were the foundation of agriculture for thousands of years. Many of the centers of genetic diversity where they evolved were isolated by mountains or other topographical features. As a result, when Vavilov made his explorations during the 1920s, he found that agriculture continued uninterrupted much as it had for centuries. During the next fifty years, scientists explored many of these regions, raiding them for the genes that in many cases became the foundation for our "super crops."

Yet as early as the 1930s, scientists became uneasy about the future of these "genetic reservoirs." In that year, a prophetic article in the U.S. Department of Agriculture's yearbook observed:

> In the great laboratory of Asia, Europe and Africa, unguided barley breeding has been going on for thousands of years. Types without number have arisen over an enormous area. The better ones have survived. Many of the surviving types are old. Spikes from Egyptian ruins can often be matched with ones still growing in the basins along the Nile . . . The progenies of these fields with all their surviving variations constitute the world's priceless reservoir of germplasm. It has

waited through long centuries. Unfortunately from the breeder's standpoint, it is now being imperiled. When new barleys replace those grown by the farmers of Ethiopia or Tibet, the world will have lost something irreplaceable.

DRAINING THE GENETIC RESERVOIR

What scientists feared for barley has come to pass for many other crops as well. As the world has shrunk under the influence of improved transportation and communication, remote areas have become more accessible. At first the new varieties trickled in, displacing the old land races here and there. Then, with the advent of the Green Revolution, the new high-yield crops were thrust upon Third World farmers with the entirely laudable intention of ending hunger. The scientists who focused on boosting productivity paid little attention to the old crops that were being abandoned; yet when plant breeders returned to areas of traditional diversity to dip into the genetic reservoir, many of the crops they sought were gone. "Suddenly, we are discovering that Mexican farmers are planting hybrid corn seed from an American mid-western seed firm, that Tibetan farmers are planting barley from a Scandinavian plant breeding station, that Turkish farmers are planting wheat from the Mexican wheat program," writes Dr. Garrison Wilkes, in an article first published in 1977 in the *Bulletin of Atomic Scientists*. "Each of these classic areas of crop specific genetic diversity is rapidly becoming an area of genetic uniformity."

Genetic uniformity has been a goal of plant breeders, though uniformity makes a crop susceptible to environmental stress. A new disease that attacks one plant attacks the entire field and, when a crop has been widely distributed, an entire region. Since new diseases are constantly evolving, scientists have found that many of the new "super crops" can only survive for a few years until disease catches up with them. The average

White Creaseback Pole bean. *Exceedingly productive; the long pods being produced all over the vines, in clusters of from four to twelve. The handsome green pods grow from 5 to 6 inches long, perfectly round, with a crease in the back . . . hence the name. The pods are perfectly stringless, very fleshy, and as string beans are of superb quality.* BP

life span of a new wheat variety, for example, is only five years; then a newly evolved fungus attacks it. Unlike a land race, some of whose plants would survive no matter what nature dished out, the new crops evolve only with the help of people, who must constantly introduce new genes.

So far, plant breeders have responded to new pests and other environmental changes by going back to the centers of diversity to locate new genetic material, but now they are less and less likely to find what they want. Unlike wild plants, which may survive for a time even if human beings alter their environment, domesticated plants cannot survive unless people prepare the ground, eliminate competitive plants, and harvest the seed. When a crop is abandoned by a native farmer, its irreplaceable genetic characteristics often disappear in a single season.

This places plant breeders in a catch-22 situation that is well illustrated by the story of Philippine rice. Several years ago, Philippine farmers gave up native strains of rice that had been grown in the region for centuries in favor of a "miracle" variety called IR-8. When IR-8 was decimated by tungro disease, breeders recommended that farmers grow IR-20, a strain that turned out to be vulnerable to brown hopper insects. So the breeders suggested IR-26, which resists virtually all Philippine diseases and insects. However, IR-26 had a fragile stem; so the breeders decided to cross it with a native Taiwanese variety that could withstand high winds. Yet when they sought out the native variety, they found it had been virtually eliminated because the Taiwanese farmers had switched to IR-8.

Problems of this sort led to the establishment, in the Philippines, of the International Rice Institute, which is attempting to collect the 100,000 varieties of rice grown in Asia as well as wild strains. The Institute is part of an international network of sixty germplasm banks operating under the direction of the Food and Agriculture Organization. United Nations concern about the germplasm problem dates back to the early 1960s. By 1973, the International Board for Plant Genetic Resources had been established to oversee the development of seed banks, as well as plant exploration, seed collection, and germplasm preservation around the world. Though the UN effort is important, it has not adequately sampled the materials that are still being lost. "It would be nice to think that all the genetic diversity we will ever need is safely stored away in gene banks for future use," writes Jack Harlan, professor of plant genetics at the University of Illinois, in *Science* magazine. "Unfortunately this is hardly the case. Some of our collections are large even when the numerous duplications are accounted for, but none is really complete, and sources of diversity are drying up all over the world."

For plant breeders, the sources of diversity include both the land races grown by native farmers and the *wild relatives* of domesticated species. Wild relatives of domesticated plants are often dismissed as weeds because they never evolved into a form that humans enjoy eating. Queen Anne's lace, for example, is ignored because it never developed the fleshy root of its cousin the garden carrot. However, weeds are survivors, often displaying tenacious resistance to insects and diseases, and because they are related to domesticated crops, the genes for those characteristics can often be transferred to modern varieties.

The effort by plant breeders to preserve wild relatives of domesticated plants overlaps with the efforts of conservationists to preserve wild plants in general. Unfortunately, the drive to preserve wild plants has often been caricatured by the media, in part because even the most educated often find it difficult to grasp the idea that plants are endangered. Even those who sympathize with the plight of whales and whooping cranes are sometimes impatient when the Furbish's lousewort or its equivalent stands in the way of human progress. Why should a mere weed be allowed to interrupt human plans? they protest. Yet as Emerson so aptly put it, a weed is "a plant whose virtues have not yet been discovered."

THE UNKNOWN COSTS OF EXTINCTION

Despite their potential, "weeds" and other wild plants are becoming extinct at a distressing rate. Extinction has long been recognized as an inevitable part of evolution—scientists estimate that of the half-billion species that have lived, 90 percent have become extinct. But today, the rate of extinction has accelerated dramatically. Between 1600 and 1900, experts estimate that a species became extinct every four years. During the first seventy-five years of the twentieth century, one was lost each year. Today, scientist Norman Myers estimates that at least one species is disappearing each day. And by the late 1980s, if present trends continue, one species will be lost every hour.

Myers is speaking of animals as well as plants, and endangered animals do tend to grab the headlines. Many people find it easier to sympathize with the last tribe of African cheetahs than with an obscure plant they've never heard of. Yet the truth is that plants contribute more to human well-being than do animals. Plants are at the bottom of the food chain; so dozens of other species depend on them. Dr. Peter Raven of the Missouri Botanical Garden estimates that each plant species that becomes extinct leads to the extinction of ten to thirty other organisms that are dependent upon it. Since the loss of those organisms will, in turn, affect others, the fabric of life, as one observer puts it, "will not just suffer a minor rip; sections of it will be torn to shreds."

Aside from the ecological implications of plant extinction, we may also be allowing plants with valuable properties to slip through our fingers. Many plants dismissed as useless in the past are now vital to our well-being. For example, *Hevea bras-*

Essex Hybrid squash. *A new and excellent variety, a cross between the Hubbard and American Turban, having the color, shape and good qualities of the Turban, with the dryness and hard shell of the Hubbard. It is one of the finest-grained, richest-flavored and sweetest of all squashes, and will keep till the following June. The flesh is very rich-colored, thick and solid, and it is heavier than most other sorts of the same size.* DM

iliensis, a member of the Euphorbia family, which was considered a nuisance by tropical developers a hundred years ago, supplies a large percentage of the world's rubber today. The rosy periwinkle, an "insignificant" tropical flower, contains a chemical that is now used to treat leukemia in children. *Zea diploperennis*, a primitive relative of corn being grown in the Mexican mountains, may make it possible for scientists to breed perennial corn. Before their valuable properties were discovered, all of these plants were considered weeds and would have been allowed to become extinct without a moment's thought. The fact is that relatively few of the world's plants have yet been analyzed for useful properties, though plants have supplied humans with gums, oils, dyes, pesticides, drugs, and, of course, food.

Directly or indirectly, plants supply everything that humans eat; yet humans have limited their diets to a small fraction of nature's bounty. Of the estimated 80,000 edible plants, 3,000 have been eaten in the past; only 150 are cultivated extensively today; and a mere 20 supply 90 percent of the food consumed by people. One compelling reason for preserving wild and semidomesticated plants is to broaden this disturbingly narrow base for food. Several years ago, a study by the National Academy of Sciences uncovered fifty-four plants that would be good alternatives to our current food supplies, either because they grow well in difficult climates or because they contain extra protein.

The tropics, for example, are filled with food crops that have been largely ignored since colonial times, when colonists imposed their own tastes on the indigenous people. Today, in tropical countries, large amounts of money are spent to grow corn while ignoring native crops such as amaranth, a native American grain whose seeds and leaves are unusually rich in protein.

Many of the crops "discovered" by the National Academy

of Sciences have long been appreciated by "primitive" people. The winged bean, for example, is raised in New Guinea, where it is considered a poor man's crop. Today, researchers are enthusiastic about this "supermarket on a stalk" because virtually the entire plant can be consumed. The immature pods taste like green beans, mature pods resemble garden peas, the leaves are like spinach, the flowers taste like mushrooms, the sprouted beans are like tofu, the roots are richer in protein than potato, and the seeds produce unsaturated oil as well as a flour rich in protein. The winged bean has become a sensation similar to the soybean, which has a venerable history in China. Brought to the United States by Benjamin Franklin, the soybean was neglected until the 1920s, when the world needed a new source of oil and protein.

Many other remarkable plants are waiting for their worth to be recognized. The ground nut, for instance, was shared with the Pilgrims by the Wampanoag tribe. Its tubers, which are strung on the roots like beads, are as delicious as our potatoes but have three times the protein. Tepary beans, a traditional crop for the Papago of Arizona, are also rich in protein. Additionally, the plant is ideally adapted to dry climates since it produces beans with only one or two rainfalls. Amaranth, winged beans, ground nuts, and tepary beans have, at least, been identified by humans as useful sources of food; yet among the plants that are being allowed to become extinct, there may be many whose food potential is still undiscovered.

Aside from food, plants have provided most of the wonder drugs that have prolonged life so dramatically in the twentieth century. Chemicals synthesized from higher plants are major ingredients of almost a quarter of the prescriptions written annually in the United States. Scientists estimate that 20 percent of all plants contain alkaloids, chemical defense systems that protect the plants from parasites and predators. Though only 2 percent of the world's plants have been screened for alkaloids,

Green Globe Savoy cabbage. *This does not make a firm head but the whole of it being very tender and pleasant-flavored, is used for cooking; leaves wrinkled and dark green; is very hardy and improved by frost.* DM

they have yielded more than 1,000 drugs, including heart stimulants, painkillers, muscle relaxants, and local anesthetics. Alkaloids now under investigation show so much promise in treating cancer that the National Cancer Institute has funded a major effort to collect plants so that their component chemicals can be extracted and analyzed.

Similarly, the birth control pill was first synthesized from a South American yam, and efforts by the World Health Organization to find an even safer contraceptive have concentrated on tropical forests, where tribal peoples have used hundreds of plant species for antifertility. Again, all these benefits have accrued from known plants; yet many of the plants that are being allowed to become extinct have never been tested. And, even if they had been tested and found not to meet today's needs, it is possible that some of them might provide cures for plagues and problems in the future. It is disturbing to think that the cure for a lethal new disease such as AIDS might have been found in a plant that, through carelessness, has already become extinct.

Plants are used for more than food and drugs, however. They have also been employed extensively in industry. "The plant kingdom represents a virtually untapped reservoir of new chemical compounds," according to Dr. Richard E. Schultes, a Harvard botanist. For example, during the recent energy crisis, the U.S. government screened 6,400 plants to identify petroleum substitutes. Among the 460 plants that showed promise were the buffalo gourd and the jojoba shrub, two ancient crops from the American Southwest.

Obviously, we have not yet begun to tap the potential of the plant kingdom. Unfortunately, plants are becoming extinct before we can identify and catalogue them, much less analyze them for their usefulness to humans. Much of the loss is occurring in the moist tropical rainforests, where the diversity of species is unusually great. Though they represent only 10 percent of the earth's land, these moist tropical forests harbor three-quarters of the earth's species. Nevertheless, worldwide, these forests are being felled and burned at the incredible rate of seventy acres per minute. "Most of these zones supported extensive gene stocks as recently as 1960," writes Norman Myers. "Few will have much left in 1990." Though some of the moist tropical forests are being harvested by corporations eager for quick, one-time profits, much of the land is succumbing to the pressures of population. In "The Exhausted Earth," a 1981 article in *Foreign Policy*, Myers puts the matter succinctly:

> Developing countries often have difficulty keeping their citizens alive, let alone guaranteeing the survival of their wild creatures. The benefits of efforts at species conservation tend to accrue to . . . developed countries. Most people in the developing world do not live long enough to contract cancer or heart disease. To the extent that developing countries are currently trying to safeguard their species through parks and related measures, their efforts amount to a resource handout to developed countries.

Clearly, developed countries should be accepting some of the responsibility for the preservation of these global resources, but help has been slow in coming while the destruction has been accelerating.

Though much of the world's genetic heritage exists in other countries, the United States, too, has wild species in need of protection. Botanists estimate that as many as 3,000 known American species will disappear in the next few decades unless they are protected by the government. The Endangered Species Act, which was passed in 1940, didn't protect plants at all until 1973 and presently covers only sixty-one plant species. In addition, when it comes to plants, the Americas are still a "new world." During the last fifteen years, scientists in Arizona, California, and Florida have discovered species so unique that three new genus classifications had to be created for them. It is impossible to know how many other endangered plants fail to show up on official lists because they have not yet been identified and catalogued by scientists.

Unfortunately, plant extinction has a long history in this country. In the seventeenth century, John Bartram, one of our most famous botanists, found that several species he had noted on expeditions had vanished when he returned to their locales. One of these early casualties was a plant named Franklinia (*Gordonia altamaha*). Bartram initially found a tiny stand of this rare plant, but it was later exterminated—partly because the land was cleared for agriculture and partly because overenthusiastic collectors were determined to have a sample of the plant. Today, the same problem is being repeated on a much larger scale. Though many endangered plants have not been tested for useful properties, some have already proven their value. "What tends to be overlooked is that there are over 100 wild species of plants related to New World crops that are currently threatened by extinction within our boundaries," notes ethnobotanist Gary Nabhan in a survey commissioned by Meals for Millions/Freedom from Hunger Foundation. "Few of their populations fall within nature conservancy areas, and hardly any have had some of their seeds collected for preservation in seed banks."

PREVENTING THE QUIET CATASTROPHE

In short, the problem of plant extinction exists at home and abroad, among wild and domesticated plants. In the day that it might take to read this book, at least one plant will probably have disappeared from the earth. No one will mourn its passing because, in our ignorance, we probably did not know that it existed. Nor do we know whether it contained the genes that would have helped one of our crops resist acid rain, or an al-

Mountain Sweet watermelon. *A large, long, oval variety, often contracted towards the stem in the form of a neck; skin striped and marbled with different shades of green; rind rather thin, measuring scarcely half an inch in thickness; flesh scarlet and solid quite to the centre . . . A popular and extensively cultivated variety, quite hardy, productive and of good quality.* FB

kaloid that would have cured skin cancer, or an oil that would have fueled our engines. The plant that died today may not have had economic value, and perhaps humanity will get along fine without it. Yet, added to the plant we lost yesterday, and the seven we lost last week, and the one we'll lose tomorrow, that plant begins to take on ominous significance. A world rich in genetic resources can probably afford to lose a few plants, but we have long since passed the margin of safety. We are recklessly extinguishing plants without regard for what they might contribute or how their loss will affect other species.

Because the erosion of plant resources proceeds quietly, without conspicuous consequences, it is difficult to mobilize public opinion. Even conservationists often do not know where to make a stand. The extermination of a single plant may be justified when weighed against other human priorities; yet the extermination of thousands, indeed millions, of species is quietly catastrophic. Genetic diversity is the raw stuff of evolution. Life on our planet has survived ice ages and other environmental stresses because life forms were so abundant and diverse. Though some did not adapt to new conditions, others had the genetic predisposition to survive and thrive. By draining the genetic reservoir, we make it less likely that plants—and, ultimately, we—will be able to adapt to the conditions of the future.

Given the scope of the problem, backyard gardeners may feel that their participation is inconsequential. Not so, according to Bruce McBryde of the U.S. Fish and Wildlife Service. In an article entitled "Why Are So Few Endangered Plants Protected," published by *American Horticulturist*, he writes, "The foremost change necessary to be certain our endangered plants survive is the participation of all gardeners, horticulturalists, botanists, plantsmen—all who have made plants a significant part of their lives."

There is no question that the nation's 35 million gardeners

Scarlet China radish. *Form rather conical, and very smooth; of a lively rose color; flesh firm, like the Black Spanish but more pungent.* DM

could form a potent constituency supporting public and private efforts to preserve genetic diversity. Our vigilance could assure the continued funding and strengthening of federal efforts such as the National Plant Germplasm System and the Endangered Species Act. Our insistence could require more vigorous U.S. involvement in the international movements to preserve the genetic diversity of both land races and moist tropical forests. Our contributions could help solidify the position of organizations that are working to preserve domestic and wild plants at home and abroad.

This is hard work, but the incentive to do it grows in our gardens. There, genetic diversity becomes tangible in a cornucopia of colors, shapes, flavors, and growing habits. Those who tend heirloom fruits and vegetables know firsthand the generosity of nature. We have inherited a stunning legacy, a miraculous diversity of plants produced by ages of evolution. As a race, we seem intent upon destroying our birthright. As individual gardeners, we have an opportunity to save a rare bean, an incomparable apple, a disease-resistant corn. It is a beginning.

Seed Exchanges

THE ORGANIZATIONS LISTED BELOW ARE DESCRIBED in Chapter 3. All are dedicated to locating, exchanging, and preserving edible plants. Though they may be sources of seed for heirloom varieties, they are *not* seed companies. In fact, most are rather fragile organizations, run by one or two committed volunteers who have jobs and families competing for their time. If these organizations are to grow, those who participate must be equally committed. Before obtaining seeds or plants for an old variety from any of these groups, make a pledge to yourself to keep that variety going and to share it with others. For membership information, contact the organizations directly—and don't forget to enclose a self-addressed, stamped envelope.

Blue Ridge Seed Savers
P.O. Box 106
Batesville, VA 22924
Members of this regional organization save seeds from varieties that grow well in the Blue Ridge Mountains. Anyone can attend seed-swapping meetings. A subscription to the newsletter costs $2.

California Rare Fruit Growers, Inc.
Fullerton Arboretum
California State University
Fullerton, CA 92634
This group's interest is exotic fruits. A newsletter promotes unusual new fruits and reports on members' experiments in growing them.

CORNS
% Carl Barnes
Route 1, Box 32
Turpin, OK 73950
CORNS is dedicated to the preservation of old varieties of corn, in-
cluding teosinte, pod corn, flint corn, dent corn, popcorn, and sweet
corn. Members grow out old varieties, so they must be experienced
and knowledgeable about corn.

Henry Doubleday Research Association
Convent Lane
Bocking, Braintree, Essex
England
The primary purpose of this organization is to conduct research in organic gardening, but it is now deeply involved in the preservation of
heirloom varieties. Members can take advantage of a plant-finder service and can withdraw seeds from the Association's library of old varieties as long as they return fresh seed. Annual dues are £8.

Home Orchard Society
2511 S.W. Miles Street
Portland, OR 97219
Members are amateur fruit growers who live, for the most part, in the
Pacific Northwest. The Society publishes a quarterly newsletter and
sponsors meetings and workshops on fruit growing.

International Association for Education, Development and Distri-
bution of Lesser Known Food Plants and Trees
P.O. Box 599
Lynnwood, CA 90262
This group was organized to promote the cultivation and consump-
tion of little-known but nutritious edible plants.

KUSA Research Foundation
P.O. Box 761
Ojai, CA 93023
The Foundation is dedicated to the preservation of endangered grain
varieties.

Native Seeds/SEARCH
3950 W. New York Drive
Tucson, AZ 85745
This new organization is committed to researching, conserving, and

distributing heirloom Native American seeds, especially those adapted to marginal, desert conditions.

North American Fruit Explorers
% Robert Kurle
10 S. 055 Madison Street
Hinsdale, IL 60521
Membership in this organization of fruit enthusiasts costs $5 per year and includes a subscription to the quarterly publication *Pomona*. Members can also participate in plant exchanges.

Northern Nut Growers Association
4518 Holston Hills Road
Knoxville, TN 37914
Members seek out unusual nut trees, report on their success with different varieties, and exchange plant materials.

Plumas Seed Savers
% Cindy Robinson
P.O. Box 1917
Quincy, CA 95971
This is a new organization of California gardeners who meet regularly to exchange seed.

Scatterseed Project
% Khadighar
P.O. Box 1167
Farmington, ME 04938
Scatterseed Project was founded by Will Bonsall, a seed collector who would like to see the unusual varieties he has accumulated more widely grown and appreciated. Seeds for heirloom vegetables are available to those who will replenish and return seed stocks.

Seed Savers Exchange
203 Rural Avenue
Decorah, IA 52101
This is the largest and best organized of the grassroots groups exchanging seed. Members must have seeds to exchange, but anyone can subscribe to the Fall Harvest Edition and winter yearbook for $6. The organization's Growers Network distributes seeds from rare vegetable varieties to gardeners who agree to replenish and return seed. The Exchange also publishes a *Vegetable Variety Inventory*, which lists all heirloom varieties that are still sold by seed companies.

Stronghold, Inc.
3618 Gleneagles Drive
Silver Spring, MD 20906
This organization is dedicated to the preservation of the American chestnut.

Magazines that publish letters from readers wishing to exchange or locate old varieties include:

Gardens for All
180 Flynn Avenue
Burlington, VT 05401

Family Food Garden
464 Commonwealth Avenue
Boston, MA 02215

APPENDIX II

Seed Companies

THE FOLLOWING LIST PROVIDES ADDRESSES FOR SEED companies described in Chapter 4, as well as for additional companies that sell standard, open-pollinated varieties that have been phased out by other firms. Some of these companies fill an entire catalogue with heirlooms; others make gardeners hunt between the hybrids. Some businesses are newly founded; others have been run by the same family for the past seventy-five years. Some sell varieties that are particularly well suited to a particular region; others specialize in a single fruit or vegetable. All deserve to be better known by gardeners who want to grow and preserve heirloom varieties.

Abundant Life Seed Foundation
P.O. Box 772
Port Townsend, WA 98368
This nonprofit organization sells seeds of native plants and vegetables that are adapted to the Pacific Northwest. Its catalogue includes many heirlooms at very reasonable prices, as well as hard-to-find books such as Vilmorin's *The Vegetable Garden*. An annual subscription to the catalogue and four newsletters costs $2.

Alston Seed Growers
P.O. Box 266
Littleton, NC 27850
This very small seed company sells a few heirloom varieties, including Old Red Field corn, Old Yellow Hickory King corn, African Zulu

maize, Pencil Cob corn, and Everlasting Old Garden tomato, a tomato that grows year after year with minimal care.

Baum's Nursery
R.D. 2
Fairfield, CT 06810
This company offers an usually large selection of heirloom apples.

Butterbrooke Farm Seed Coop
78 Barry Road
Oxford, CT 06483
At Butterbrooke Farm, "multiplication of seed from heirloom varieties is given first priority." The coop sells a small selection of open-pollinated varieties adapted to New England, as well as a booklet called *How to Save Seed from Your Own Garden Produce*. Those who pay a $5 membership fee receive a newsletter and the opportunity to purchase heirloom varieties that are in short supply, such as Aunt Mary's sweet corn, White Snowball tomato, and Vine pomegranate, sometimes called "pocket melon."

Centre for Community Self-Sufficiency
P.O. Box 797
Bolinas, CA 94924
This nonprofit organization has an interest in antique apple varieties. It sells year-old trees of Rhode Island Greening, Hudson's Golden Gem, Cox's Orange Pippin, and several others.

Comstock, Ferre & Co.
263 Main Street
Wethersfield, CT 06109
Founded in 1820, this company lists some of what it calls "old reliables," such as Telephone peas, Black Spanish radishes, and Oxheart tomatoes. Gardeners have to know what they are looking for since the catalogue gives no hint about which varieties are heirlooms.

Converse Nursery
Amherst, NH 03031
More than 170 apple varieties are being preserved by this nursery, though not all are available every year. Trees are grafted on E.M. VII Rootstock; so trees grow to between ten and twelve feet.

Crocket Seeds
336 E. Main Street
Metamora, OH 43540

Crocket's specialty is popcorn—more than a dozen varieties, including some heirlooms, such as Strawberry, Tiny Tender Black, and Blue Thumb. The seed list for vegetables and flowers, inherited from the Natural Development Company, isn't heavy on heirlooms, but Crocket does sell Turkey wheat, a "grandparent of current Kansas wheat."

Fern Hill Farm
Jessup Mill Road
Clarksboro, NJ 08020
The Dr. Martin Pole Lima bean is the only variety sold by Fern Hill Farm. The origin of the bean is uncertain, but its followers love it for its large size and superior flavor.

Fred's Plant Farm
P.O. Box 707
Dresden, TN 38225
Most seed companies sell one or two sweet potatoes, but not Fred. He offers eighteen varieties, including Nuggett, Southern Queen, Copperskin, and Jasper.

G. Seed Company
P.O. Box 702
Tonasket, WA 98855
One of the new seed companies springing up to satisfy the demand for heirloom varieties, G. Seeds offers a nice selection of heirloom beans, corn, tomatoes, and other vegetables. Dates of introduction are included for heirloom varieties, and the company is willing to swap for varieties it doesn't have. By the way, the *G* in the company's name stands for "good."

Garden City Seeds
625 Phillips
Missoula, MT 59802
This small regional seed company specializes in open-pollinated varieties adapted to northern states.

Gleckler Seedsmen
Metamora, OH 43450
This family-owned company seeks out unusual foreign vegetables and makes them known to American gardeners. Though the company's emphasis isn't on American heirlooms, most of its varieties are open-pollinated. The tomato selection includes such old varieties as Goldie, Sunray, and Dutchman.

Grace's Garden
10 Bay Street
Westport, CT 06880
In her search for novelties and record-size vegetables, Jane Grace has stumbled over some heirlooms, including the husk tomato, which is the wild ancestor of ordinary tomatoes; *petit pois* peas, and Belgium white carrots.

Greenleaf Seeds
P.O. Box 89
Conway, MA 01341
A company that is "the result of an ever-enlarging garden," Greenleaf offers seeds for many unusual vegetables, including Rat's Tail radish, skirret, and Narrowleaf celtuce. Many of the older seeds are imported from foreign countries.

Grootendorst Nurseries
15310 Red Arrow Highway
Lakeside, MI 49116
Grootendorst has taken over the work of the Southmeadow Fruit Gardens and continues to sell the country's largest selection of antique apples as well as many other fruits. The catalogue, which costs $5, is one of the best available sources of information about old fruit varieties.

Gurney Seed & Nursery Co.
Yankton, SD 57078
One of the giants in the mail-order seed business, Gurney continues to stock some of the old varieties, including Soldier beans, Striped cushaw squash, and Lady Finger potatoes.

Hart Seed Company
Main and Hart Street
Wethersfield, CT 06109
This is another family-owned seed company with a large number of open-pollinated heirlooms, including Green Mountain potatoes.

H. G. Hastings Co.
P.O. Box 4274
Atlanta, GA 30302
Hastings carries varieties suited to the South, including such heirlooms as Early Adams corn and Christmas lima beans.

Hidden Springs Nursery
Route 14, Box 159
Cookeville, TN 38501
This nursery carries heirloom fruit trees including a number of regional varieties.

Horticultural Enterprises
P.O. Box 34082
Dallas, TX 75234
This company sells thirty different peppers in varied shapes, colors, and intensities.

Internode Seed Company
16 Pamaron Way
Novato, CA 94947
This seed company is saving many old varieties with the intention of selling seed when their supplies are large enough. Among the varieties to watch for are Estem squash, White Egg turnip, Short Horn carrot, Netted Gem muskmelon, and Everbearing cucumber.

Johnny's Selected Seeds
Albion, ME 04910
One of the most successful alternative seed companies, Johnny's sells seeds for vegetables that will do well in short-season states such as Maine. The informative catalogue includes many open-pollinated heirlooms.

J. W. Jung Seed Company
335 South High Street
Randolph, WI 53956
This family-owned seed company is making an effort to "reintroduce productive old-timers." It specializes in varieties adapted to north-central states.

D. Landreth Seed Company
Leadenhall and Ostend Streets
Baltimore, MD 21230
The oldest seed company in America, Landreth sold seed to Thomas Jefferson and George Washington. Contemporary catalogues often include instructive excerpts from old catalogues but few of the old varieties.

Lands-End Seed
Crawford, CO 81415

Heirloom varieties that are adapted to high altitudes are the specialty here. Some, such as Great White Souper beans, have been grown on the ranch for over 80 years.

Lawson's Nursery
Route 1, Box 294
Ball Ground, GA 30107
Lawson's is a specialist in old-fashioned fruit trees. Apple varieties include Mother Apple, Sops of Wine, and Wolf River.

Liberty Seed Company
P.O. Box 806
New Philadelphia, OH 44663
This new seed company serves gardeners in the Northeast and north-central states.

Long Island Seed and Plant
1368 Flander's Road
Riverhead, NY 11901
This company specializes in "genetically diverse seed blends." Though the firm sells primarily to growers, it will send home gardeners a list of old, open-pollinated vegetables that are available to them. Customer newsletter includes a seed exchange.

Mayo Seed Company
P.O. Box 10247
Knoxville, TN 37919
Family-owned since 1878, the Mayo Seed Company continues to sell heirloom beans, such as White Greasy Cornfield bean, to satisfy its Tennessee customers who feel that "stringless beans have had the flavor bred out of them."

National Seed Order
P.O. Box 932
Woodstock, NY 12498
This company was started to "beat the price of fancy-package varieties." It still sells untreated seed for open-pollinated varieties for twenty-five cents a packet plus postage.

Neal's Open-Pollinated
417 N. 8th Street W.
Mt. Vernon, IA 52314
The open-pollinated corn varieties sold by this company have been in the Neal family since the turn of the century.

New York State Fruit Testing Association
Geneva, NY 14456
Not really a seed company, NYSFTA distributes varieties that are being developed at the New York State Agricultural Station. The Association also has a selection of old apple and pear varieties, which are available to members who pay $5 dues per year.

Nichols Garden Nursery
1190 North Pacific
Albany, OR 97321
Most famous for its herbs, Nichols also carries a few heirloom varieties, including Oregon Giant beans, Montezuma Red beans, and Guatemalan Blue squash.

Pine Tree Seed Company
P.O. Box 1399
Portland, ME 04104
Pine Tree is a company in search of heirlooms, especially those that "use space efficiently."

Plants of the Southwest
1570 Pacheco Street
Santa Fe, NM 87501
This company's wonderful catalogue features native plants and vegetables that can be grown in the arid Southwest. A short section includes ancient Indian heirlooms, such as tepary beans, Papago corn, and devil's claw.

Porter & Son
1510 E. Washington
Stephenville, TX 76401
This company is a good source for heat-resistant varieties, including a few heirlooms. It is also a source of seed for Cob melon.

Prairie State Commodities
P.O. Box 6
Trilla, IL 62469
This firm offers a small selection of grains suited to the Midwest, including open-pollinated field corns, cane sorghum, and buckwheat.

Redwood Seed Company
P.O. Box 361
Redwood City, CA 94064
Redwood offers a large selection of open-pollinated vegetables as well

as other edible and ornamental plants. The owners are glad to exchange seed with any customer who has an heirloom variety the company doesn't already sell.

Seeds Blum
Idaho City Stage
Boise, ID 83707
Seeds Blum was born out of a concern for heirlooms. Jan Blum raises her own seed for many old varieties that are being dropped by larger seed companies. She also runs a seed exchange and a plant-finder service.

Sonoma Antique Apples
4395 Westside Road
Healdsburg, CA 95448
As its name suggests, this nursery specializes in old-time apples.

Southern Exposure Seed Exchange
Route 1, Box 150
Esmont, VA 22937
This is a new seed company specializing in heirlooms as well as varieties that are disease-resistant or otherwise adapted to conditions in the Middle Atlantic states.

Suter, Herman L.
3220 Silverado Trail, North
St. Helena, CA 94574
Mr. Suter offers a selection of more than seventy heirloom apple varieties. He no longer sells trees but will sell scion wood to those who can make their own grafts.

Taos Pueblo Native Seed Company
P.O. Box EEE
Taos, NM 87571
This seed company sells only Taos Pueblo Blue corn, though it hopes to have seed from other Native American crops in the future.

Territorial Seed Company
P.O. Box 27
Lorane, OR 97451
This company offers over 150 varieties specially suited to the unique growing conditions in the Pacific Northwest.

Vermont Bean Seed Company
Garden Lane
Bomoseen, VT 05732
Though this company has expanded its list to include other vegetables, it still offers the largest selection of heirloom beans and peas.

Vita Green Farms
217 Escondido Avenue
Vista, CA 92083
This family-owned company sells only herb and vegetable seeds, including many grown in the family garden during the 1930s.

Westwind Seeds
2509 N. Campbell Avenue, No. 139
Tucson, AZ 85719
This collectively owned company offers inexpensive seed for varieties adapted to the arid Southwest.

Willhite Seed Company
P.O. Box 23
Poolville, TX 76076
Melons are the specialty here—over sixty varieties of cantcloupes and watermelons.

A World Seed Service
P.O. Box 1058
Redwood City, CA 94064
This seedsman states flatly, "We sell only open-pollinated varieties—the older the better." The catalogue is filled with unusual edible and ornamental plants from around the world.

Worley Nursery
Route 1
York Springs, PA 17372
Worley Nursery's stock includes fifty heirloom apple varieties.

Living Historical Farms and Museums

THE LIVING HISTORICAL FARMS AND MUSEUMS LISTED below have or would like to have heirloom gardens. Those with exemplary programs are described in more detail in Chapter 5. The list should serve two purposes. First, those who want to learn more about heirlooms can visit these museums and see old varieties growing. Second, many of the institutions need help finding, growing, and propagating heirlooms; so experienced gardeners may want to volunteer their time and expertise. The addresses in the listings are, for the most part, mailing addresses. For directions to many of these museums, as well as updated hours, request a copy of *Travel Historic Rural America* ($5.95) from the American Society of Agricultural Engineers, P.O. Box 410, St. Joseph, MI 49085. Or write directly to the farm or museum. Another source of information about these institutions is the Association of Living Historical Farms and Museums, % The Smithsonian, Washington, DC 20560.

Acadian House Museum
P.O. Box 497
St. Martinville, LA 70582
The extensive gardens around this plantation home contain many rare and unusual plants that would have been used by its occupants in the eighteenth century. The museum preserves heirloom varieties of peppers, squashes, okra, cotton, and other crops. One particularly interesting crop is mirliton or vegetable pear, an heirloom in Louisiana that is seldom grown elsewhere.

Accokeek National Colonial Farm
3400 Bryan Point Road
Accokeek, MD 20607
Established in 1958 to preserve the view opposite Mount Vernon, Accokeek depicts a middle-class, eighteenth-century tobacco plantation. The museum, which plans to acquire two or three heirlooms per year, now preserves Virginia Gourd Seed corn, Red May wheat, Champion of England peas, and several bean varieties. Research reports on heirloom vegetables and other topics are issued regularly.

Blackberry Historical Farm
R.R. 3, Box 591
Barnes Road
Aurora, IL 60504
Under development, this site will represent a pioneer farm in northern Illinois in the 1840s. The curator is looking for historically appropriate varieties.

Blue Ridge Institute
Ferrum College
Ferrum, VA 24088
Staff members at this newly developed museum are looking for vegetables compatible with an 1800 German-American farmstead.

Booker T. Washington National Monument
Route 1, Box 195
Hardy, VA 24101
The Borroughs Plantation is recreated as it might have been around 1860, when Booker T. Washington lived there as a slave. Heirloom varieties, including Prince Albert peas, Gourd Seed corn, and Sugar Crowder peas, were selected based on a research report by Edwin Bearss entitled "The Borroughs Plantation as a Living Historical Farm"(1969).

Buckley Homestead
3606 Bleshaw
Lowell, IN 46356
This newly developed living historical farm will have gardens that would have been appropriate in 1850 and 1910.

Claude Moore Colonial Farm at Turkey Run
6310 Old Georgetown Pike
McLean, VA 22101

At Turkey Run, a "family" of volunteers demonstrates what life would have been like on a low-income homestead during the late colonial period. The farm's heirloom varieties are dent corn and Oranoko tobacco. Other crops are represented by modern varieties selected to match descriptions from the eighteenth century.

Clayville Rural Life Center and Museum
R.R. 1
Pleasant Plains, IL 62677
Operated by Sangamon State University, the Clayville Rural Life Center and Museum revolves around a restored inn that was a stagecoach stop in the 1850s. The extensive kitchen garden is planted exclusively with varieties known to exist in the mid-1800s. The center's *Seed Varieties of the 1850's* (request Resource List #10) includes a seed list prepared by Simon Francis in 1857 and a list of varieties planted at Clayville, along with commercial sources for seed.

Colonial Pennsylvania Plantation
Ridley Creek State Park
P.O. Box 385
Edgemont, PA 19028
The gardens at this colonial plantation include herbs and vegetables typical of the period, though little attempt has been made to acquire authentic varieties. Staff members have done extensive research, however, and are beginning to save seed from open-pollinated varieties; so they might be receptive to donations of old Pennsylvania varieties.

Conner Prairie Pioneer Settlement
30 Conner Lane
Noblesville, IN 46060
This outdoor museum recreates the year 1836 in a central Indiana farming community. Staff members are looking for seeds appropriate to the period.

Dayton Museum of Natural History
2629 Ridge Avenue
Dayton, OH 45414
As part of the excavation and restoration of a Native American fort, the museum has planned extensive gardens, including many varieties believed to have been grown in the twelfth century. The museum raises its own seed for several varieties of corn, including Iroquois, Papago, Longfellow Yellow Flint, Tama Flint, and Tamaroa Flint.

Fort Vancouver National Historic Site
National Park Service
Vancouver, WA 98661
Fort staff members are trying to reconstruct the vegetable garden to be as it was in 1840, when the Hudson Bay Company of Canada operated the fort.

Four Mile Historic Park
715 S. Forest Street
Denver, CO 80222
The site recreates life in Colorado in 1867, and the gardens have varieties appropriate to the period.

Genesee Country Museum
P.O. Box 1819
Rochester, NY 14603
This open-air museum includes more than forty buildings and several heirloom gardens. Seeds for the thirty-odd varieties that are planted in the museum gardens are made available to the public each spring. In the fall, gardeners who have grown heirloom varieties are encouraged to display them at a nineteenth-century agricultural fair. For details about the seeds or the fair, write to the museum.

George Washington Birthplace National Monument
Washington's Birthplace, VA 22575
This site recreates the Tidewater plantation on which George Washington was born. Garden vegetables, field crops, and herbs are those that would have been grown between 1730 and 1750.

Georgia Agrirama
P.O. Box Q
Tifton, GA 31794
The Agrirama, which depicts rural Georgian life between 1870 and 1899, has always planted seeds from crops appropriate to that period. Now the staff is making an active attempt to locate heirloom varieties that are no longer available from seed companies.

Hans Herr House
1849 Hans Herr Drive
Willow Street, PA 17584
As the oldest house in Lancaster County, the Hans Herr House recreates the conditions of 1719. The gardens include vegetables from the collection put together by the Genesee Country Museum (see above),

and the many old apples in the orchard include Smokehouse, Winter Banana, Maiden Blush, Watermelon, Red Astrachan, and Tolman Sweet.

Heckler Plains Farmstead
474 Main Street
Harleysville, PA 19438
Located on thirty-six acres in the town park, the Heckler Plains Farmstead depicts life on a nineteenth-century farm. The garden includes both herbs and vegetables grown between 1800 and 1850.

The Hermitage
Hermitage, TN 37076
The Ladies Association at this historic home is trying to locate plants that would have been grown in Tennessee before 1845.

The Homeplace 1850
T.V.A.–L.B.L.
Golden Pond, KY 42231
The Homeplace 1850 maintains several heirloom field crops, including Swedish oats, White Swedish oats, Red May wheat, White Gourd Seed corn, and White and Yellow Flint corn. The heirloom orchard includes plums, peaches, and apples such as Honey Cider, Horse, Red June, and Limbertwig.

Kipahulu District, Living Farm Area
P.O. Box 97
Hana, HI 96713
An unusual living historical farm, Kipahulu is dedicated to the preservation of plants used by the Hawaiians before Captain Cook arrived on the Islands in 1778. Since the Hawaiians had no written language, researchers have had to depend upon archeological findings and oral history to decide which plants should be preserved.

Lincoln Boyhood National Memorial
Lincoln City, IN 47552
This farm, once owned by Abraham Lincoln's father, has been restored to be much as it was when Lincoln was a boy. The crops planted have been scrupulously documented in *Pioneer Farming in Indiana: Thomas Lincoln's Major Crops, 1816–1830*. Heirloom field crops include Yellow Gourd corn, Old Red Chaff Bearded wheat, Common White oats, Riga flax, Tennessee Green Seed cotton, and Old Connecticut pumpkins. Fruit varieties include American Golden Russet,

Rawle's Janet, Rambo, Wine, and Pennock apples, as well as several peach, plum, and pear varieties.

Lincoln Log Cabin Historic Site
R.R. 1, Box 175
Lerna, IL 62440
This living-history program illustrates life on an 1840s farm. The selection of heirloom seeds for the garden was based on research done by the Clayville Rural Life Center and Museum.

Living History Farms
2600 N.W. 111th Street
Des Moines, IA 50322
The Living History Farms represent five periods in the history of Iowa—an Iowa tribe settlement from 1700, a pioneer farm from the 1840s, a Victorian town, a farm from 1900, and a contemporary farm. The entire 600-acre farm includes orchards, herb gardens, and vegetable beds, though the museum is not preserving its own heirloom varieties.

Meadow Farm Museum
P.O. Box 27032
Richmond, VA 23273
One of the newer living historical farms, Meadow Farm depicts life in southern Virginia between 1820 and 1850. The heirloom vegetables come mostly from the collection developed at Genesee Country Museum, but there are some surprises, such as Early Adams corn, Black Hawk raspberries, and Russet Burbank potatoes.

Missouri Town 1855
22807 Woods Chapel Road
Blue Springs, MO 64015
Staff members at this living-history site are interested in obtaining and propagating heirloom varieties from the 1850s.

Monticello
P.O. Box 316
Charlottesville, VA 22902
Excavations begun in June, 1979, have led to the restoration of Thomas Jefferson's orchard and vegetable gardens. The new gardens follow as closely as possible the plan for 1812 described in Jefferson's *Garden Book*. Of the forty-three vegetables planted that year, many will be represented by authentic heirloom varieties. The rest will be

modern varieties that resemble those described by Jefferson and his contemporaries.

Mount Vernon
Mount Vernon, VA 22121
To its many other horticultural projects, Mount Vernon has now added an interest in heirloom vegetables. Gardener J. Dean Norton is seeking information about varieties grown during George Washington's time.

Naper Settlement
201 West Porter Avenue
Naperville, IL 60540
Located in a Chicago suburb, this living historical site recreates the 1830s. The flower and herb gardens at the site are appropriate for the period, and staff members are seeking appropriate vegetable varieties.

New Hampshire Farm Museum
P.O. Box 644
Wilton, NH 03851
Located on the historic Jones Farm, the New Hampshire Farm Museum preserves New Hampshire's agricultural heritage by collecting farm implements and sponsoring special programs, such as Maple Syrup Day. The museum has a small collection of seeds and hopes to replenish them in an heirloom garden.

Old Bethpage Village Restoration
Round Swamp Road
Old Bethpage, NY 11804
More than forty-five historic structures contribute to the illusion that this is a small Long Island village of the pre–Civil War era. The village maintains one garden containing vegetables that might have been grown by a Dutch family in 1760 and four gardens containing nineteenth-century varieties. The annual agricultural fair, held each fall, includes awards for heirloom varieties of fruits and vegetables.

Old Salem
600 S. Main Street
Winston-Salem, NC 27108
This restoration recreates a German settlement from the 1760s. In an attempt to make the gardens more authentic, the staff horticulturist is seeking old bean varieties.

Old Sturbridge Village
Sturbridge, MA 01566
One of the most famous of the living historical farms, Old Sturbridge Village evokes rural life in New England between 1790 and 1840. The orchard, which is managed in cooperation with the Worcester County Horticultural Society, contains more than a hundred heirloom apple varieties. In addition, three of the village gardens include vegetables appropriate to the period.

Old World Wisconsin
Route 2, Box 18
Eagle, WI 53190
This museum makes a special effort to capture the ethnic heritage of the various immigrant groups that settled Wisconsin. The nine gardens represent what would have been grown by Danish, Swedish, and Finnish gardeners in different periods. When heirloom gardener Jim Johnson was in charge, the gardens were filled with heirloom varieties, but now they have been replaced by contemporary lookalikes.

Oliver H. Kelley Farm
15788 Kelley Farm Road
Elk River, MN 55330
This museum preserves the home of Oliver H. Kelley as it would have been when he was doing experimental "book farming" between 1850 and 1876. Authentic varieties are grown in the fields, orchards, and vegetable gardens. The museum also distributes seeds of heirloom varieties and encourages local gardeners to display their vegetables at a fall agricultural fair.

Pennsbury Manor
Morrisville, PA 19067
Pennsbury Manor, which was reconstructed in the 1930s to celebrate Pennsylvania's 150th anniversary, resembles an English country manor garden of the late 1600s. The staff is in the process of introducing authentic flowers, vegetables, and field crops based on letters from William Penn and other period documents.

Pioneer Farm
11418 Sprinkle Cut-off Road
Austin, TX 78754
When Pioneer Farm started its heirloom garden in 1982, staff members drew upon plant materials collected by three local heirloom gardeners. In keeping with their goal of preserving "locally adapted va-

rieties of plants," they are now growing and saving seed from two varieties of corn, six varieties of beans, and seven varieties of grapes. The gardens may be seen by appointment.

Plimoth Plantation
P.O. Box 1620
Plymouth, MA 02360
Founded in 1949, Plimoth Plantation is one of the oldest living historical farms. The staff maintains several hundred varieties of herbs, vegetables, flowers, shrubs, and trees, "all period correct for the 17th century." Seed is saved for some vegetable varieties.

Sleepy Hollow Restorations
150 White Plains Road
Tarrytown, NY 10591
Staff members at this historic site, which represents the years between 1725 and 1860, are seeking vegetable and fruit varieties dating from that period.

Strawberry Banke
Marcy Street
Portsmouth, NH 03801
Thirty-five shops and homes are preserved at this ten-acre living-history site. The buildings represent the seventeenth, eighteenth, and nineteenth centuries. The garden of the John Sherburne home, believed to be one of the oldest in the country, is being planted with authentic old varieties.

Author's note: Information for this list was gathered through a survey of more than a hundred living historical farms and museums. The author would appreciate information concerning other institutions that are maintaining or starting heirloom gardens.

APPENDIX IV

Bibliography of Selected Historical Sources

THE FOLLOWING LIST OF SELECTED HISTORICAL sources includes books recommended by heirloom collectors, but it is not comprehensive. Many horticulture books were written during the nineteenth century, and many contain excellent descriptions of fruits and vegetables.

Barry, Patrick. *The Fruit Garden*. New York: C. M. Saxton & Co., 1851 (rev. ed., 1883). Variety descriptions for 133 apples, 182 pears, and many smaller fruits.

Beach, S. A. *The Apples of New York*. Albany, 1905. Two beautiful volumes with color plates and detailed descriptions of varieties known at the time.

Bridgeman, Thomas. *The Young Gardener's Assistant*. New York: C. M. Saxton & Co., 1829. The catalogue of garden and herb seeds is taken from Grant Thorburn, a seedsman of the period.

Buist, Robert. *The Family Kitchen Gardener*. New York, 1860. This book includes "plain and accurate descriptions of all the different species and varieties of culinary vegetables" as well as comments based on Buist's own experience as a grower.

Burr, Fearing, Jr. *Field and Garden Vegetables of America*. Boston: Crosby & Nichols, 1865. This is the first comprehensive description of the varieties popular in this country. More than 1,000 varieties are described in great detail.

Cole, Samuel W. *The American Fruit Book*. Boston, 1849. In addition to the usual information about cultural techniques, Cole includes variety descriptions for 177 apples, 119 pears, and many smaller fruits.

Coxe, William. *A View of the Cultivation of Fruit Trees*. Philadelphia, 1817. The first American book on apples with detailed varietal descriptions and engravings.

Deane, Samuel. *The New England Farmer*. Worcester, Mass., 1797. One of the earliest American works on horticulture, this book discusses many varieties popular at the time.

Downing, A. J. *The Fruits and Fruit Trees of America*. New York, 1845. This classic work by a nineteenth-century nurseryman went through twenty editions. Downing maintained a nursery with more than 3,000 varieties so that the descriptions in his book would be accurate. The book is a major source of information about nineteenth-century varieties of apples, pears, peaches, plums, strawberries, apricots, cherries, currants, and melons.

Elliot, Franklin. *Elliot's Western Fruitbook*. New York, 1859. A useful reference for Western gardeners. Elliot was the first author to discuss orchards throughout the entire country and to attempt to analyze varieties according to the regions in which they performed well.

Fessenden, Thomas. *New American Gardener*. Boston, 1834. This very popular gardening book went through thirty editions. The "practical directions" are interspersed with some information about vegetable varieties.

Field, Thomas W. *Pear Culture*. New York, 1859. One of the few nineteenth-century references on pears, with detailed descriptions of 57 varieties and tabular information on 150 more.

Hedrick, Ulysses P. *The Cherries of New York* (1915), *The Grapes of New York* (1908), *The Peaches of New York* (1917), *The Pears of New York* (1921), *The Plums of New York* (1911), *The Small Fruits of New York* (1925). All Albany, N.Y.

Hedrick, Ulysses P., ed. *The Vegetables of New York* (Vol. I). Albany: New York State Agricultural Experiment Station. Four volumes: *Peas of New York* (1928), *Beans of New York* (1931), *Sweet Corn* (1935), and *The Cucurbits* (1937). Ulysses P. Hedrick was a director of the New York State Agricultural Experiment Station and, as this list suggests, a prolific writer. Each of these books is an excellent, well-illustrated reference work.

Henderson, Peter. *Gardening for Profit*. New York, 1887. This book was written by a market gardener, so it includes lots of information about efficient and economical culture. Also includes opinionated descriptions of varieties Henderson thought most valuable for market.

Hovey, Charles. *The Fruits of America*. Boston, 1853. A stunning collector's item that includes "richly colored figures and full descriptions of all the choicest varieties cultivated in the United States."

Kenrick, William. *The New American Orchardist*. Boston, 1835. Contains thorough descriptions of fruit varieties grown on the East Coast early in the nineteenth century.

Landreth, Burnet. *Market Gardening and Farm Notes*. New York, 1893. Another in the series of books written by nineteenth-century seedsmen. It includes Landreth's "experiences and observations" on vegetables.

Manning, Robert. *Book of Fruits*. Salem, Mass., 1838. Many nineteenth-century books on fruit sound alike because the authors freely copied each other's varietal descriptions. Manning was the first pomologist to rely solely on his own observations. Covers apples, pears, peaches, plums, and cherries suited to New England.

Prince, William. *A Short Treatise on Horticulture*. New York, 1828. Describes varieties at the Linnean Botanical Garden as well as promising "new" fruits.

Quinn, P. T. *Money in the Garden*. New York, 1871. Slanted toward market gardeners, with descriptions of varieties recommended by Quinn.

Ragan, W. H. *Nomenclature of the Apple* (1905), *Nomenclature of the Pear* (1907). Both, Washington, D.C. Major reference works, sponsored by the U.S. Department of Agriculture, which describe every variety of apple and pear mentioned in American publications after 1804. The volume on apples, which lists a staggering 8,000 varieties, was reprinted in 1926.

Sturtevant, Peter L. *Sturtevant's Notes on Edible Plants*. Albany, 1919 (reprinted by Dover, 1972). Edited by U. P. Hedrick, this reference work makes fascinating reading. Though Sturtevant gives relatively little information about nineteenth-century varieties, he summarizes virtually everything that was known about the history of vegetables in 1900.

Thomas, John J. *The Fruit Culturist*. New York: Auburn and Geneva, 1846. Detailed descriptions of three dozen apple varieties, with a longer reference list of 283 varieties.

Thorburn, Grant. *The Gentleman's and Gardener's Kalendar*. New York, 1821. Advice on gardening from one of the nineteenth century's most important seedsmen.

Sources for Old Horticultural Books and Seed Catalogues

BOOKSELLERS

Any bookseller who specializes in rare books may have horticultural texts that would be valuable to heirloom gardeners. For a list of members of the Antiquarian Booksellers Association of America, send a self-addressed envelope with fifty-four cents postage to the ABAA, 50 Rockefeller Center, New York, NY 10020. A few booksellers specialize in horticultural works. The following publish catalogues of works they have available and will search out specific volumes for their customers. Some of these dealers also carry old seed catalogues.

Henry Hurley, Bookseller
Route 12
Westmoreland, NH 03467

Ian Jackson
P.O. Box 9075
Berkeley, CA 94709

Elizabeth Woodburn
Booknoll Farm
Hopewell, NJ 08525

Savoy Books
Chapel Road
Savoy, MA 01256

Second Life Books
Quarry Road   P.O. Box 242
Lanesborough, MA 01237

LIBRARIES

The following list includes libraries that have been designated as regional repositories for historical materials by the Council of Botanical and Horticultural Libraries. Most of these libraries have very good collections of seed catalogues, though access may be limited because the old catalogues are fragile. The list is not complete, but librarians at these institutions should be able to refer gardeners to other collections in their regions.

Massachusetts Horticultural
    Library
300 Massachusetts Avenue
Boston, MA 02115

National Agricultural Library
Beltsville, MD 20705

Business Americana Collection
The Smithsonian
Washington, DC 20560

Pennsylvania Horticultural
    Library
325 Walnut Street
Philadelphia, PA 19106

Longwood Library
Longwood Gardens
Kennett Square, PA 19348

Bailey Hortatorium
Cornell University
Ithaca, NY 14850

Anderson Horticultural
    Library
3675 Arboretum Drive
Chanhassen, MN 55317

Shields Library
University of California
Davis, CA 95616

Federal Repositories for Fruits and Vegetables

THE INSTITUTIONS THAT FOLLOW SHOULD NOT BE considered sources for heirloom fruit and vegetable varieties. As Chapter 6 makes clear, the National Plant Germplasm System is strained to the limit by its efforts to obtain, document, and maintain its collections. In some cases, heirloom gardeners may be able to contribute rare varieties to these collections; in other cases, scientists at these institutions may be able to direct private collectors to other sources for varieties they seek. Either way, the resources of these organizations should be used very sparingly by heirloom gardeners since their purpose is not to make unusual varieties available to a few but to preserve them for us all.

One way to keep up on the varied activities of the National Plant Germplasm System is to subscribe to *Diversity*, a bimonthly publication for "the plant genetic resources community." The publication covers political and scientific developments related to conservation of plant resources and costs $35 a year. For subscriptions, write to: *Diversity*, Laboratory for Information Science in Agriculture, P.O. Box 2160, Arlington, VA 22202.

SEED BANKS

National Seed Storage Laboratory,
Fort Collins, CO 80521
Dr. Louis Bass, Director
This facility is the primary seed bank in the United States, with

responsibility for preserving seed samples of nearly 200,000 seed-bearing plants, including (as of October 1981):

Vegetable	Number of Varieties
Bean	480
Beet, garden	85
Broccoli	61
Cabbage	168
Carrot	118
Corn, sweet	115
Cucumber	207
Lettuce	215
Melon	232
Onion	172
Parsnip	11
Pea	287
Pepper	201
Pumpkin and summer squash (*C. pepo*)	84
Radish	282
Squash, cushaw (*C. mixta*)	5
Squash, winter (*C. maxima*)	88
Squash, winter crookneck (*C. moschata*)	32
Tomato	3540
Watermelon	199

Small Grains Collection
Plant Genetics and Germplasm Institute
Beltsville, MD 20705
This collection includes seed for wheat, oats, barley, rye, and other small grains.

REGIONAL PLANT INTRODUCTION STATIONS

Northeast Plant Introduction Station
New York State Agricultural Station
Geneva, NY 14456
Dr. Desmond Dolan, Coordinator
Primary responsibility for testing and maintaining plant introductions of broccoli, cauliflower, onions, peas, kohlrabi, *Cucurbita maxima*, celery, and brussels sprouts.

Midwest Plant Introduction Station
Iowa State University
Ames, IA 50011
Dr. Willis Skrdla, Coordinator
Primary responsibility for testing and maintaining plant introductions of corn, beets, cucumbers, and tomatoes.

Western Plant Introduction Station
Washington State University
Pullman, WA 99164
Dr. S. M. Dietz, Coordinator
Primary responsibility for testing and maintaining plant introductions of beans, cabbage, lentils, lettuce, chickpeas, and faba beans.

Southern Plant Introduction Station
Experiment, GA 30212
Dr. G. R. Lovell, Coordinator
Primary responsibility for testing and maintaining plant introductions of melons, cowpeas, millet, peanuts, sorghum, and peppers.

Interregional Potato Introduction Station
Sturgeon Bay, WI 54235
Primary responsibility for testing and maintaining potato germplasm.

CLONAL REPOSITORIES

In operation:
Corvallis, Oregon: pears, filberts, hazelnuts, and hops
Davis, California: grapes, peaches, plums, and nuts
Miami, Florida: subtropical fruits and sugar cane
Brawley, California: date palms
Mayaguez, Puerto Rico: tropical fruits
Geneva, New York: apples and grapes

Planned:
Riverside, California: citrus fruits
Kona, Hawaii: subtropical fruits
Byron, Georgia: stone fruits and Southern apples
Orlando, Florida: oranges
Brownwood, Texas: pecans and hickory nuts

General Bibliography

Author's note: The following books and articles are among those the author found valuable and are recommended for further reading. Books on specific topics of interest to heirloom gardeners are listed in the relevant chapters—books about seed saving in Chapter 9, historical references in Appendix IV, etc.

Becker, Robert, with Lynne Belluscio and Roger Kline. *The Heirloom Vegetable Garden*. Cornell University Cooperative Extension, Distribution Center, 7 Research Park, Cornell University, Ithaca, NY 14850.

Bettes, E. M., ed. *Jefferson's Garden Book*. Philadelphia: American Philosophical Society, 1944.

Culpeper, Nicholas. *Culpeper's Complete Herbal*. 19th century. Reprint. New York: Sterling, 1959.

Ehrlich, Paul. *Extinction: The Causes and Consequences*. New York: Random House, 1981.

Fowler, Cary. *Reaping What We Sow—Seeds and the Crisis in Agriculture*. The Rural Advancement Fund, P.O. Box 1029, Pittsboro, NC 27312.

Fowler, Cary, et al. *Seed Banks Serving People, Highlights of a Workshop*. 1982. Meals for Millions, P.O. Box 680, Santa Monica, CA 90406.

Frankel, O. H. *Conservation and Evolution*. Cambridge: At the University Press, 1981.

General Accounting Office. *Better Collection and Maintenance Procedures Needed to Help Protect Agriculture's Germplasm Resources*. Washington, D.C.: Superintendent of Documents, 1981.

General Accounting Office. *The Department of Agriculture Can Minimize the Risk of Potential Crop Failures*. Washington, D.C.: Superintendent of Documents, 1981.

Gerard, John. *Herbal or General History of Plants*. 19th century. Reprint. New York: Dover Publications, 1975.

Harlan, Jack. "The Genetics of Disaster." *Journal of Environmental Quality* 1, no. 3 (1972):212–215.

Harlan, Jack. "Our Vanishing Genetic Resources." *Science*, May 1975, pp. 619–621.

Hedrick, Ulysses P. *A History of Horticulture in America to 1860*. New York: Oxford University Press, 1950.

Hyams, Edward. *Plants in the Service of Man*. Philadelphia: Lippincott, 1971.

Jabs, Carolyn. "Seed Savers." *Country Journal*, June 1981, pp. 34–39.

Johnson, Jim. *Heirloom Vegetable Guide*. Jim Johnson, 7705 Normandy, Oconomowoc, WI 53066.

McMahon, Bernard. *McMahon's American Gardener*. New York: Funk & Wagnalls, 1967.

Mooney, P. R. *Seeds of the Earth*. London: International Coalition for Developmental Action, 1979.

Myers, Norman. *The Sinking Ark*. Elmsford, N.Y.: Pergammon Press, 1979.

Nabhan, Gary. "Kokopelli—The Humpbacked Flute Player: Conserving Agricultural Diversity as a Community Responsibility." *Co-Evolution Quarterly*, Spring 1983, pp. 4–11.

National Academy of Sciences. *Genetic Vulnerability of Major Crops*. Washington, D.C.: National Academy of Sciences, 1972.

National Academy of Sciences. *Conservation of Germplasm Resources*. Washington, D.C.: National Academy of Sciences, 1978.

Raven, Peter, ed. *Conservation of Threatened Plants*. New York: Plenum, 1976.

Teweles, L. Wm. & Co. *The Global Seed Study*. L. Wm. Teweles & Co., 1978.

U.S. Department of Agriculture. *Yearbook of Agriculture: Seeds*. Washington, D.C., 1961.

U.S. Department of Agriculture, Science and Education Department. *The National Plant Germplasm System*. Washington, D.C., 1981.

Vilmorin-Andrieux, MM. *The Vegetable Garden*. Berkeley: Ten Speed Press, 1981.

Whealy, Kent. *Seed Savers Yearbook*. Princeton, Mo.: Seed Savers Exchange, 1979–1983.

Whealy, Kent. *Fall Harvest Edition*. Princeton, Mo.: Seed Savers Exchange, 1981–1982.

Wilkes, Garrison. "The Endangered Genetic Base of the World's Food Supply." *Bulletin of the Atomic Scientist*, February 1977, pp. 8–14.

Wilkes, Garrison. "Breeding Crisis for Our Crops—Is the Gene Pool Drying Up?" *Horticulture*, April 1977, pp. 53–59.

Wilkes, Garrison, and Wilkes, Susan. "The Green Revolution." *Environment*, October 1972, pp. 32–39.

Withee, John. *Growing and Cooking Beans*. Dublin, N.H.: Yankee Press, 1980.

Index